OUT OF THE WASTELAND:
STORIES FROM THE
ENVIRONMENTAL FRONTIER

Published by
Community Environmental Council, Inc.
Santa Barbara, California
cecsb.org

ISBN: 0986173002
ISBN 13: 978-0-9861730-0-4
Library of Congress Control Number: 2015933249

Cover and book design by
PHAROS Creative LLC
pharos.net

OUT OF THE
WASTELAND
Stories From The Environmental Frontier

PAUL RELIS

Community
Environmental
Council

To Kathy.

TABLE OF CONTENTS

FOREWORD

In the age of the global, the local has more power than ever. Small towns and multinationals can match. But in the global era, the local also has access to all the world. An idea in California can inspire Beijing. A kind and careful intuition anywhere can almost instantly become the blessing of everywhere. As I travel the world, from Bolivia to North Korea to Ethiopia to Paris, I see how collaboration is ever-more invisible and planetary as random minds addressing the same questions in all corners of the globe help and quicken one another toward a collective solution.

I always think of this process when I think of Paul Relis, his wife Kathy, and all their heroic and devoted colleagues at the Community Environmental Council. For more than forty years now, I've been watching them nurture tiny seeds into great oaks that sustain our local community and countless others across the globe, and I've seen what began as a little office spread its roots and fruits into every corner of the world. Whenever I reflect on their shining and uplifting example, I feel that this is exactly what the New World can still offer the rest of us: a mix of rigor and confidence, hard work, and clearly defined and calibrated hopes. It is as if—as in this book—a sense of the future and its possibilities is held up by a sense of the past and its realities, so that ideas are passed from generation to generation, gaining substance and new applications with each transmission.

Indeed, the striking and often unexpected thing about every hero I've met, from the Fourteenth Dalai Lama to Desmond Tutu—and every hero I've read about, from Mahatma Gandhi to Martin Luther King—is that they work for change in the very real world not by dreaming but by acting, in down-to-earth, practical, visible ways; as Tutu writes in one of his books, he doesn't like to be called an "optimist," because at heart and at best he's a realist. That's exactly what I've always sensed about Paul, the hero of everyone I know in Santa Barbara, for his ability to spin out a local story with a global vision, and to open out onto larger vistas by tending so precisely to what's here, right now, before him. When he took up a position in the state government of California, it was as if he was bringing into the most uncompromisingly tough world his realistic, empirical, carefully tended sense of how change could work and bring benefits, both visible and invisible, to everywhere.

For decades now, I've been hoping that he would share his story and his vision with the rest of us; nobody I've met in California has better and more beautifully embodied the spirit of individual enterprise and collective thinking, and no one I know has proceeded as quietly and dauntlessly along his path with such lucid determination and such keen and friendly alertness to the world as he has. I have learned what little I know about waste management from Paul, and I have learned a lot about Sweden and Israel and China and the ecological tradition from him.

But more than that, I have learned about what it is to lead a human life. Family, community, globe, and council have all become one in his example, and what he and his loved ones and colleagues do has become my personal model of what the globe can become in an age of multinational affiliations and universal responsibility. It's hard for me to believe that the smiling, bright-eyed couple I met in my teens, working out of a largely empty space, have become heroes and teachers for so many of us. A vision that began amid the oil fields of Long Beach can reach into the unimagined depths (and the unexpected oil spills) of the twenty-first century. An idea that came to light in Santa Barbara in the late sixties, diligently nurtured and pursued with untiring and unswerving practicality, can become a solid, sustainable, and living—but still human, local, and kind—solution for the planet. Read Out of the Wasteland, and you may find the courage to extend and enrich the lives of your community as well. What you have and what you once dreamed of may come to seem like one and the same thing.

PICO IYER
SANTA BARBARA, MAY 2014

January 28, 1969.
Offshore erupts in the Santa Barbara Channel.
This oil spill is heard round the world.

PROLOGUE

Until one commits oneself, there is hesitancy, the chance to draw back, always ineffectiveness. Concerning all acts of initiative (and creation), there is one elementary truth, the ignorance of which kills countless ideas and splendid plans, that the moment one definitely commits oneself, Providence moves too. All sorts of things occur to help one that would never otherwise have occurred. A whole stream issues from the decision, raising in one's favor all manner of unforeseen incidents and meetings and material assistance, which no man could have dreamt would have come his way. Whatever you do or dream you can, begin it. Boldness has genius, power, and magic in it.

WILLIAM MURRAY, THE SCOTTISH HIMALAYAN EXPEDITION

Most of us have had a special encounter with nature—with a field near your home, a park, a garden patch, a river or a rivulet, a mountain or a hilltop that embeds itself in you, becomes part of you like your DNA. I like to think of it as the DNA of place. When you call it up in the mind's eye, it's always as available to you as it was when you first experienced it. Such places are the wellsprings of our love of nature, our kinship with her. They are, in many ways, the source of who we are.

Among the first images I absorbed as a child of three were the oil refineries near our home in Lomita, California. It was 1949. Our military-issue housing was perched on a hillside facing refineries, their tall, dark stacks silhouetted against the sky. When darkness fell, brilliant orange-and-blue flames from the flares licked the night.

When I was four years old, my family moved to the little island community of Naples at the southern end of Long Beach, California, nestled between the elegant Alamitos Bay fronted by affluent bayside homes, sail-boats and motor yachts, and the red brick–lined Marine Stadium, built for the 1932 Los Angeles Olympic Games rowing events. The side of Naples that I lived on didn't enjoy a waterfront view. We fronted a still-operating rail line that brought an occasional train rumbling through the neighbor-hood with hobos on board. The open land was hardscrabble, dusty in the long dry season, giving way to deep green grasses when the winters were wet.

Our home was a small stucco single-family structure, the kind that housed many of California's middle-class families in those days; barely a stone's throw away was the Marine Stadium. Beyond the stadium were oil fields that spread out below oil derrick–covered Signal Hill, which looked like a giant pimple rising out of a flat landscape. It was here that California's largest oil discovery was made in 1921. It became one of the richest oil fields in the world.[1]

My friends and I played in the flatlands below Signal Hill amid the heaving and squeaking iron horses and the vast network of pipes and roads that are the nerves of an oil field. We called this backyard "the badlands." In this desiccated world where the land had literally been stripped clean of life, but for the occasional tumbleweed, I discovered a little miracle. There was a large water pipe running through the field that had a leak in it. It must have leaked for a very long time because it had created a small pond defined, at a distance, by a stand of tall, deep-green tule reeds with brown fuzzy tips. As I came to the pond's edge, I entered a magical world. There were tree frogs clinging to the reeds, frogs of varying colors, green, brown, and mottled, that blended in most perfectly, making them almost invisible. When I sat still, the frogs would begin to croak. Brilliant blue mayflies skimmed the water's surface, blue-headed dragonflies buzzed overhead, and red-winged blackbirds squawked in the reeds that bent to the prevailing coastal winds as the iron horses squeaked and creaked in the background.

Throughout my boyhood I would visit this place that I named, with a boy's matter-of-factness, the "frog place." I kept its location a secret, shar-ing it only with a few of my closest friends and my brother. As I would approach the frog place, powerful and complicated feelings would overwhelm me, mostly joyous but sometimes fearful—fearful that I would find it destroyed like so many natural wonders of my childhood that had been obliterated by development.

The magnificent Newport Coast, Southern California as it appeared in the 1950s.

Less than a mile from my home, there were truly wild lands—sand dunes and estuaries that were full of fish and wildlife. My brother and I reveled in it—we fished the shallow waterways and flushed crawdads that we used as fishing bait; we learned to skim-board, surf, and fish the open ocean that was teeming with bass, yellowtail, bonita, and barracuda.

A few miles distant were vast tracks of farmlands and orange groves. Driving south of Long Beach, past the Huntington Beach oil fields and Newport Beach, one came upon a largely untouched California coast, images of which are preserved best by the plein air painters of the early twentieth century whose idyllic images had drawn throngs from around the country to migrate to California. There were waves of golden summer-bleached grasses and the irrepressible fire-resistant landscape we call the chaparral. In the deeper recesses of the coastal canyons were sycamores and large live oaks, jackrabbits and coyotes. Red-tailed hawks and vultures flew overhead. If you were still, you could hear the red-winged blackbirds squawking in the tule reeds in the wetlands at the canyon mouths and the unmistakable meadowlark, its crisp, melodic, unforgettable song breaking the silence when the blackbirds were away.

Within a decade, by the early 1960s, most of these treasures were gone—dredged away to make way for marinas and shopping centers, subdivisions and strip malls. The farms and orange groves became housing tracts. Through a young boy's eyes, I saw the bulldozers ripping up the rich earth and felt something deep and disturbing. I didn't have words for these feelings; all I knew was that the world I loved was getting ripped apart. And it hurt.

That sense of hurt returned to me on January 28, 1969, when the oil spill blanketed the Santa Barbara, California, coastline. Black, thick, and suffocating, it took the very life out of a vibrant and diverse marine environment, reducing it to a marine moonscape. What to make of this? What could be done about it? What did this catastrophe portend for our future?

These questions became my singular focus and began a personal transformation, from being a young person who "observed" history to someone who was stirred to make it. It began with a meditation of sorts, not the kind of inward meditation one associates with personal growth, but on a specific phenomena that affected my home, my friends, my community, and my sense of the future. It was a meditation on a liquid called oil.

To my chagrin, I quickly realized that oil made possible so much of what I loved. It fueled the grand road trips of my boyhood to the Salmon River country of Idaho, the Grand Tetons, Mesa Verde, Yellowstone, Glacier, Banff, and Lake Louise. Oil allowed me to surf the coast of California and make the long drive through the night to ski the Sierra by morning. Oil made my mobility possible. I could, on a whim, drive to the Big Sur or further north to UC Berkeley, where many of my contemporaries were studying, or make a spur-of-the-moment road trip to watch the sun rise over the Grand Canyon. Oil fueled my mobility and my mobility made me free!

Oil powered the tractors that tilled the soils and nourished the crops. Oil made suburban life possible. Oil lit up and warmed our lives, heating our buildings and running all the machinery of the modern world. Oil kept the lights on. Oil ran the ships delivering manufactured goods across the seas; it fueled the planes that made world travel possible; it was the source of our military might. Oil ran our national laboratories and our hospitals. Oil was at the heart of modern chemistry, and it was making possible the plastics and other materials that we all had come to depend on. Try as I might to find something modern that was not tied to oil, I could not. In a word, oil and modern life were one.

All true and irrefutable, but before me on the beaches of Santa Barbara there was oil seen in a different light—oil as life-destroyer, oil as a killer of the marine kingdoms, oil as a ruination of our local economy, oil depriving us of our recreation, oil taking away the beauty of our world. The exploitation of oil had produced the desiccated landscape of my childhood, the badlands of pipes, iron horses, metal towers, and acrid smells; it led to the foul air that hampered my breathing and made me sick to my stomach after tennis matches and surfing; it was the haze that hung over my hometown of Long Beach and all of Southern California, robbing us of the beauty of Southern California, fronted by the sea and backed by the majestic San Gabriel and San Bernardino mountain ranges. So this was oil—its shadow side—in all its nakedness. Yes, our civilization was built on oil's exploitation, but depending on it out into the future looked to me like our possible demise.

AWAKENING

Santa Barbara citizens revolt against the oil industry in the aftermath of the Santa Barbara Oil Spill.

An explosion of new policies, laws, and regulations came in the wake of the oil spill, including the National Environmental Policy Act, the Clean Air and Water Acts, the creation of the US Environmental Protection Agency, not to mention Earth Day—the largest secular holiday in the world.[2] This outpouring of environmental interest and commitment established the United States as the world's unquestionable leader in environmental protection.

Locally the oil spill transformed Santa Barbara from the staid and conservative community it was into one of the most environmentally progressive communities in the world. Santa Barbara galvanized itself into a ferocious critic of the government and the oil industry alike. Through its elected officials and the long hand of its influential citizenry, it subjected both the oil industry and the federal agencies to a searing critique of roles and responsibilities. The response to the spill was pathetic by the powers that be. It was dismaying; it demonstrated that neither the government nor the industry had developed the means to contain the spill, let alone knew how to clean it up. Booms were lacking to prevent it from spreading, and there was little in the way of equipment to collect it. On shore the best that industry and government had to offer was to spread straw with an army of hired hands to try to sop it up. Why, for God's sake, didn't the coast guard have a credible oil spill containment plan in place that could be enforced on the industry? And what about Union Oil, the company that had caused the spill? What recourse was to be taken against them for all but destroying the local tourist economy, for the actual destruction of marine life, and for depriving the people of Santa Barbara of the enjoyment of their shoreline?

In the spotlight of the national media, with pictures of dead and dying marine birds and fish splashed across the newspapers, the federal government was compelled to act. On March 21, 1970, President Nixon came to see the spill and clean-up efforts.[3] During his visit, he spoke to Santa Barbara residents, saying that the Santa Barbara incident had frankly touched the conscience of the American people.

As Santa Barbara grappled for answers and a sense of direction, the reality of what had happened and what could be done about it began to sink in. Environmental catastrophes could happen and, in short order, ruin the economy of a community. The oil spill revealed that government had little knowledge of the environmental consequences of such events. This raised larger questions. What protections could communities expect from their government when confronted with a massive environmental disaster? Could offshore oil continue to be developed safely? Were there other environmental catastrophes in the offing, not just from oil development, but from other industrial activities?

Public protests against the oil industry were building, and "get oil out" became a rallying cry. The Santa Barbara wharf—then a working wharf of the oil industry—was shut down by hundreds of protestors who had mobilized to stop the oil trucks from entering or leaving. The rage was palpable, and people were willing to lie down in front of the big, lumbering oil rig trucks and risk their lives in defense of their place. There was the very real prospect that one of the truck drivers would become incensed by the protests and drive forward. In the face of this spirited determination, the oil industry soon retreated from using the Santa Barbara wharf for servicing its offshore rigs.

On January 28, 1970, the first anniversary of the Santa Barbara oil blowout was commemorated at Santa Barbara City College. Some thirty organizations within the community gathered and declared with one voice that the oil spill "must be used to mark man's efforts to turn away from the ultimate folly of self-destruction." The event was keynoted by Dr. Roderick Nash, who had been recruited from Harvard to establish UCSB's new Environmental Studies Department. He authored for the occasion the "Santa Barbara Declaration of Environmental Rights,"[4] which rings with truth today:

> All men have the right to an environment capable of sustaining life and promoting happiness. If the accumulated actions of the past become destructive of this right, men now living have the further right to repudiate the past for the benefit of the future. And it is manifest that centuries of careless neglect of the environment have brought mankind to the final crossroads. The quality of our lives is eroded and our very existence threatened by our abuse of the natural world...
>
> We, therefore, resolve to act. We propose a revolution in conduct toward an environment which is rising in revolt against us. Granted that ideas and institutions long established are not easily changed; yet today is the first day of the rest of our life on this planet. We will begin anew.

The event drew many political leaders and activist academics such as Dr. Paul Ehrlich of Stanford. They spoke of the need for a new environmental ethos in America and worldwide. Media coverage of the oil spill had been extensive, including commentary by Walter Cronkite on his popular and influential CBS Evening News program and front-page stories in the New York Times and Los Angeles Times. As Robert O. Easton, one of Santa Barbara's gifted novelists and environmentalists, noted, "Santa Barbara's first Environmental Rights Day had commemorated a new kind of thinking, a new kind of personal concern, a new kind of political action, and a new series of social problems. The blowout had indeed been heard around the world."[5]

THE REALM OF IDEAS

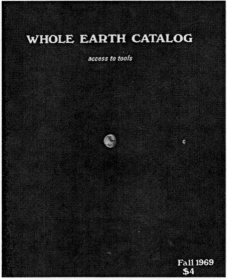

Whole Earth Catalog, *1969.*
A wellspring of ideas and tools for environmental pioneers.

Books about every facet of the environment—scientific, philosophical, and aesthetic were streaming off the presses. Writers and thinkers were traveling the world talking up their ideas; astronauts were sending back the first images from space of the earth, exalting the stunning beauty of the "blue planet" against the vastness of space. The world, so it seemed to me, was experiencing a powerful awakening to the realization that we couldn't take our natural resources for granted any longer; nor could we continue to rely so heavily on oil to fuel our modern world.

I felt compelled to find a way to contribute in some way. But to do what, and how to do it? There were no courses of study to take up; public attitudes were aroused in parts of the country but certainly not universally, and even among my friends there was interest, but not much more than that. I realized that it was up to me to set my own course, to identify people and ideas that resonated and that could inform and inspire me.

The new literature introduced me to solar, wind, geothermal, and biomass energy sources. These technologies were in their infancy, they were more experimental than proven, and those who advanced them operated on the fringes of society, in "back to the land" experiments that had proliferated around the country. Solar technology, mostly water-heating systems, were beginning to be used for home applications along with passive solar design in architecture. Solar design was talked about as the basis for a new environmental architecture, part of a future built environment to be found in homes and industrial and commercial buildings. Energy efficiency measures, such as home insulation and improved heating and cooling systems and appliances, were part and parcel of a new built environment. More physically compact towns and cities with bicycle and pedestrian paths with people living closer to work and with built-in habitat and resource protections in the surrounding environs—ideas that we associate with smart growth or sustainable cities today—these were the ideas and experiments that were beginning to percolate, though they were still outlier notions then.

My reading continued, deepening my understanding and casting light on areas of interest. In the heat of the aftermath of the oil spill I felt like a swimmer caught in a rip tide, fighting it and losing to its power. Now I began to relax and let the current take me to where I could feel the bottom and make my way to the shore.

My environmental destiny began to reveal itself. Though drawn to environmentalism as an activist protesting an oil spill, I knew that protest was not going to be my path. While deeply respecting the importance of protest in the environmental movement as a necessity in the face of callous corporate and governmental behavior and societal ignorance, I was drawn to the idea of becoming a builder of alternatives to the oil exploitation and the development path we were on. But what alternatives to explore? I needed more than books; I needed mentors.

As I saw it, many of the burgeoning ideas seemed so new and untested. Were they substantial? Could they be relied upon, or were they more expressions of unexamined idealism, like so many of the social and environmental experiments in progress around the country and in Europe? What about the alternative technologies being promoted? Were they sound or riddled with flaws? Being so young and untested myself, it was surely presumptuous of me to place such an emphasis on the veracity of ideas and technologies. I suppose I carried an intrinsic skepticism in me about buying into those making grand claims about breakthroughs—claims that we could radically change our lifestyles, shed our growing consumerism, and develop the technologies and other means of making a break from the oil age. I wanted to believe in the possibility of grand change, but like many Americans I harbored a kind of "show me" attitude born and bred into the American psyche—a product of our agrarian roots, our industrial revolution, and the hands-on public-educational approach of Thomas Dewey. No, I thought, Americans would not easily be persuaded to adopt alternatives unless they worked. Americans are innately suspicious of the kinds of dreams and idealism generated on university campuses with their liberal bias and theoretical bent. To counteract this natural skepticism, it would be necessary to demonstrate its value in practical ways. But what concepts and practical experiments were within my means to consider and implement? What could a small fledgling organization with scarcely any financial resources hope to accomplish?

What began to emerge in my mind's eye was an image of my home town becoming a center of environmental experimentation. Santa Barbara was the place I had come to as a student, one that I had grown to love. As I began to see it, Santa Barbara was small enough to be influenced and had a reach far beyond its size, fabled as it was as a tourist mecca, a place that attracted people who had built lives and fortunes around the world to come live in it and participate in its civil life.

Physically, the Santa Barbara area is a series of alluvial fans, about three miles in width at their widest, reaching the ocean as wetlands or coastal cliffs of about fifty feet in height, and in places higher, stretching about twenty miles east to west. It's backed dramatically by the majestic Santa Ynez Mountains that rise to nearly four thousand feet. A multitude of sandstone outcroppings add drama to this unique east-west running mountain

City of Santa Barbara: a jewel on the Pacific Ocean fashioned by great civic enterprise.

range that extends to Pt. Conception, where the Santa Ynez range drops into the Pacific Ocean. Within this belt lies the City of Santa Barbara, mostly built out and flanked by the elite forested enclave of Montecito, the village of Summerland, and the small town of Carpinteria in the agricultural Carpinteria Valley. To the west of Santa Barbara and located on a broad alluvial plane is the unincorporated, mostly suburban Goleta Valley. To the west of Goleta the land turns rural as the mountains and coastal shelves nearly merge. Deep canyons and dramatic sandstone outcroppings characterize this beautiful, untrammeled coastline.

It seems audacious now as I look back that I thought of Santa Barbara as my laboratory, but that's what I did. I guess audacity is one of the blessings of being young and inexperienced. Youth has its protections; in my case it acted as a veil protecting me from the normal cautions that come with experience, freeing me to roam in places I might have feared to tread.

If Santa Barbara was to serve as a laboratory, I needed a base of operations. Earlier that year (1970), my then girlfriend and soon to be my wife, Kathy, and I had visited Berkeley where the vibrant Ecology Center had been recently created across from the western gate to the UC Berkeley campus. It was a storefront building full of books and magazines related to environmental awareness and action. The physical presence of a storefront packed with young people pursuing various environmental interests made a forceful impression on me. The Ecology Center had been founded by middle-aged businessman Ray Balter. Here was this older guy in a world of young people—many of whom were adherents to the counterculture—who was so straight-looking, so organized and filled with focused purpose. At least that's how he struck me. What an interesting combination, I thought.

It was only a month or two after visiting Berkeley that Kathy and I attended a meeting of the newly formed Community Environmental Council that was held to seek ideas about what to do with $2,500 that it had received in contributions. At a loss as to what to do with this money and where to focus our attention, someone asked if anyone had any ideas. I found my hand going up. I stood up and said that Kathy and I had just visited an environmental center in Berkeley, and it seemed to me that Santa Barbara could benefit from doing something similar. No one else stood up and offered another option. In the absence of an alternative, all the attention in the room focused on us, a twenty-two-year-old and his nineteen-year-old girlfriend. We walked out of the room with a commitment of $2,500 toward developing a center and a pledge by the board of directors to help us in any way possible. I was named the new executive director of the organization. And with that we had at least a down payment on developing a base of operations.

We quickly rented a storefront building, a cavernous, deep rectangle with high ceilings connected to a back room that fronted an outdoor restaurant. It was in the heart of downtown and had plenty of room for a bookstore and a meeting space.

A wave of volunteers consisting of friends and colleagues and people who dropped in just wanting to help followed. We were blessed to have several talented artists among us who painted wonderful murals on the walls of the drab interior. Kathy had innate organizational skills and set her mind on creating the bookstore and exhibits that we would show in the storefront window. In short order we stocked the bookshelves, made the first exhibits, furnished the center with hand-me-downs from friends and volunteers alike, and organized the publication of a monthly magazine that we called the *Survival Times*.

Santa Barbara Ecology Center, 1970, first steps on the environmental frontier.

The center quickly became a mecca for young and old alike. The bookstore sold books and periodicals that encompassed the new environmental literature, with titles that belied a robust and often strident environmentalism: *The Population Bomb*[6], *The Limits to Growth*[7], *Operating Manual for Spaceship Earth*[8], and periodicals like *Mother Earth News* and the *Whole Earth Catalog*. The newly released *The Limits to Growth*, written by scientists at MIT, and the *Whole Earth Catalog* were especially informative. *The Limits to Growth* was the first comprehensive global assessment of resource constraints that the authors contended would challenge prevailing assumptions about future growth and development. It was among the first studies to employ computer modeling of the world's natural resource base; the influx of the sun's energy versus energy demands. It predicted a coming reckoning between mankind's growing appetite for food, raw materials, and energy with what the earth could provide on a sustained basis. It came as no surprise that *The Limits to Growth* provoked a quick and strong attack from oil and other industrial interests and conservative think tanks who argued that it presented a far too pessimistic view of the future, one that would surely be refuted by technological and scientific breakthroughs. That debate continues to this day.

Bill McKibben would observe some forty years later, speaking to faculty and alumni at the University of California, Santa Barbara, forty-year commemoration of the Environmental Studies Department[9], "Few events in environmental history were more significant than the publication of that slim book, which was translated into thirty languages and sold thirty million copies, more than any other volume on the environment...More clearly than anyone else, this small team of researchers glimpsed the likelihood that we would overwhelm the planet on which we lived, and in so doing make our lives much harder."[10]

The *Whole Earth Catalog* was an entirely different window on our environmental condition. It was a compendium of ideas by leading thinkers, a chronicle of emerging experiments in lifestyle and profiles of new technologies that, in its first few years of publication, was a uniquely rich source of information, inquisitive, eclectic, irreverent, and always entertaining. The *Whole Earth Catalog* reflected the idiosyncratic mind of its creator, Stewart Brand, an iconoclastic, free-thinking Stanford graduate with a love of new technology. Publications like the *Whole Earth Catalog* touched on so many facets of life—farming, Native American culture, technology, science, psychology—and connected them all, as in a web of life. Much of this literature was featured in our Ecology Center storefront window along with exhibits. One in particular stands out. We had decided to make an exhibit about the virtues of whole grains and whole-wheat bread with instructions about how to prepare it and bake it. At the time, as hard as it might be to imagine today, this exhibit caused the CEC grief from our next-door neighbors, a Danish pastry baker and his wife, whose livelihood depended on selling sweet pastries and fine white breads. This brought home in the most visceral way the complexities and challenges we faced as we introduced the Santa Barbara community to a galaxy of new ideas and options for the future. Our simple exhibit had challenged an economic enterprise that depended on established values and behavior. What we thought to be a relatively innocuous and innocent form of education was in fact to some a radical proposition, and like all things radical, threatening.

INSPIRATION

As our work progressed, interest within the community increased. In 1971 I became acquainted with Dr. Joseph Bagnall, a kind and progressive assistant dean of Santa Barbara's continuing education program and a devout Mormon from farming stock in Utah. Adult ed, as Santa Barbarans knew it, was among the very best continuing education programs in the country. Joe and I had a number of good talks, and in the course of these conversations, we hatched the idea that the continuing education program and the Community Environmental Council would jointly offer a lecture series that would bring to Santa Barbara a global perspective on environmental thinking, including a historical framework, technology developments, scientific research, design, and economics.

The continuing education program was flush with cash at the time; Joe invited me to identify any speaker I considered to be the best in his or her field to come to Santa Barbara and speak to the community. What an opportunity!

There were four individuals, four contemporaries, all at the peak of their careers, who had most influenced my thinking to date: Buckminster Fuller, E. F. Schumacher, Alan Chadwick, and Ian McHarg.

Through the lecture series that we entitled "The American Dream and the City of Man" (1972–74), I had the good fortune to spend the better part of a day with all but Ian McHarg in my role as series moderator. I also met Paolo Soleri, the visionary architect of Arcosanti, an architecturally inspired prototype experimental community in the Arizona desert; Norman Borlaug, often referred to as the inventor of the Green Revolution; Edward Teller, the renowned and formidable physicist and prime player in the Manhattan Project; and the noted American historian, Henry Steele Commager. To have these giants of their time come to Santa Barbara, and to spend time with them in conversation over dinner with Dr. Bagnall, was a great privilege. It was from these encounters that the intellectual foundation was set and from which all the subsequent work followed.

> The nearest star is ninety-two million miles away, and the next star after that is billions of miles away. This spaceship is so superbly designed that we've had men on board here for about two million years reproducing themselves, thanks to the ecological balance. The earth is a very small spaceship. It's only eight thousand miles in diameter...
>
> **BUCKMINSTER FULLER**

On Christmas Eve 1968, Earthrise, an image of the earth from space taken by astronaut William Anders[11], had a transformative effect on many people around the world. When Anders returned to Earth he made his famous statement, "We came all this way to explore the moon and the most important thing we discovered was the earth."[12] Earthrise became the most singular and compelling symbol of the new environmental awareness. And there was no bolder proponent of how mankind would have to operate in an age of astronauts, breathtakingly new technologies, and scientific discoveries than Buckminster Fuller.

By the late '60s and early '70s, Bucky Fuller had become one of the most sought-after lecturers in the United States. His image was featured on the cover of *Time* magazine in 1964[13]; his ideas captured the imagination of young and old alike. In his landmark work, *Operating Manual for Spaceship Earth*, Fuller argued that the time had come to reorder the relationship between man and the earth. The idea that we are passengers on a vast earth whose powers are beyond our control was now archaic; we had to take the controls of spaceship Earth to avoid certain destruction that would come from the unchecked development of nuclear weapons, spiraling population growth, and unsustainable demands on natural resources. In spite of his doubts about the human prospect in the face of such threats, Fuller was convinced that man had the capacity and the tools to navigate through these seemingly intractable problems and find peace and prosperity. He believed in man's abilities to analyze problems and design solutions to them—to find and develop ways of using just a small fraction of the resources currently required to provide shelter, food, and life's other essentials. He said that human history was replete with examples of "doing more with less."

Buckminster Fuller: a modern day Leonardo, inventor of the geodesic dome, buckyballs. Author of An Operating Manual for Spaceship Earth.

Fuller's inventions include the geodesic dome, the Dymaxion car (an automobile that could run on a small fraction of the fuel of conventional automobiles), and his Dymaxion house, a geodesic structure remarkably lightweight and energy efficient. Bucky called for a new "design science" unifying physics, mathematics, architecture, and engineering with chemistry, sociology, biology, and ecology. This design science would be dedicated to "making a success out of mankind." Like a modern Leonardo da Vinci, Fuller drew his images of the future—cities under geodesic domes, translucent membranes controlling climate and filtering out pollution; houses that could be packed into a station wagon or dropped by helicopter in remote sites with self-contained energy and wastewater systems. By doing more with less, mankind could shrink its impact on nature and natural resources and provide a high standard of living for the vast majority of mankind.

SMALL IS BEAUTIFUL

E. F. "Fritz" Schumacher was a Rhodes Scholar in economics who became the top economist and head of planning at the British Coal Board. Over time he became a critic of prevailing economic views of growth, development, and the use of natural resources. His thoughts on scale and economic development are of special note:

> What scale is appropriate? It depends on what we are trying to do. The question of scale is extremely crucial today in political, social, and economic affairs just as in almost everything else... In his urgent attempt to obtain reliable knowledge about his essentially indeterminate future, the modern man of action may surround himself by ever-growing armies of forecasters, by ever-growing mountains of factual data to be digested by ever-more wonderful mechanical contrivances...The best decisions will still be based on the judgments of mature-non-electronic brains possessed by men who have looked steadily and calmly at the situation and seen it whole.[14]

Schumacher's classical economic convictions were turned on their head while on a development assignment in Sri Lanka. There he came under the influence of Buddhist teachings and the indigenous ways the Sri Lankans managed their lands and nurtured their culture and their communities. This was a life-changing experience that led him to formulate an approach to economic development that strove to preserve rather than obliterate local values and customs. He called this "appropriate technology," a conscious selection of technological systems and inventions that would maintain the need for labor and keep people on the land while producing greater economic output that would raise the general standard of living. Schumacher founded in England a Center of Appropriate Technology to further this work.

In 1973 Schumacher wrote *Small Is Beautiful: Economics As If People Mattered*, which advocated economic development that would result in "health, beauty, and permanence," rather than the resource depletion, pollution, and cultural alienation that characterized Western- and Soviet-financed projects in less-developed countries. This book, now considered a classic study of decentralized, sustainable development, was highly influential in its day and was the basis for Schumacher's worldwide lectures, which drew full-capacity audiences wherever he went.

While Schumacher was in Santa Barbara, I shared with him what I was trying to accomplish at the CEC. He was kind and caring enough to reflect on my comments and then offer a response that was to set the framework for the work ahead. "You need to link government, business, academia, and the public—you can't exclude any of these. You need to find a way to connect these spheres, and only in this way will you have a complete approach to environmental work."

Paul Relis meets famed British economist E.F. Schumacher at the Community Environmental Council office, 1976.

DESIGN WITH NATURE

Canvas and pigments lie in wait, stone, wood, and metal are ready for sculpture, random noise is latent for symphonies, sites are gravid for cities, institutions lie in the wings ready to solve our most intractable problems, parables of moving power remain unformulated and yet, the world is finally unknowable.

IAN MCHARG

Ian McHarg
Noted professor of landscape
architecture at the University of
Pennsylvania and author of
Design With Nature.

Urban sprawl and widespread destruction of natural habitats characterized post–World War II America. Development in its myriad forms went unfettered. But in the aftermath of the Santa Barbara Oil Spill and other environmental catastrophes like the Cuyahoga River fire in Cleveland, experiments promoting more far-sighted and disciplined approaches to development emerged. One of the most promising of these was the work of Ian McHarg.

Ian McHarg was a Scottish-born landscape architect. Trained at Harvard, he became a professor of landscape architecture at the University of Pennsylvania and developed a prominent landscape architectural practice. In 1969, McHarg wrote *Design with Nature*[15], a pioneering and much-acclaimed book that celebrated the importance of giving nature her due in the task of building towns and cities. According to McHarg, the land itself, if studied deeply enough, reveals how it should be used by man, or whether it should be used at all. Simply put, if soils are exceptionally fertile, they are intrinsically suitable for cultivation and, if properly cared for, they can be cultivated for millennia to sustain mankind. Areas of marginal fertility, away from flood plains and geologically stable, are more intrinsically suitable for human settlement.

In *Design with Nature*, McHarg showed how the life sciences could be applied to the practice of land-use planning. He used a mapping system that consisted of sheets of transparent mylar. Each sheet of mylar was in effect a map of a natural resource such as soil, geology, habitat, or a flood plain. McHarg overlaid these maps and the composite image revealed what he called the "intrinsic suitability" of the land under study. This mapping system would prove invaluable to designers and the public alike in making decisions about specific projects and/or the design of whole new cities. McHarg's system provided new tools to combat what he saw as irrational and destructive patterns of land use sweeping the world.

THE GARDEN OF THE HEART'S DELIGHT

We are the living links in a life force that moves and plays around
and through us binding the deepest soils with the farthest stars.[16]

ALAN CHADWICK

*Schumacher called Alan Chadwick
"the greatest horticulturalist of the
20th century."*

I remember visiting the UC
Santa Cruz campus—it must have
been 1970 or 1971. Near the heart
of the campus, in an opening in the
redwood canopy, was a garden that
absolutely dazzled me. I had never seen anything like it. It was the
creation of Alan Chadwick.

In 1966 Chancellor McHenry
of the newest of the University of
California campuses, Santa Cruz,
recruited an eccentric horticulturalist and Shakespearian actor to build
a garden in the heart of the campus's
idyllic redwoods. Freya von Moltke,
a friend of Chancellor McHenry and
married to his great-grandnephew
Helmuth von Moltke, one of Prussia's
most illustrious generals, convinced the chancellor that a Chadwickian
garden would add a civilizing touch to this fresh space, an educational
experiment in itself that aspired to create a learning environment inte-

grating knowledge rather than succumb to the trend toward increased specialization.[17]

Chadwick combined his acting skills with an extraordinary horticultural mastery, which produced lectures that inspired the mind and gardens that delighted the eye. This combination worked magic on the pliant minds of idealistic students, many of whom were restive in the university environment and who hungered for more relevant knowledge.

Chadwick imbued horticulture with a sense of the sacred. Soil was never "dirt"; it was the nexus of the great life forces of earth, air, fire, and water—immeasurably alive and full of potential. The gardener's challenge and calling was to tap that potential by nurturing all of the forces that contribute to a plant's development, such as soil texture and tilth, mimicking falling rain in the application of water, and preserving moisture by creating a plant canopy by closely spacing transplants, creating microclimates within the garden. His approach to horticulture was complex and challenging. A Chadwickian garden was a mosaic of flowers, beds of vegetables, and herbaceous borders, carefully thought out and meticulously executed. It was the embodiment of a rich horticultural vision that reached back in time to the ancient Greeks and Romans, the Incas and the Chinese, and into the present cottage gardens and country gardens of France and England. The Santa Cruz garden that he and his apprentices established was a fusion of Asian subtlety and discipline and the English sensibility. E. F. Schumacher called Alan Chadwick "the greatest horticulturalist of the 20th century."[18]

The ideas and pragmatic experiments of these men informed every project that I was to pursue over the next fifteen years. Ian McHarg influenced our urban planning and land use projects; E. F. Schumacher put us on the path of linking our work with academia, government, the public, and business; Buckminster Fuller fired our interest in exploring technologies that could "do more with less"; and Alan Chadwick inspired the development of our organic garden and farming work, placing the garden physically and metaphorically as the centerpiece of the Community Environmental Council.

SANTA BARBARA STANDS FAST

What followed was one of the most contested land use battles in California history, pitting the economic and political might of a major Orange County developer, aligned with the Santa Barbara Building and Trades Council, the city's powerful newspaper, and the Chamber of Commerce against an aroused public.

PERSONAL JOURNAL ENTRY, NOVEMBER 1970

By 1970, the local environmental consciousness, fueled by the Santa Barbara Oil Spill, grew in dimension, taking on concerns about land use, air quality, and wetlands and wilderness protection.

In the fall of 1970, the strength of this growing movement was tested when the Santa Barbara County Planning Commission approved a residential-urban development of more than fifteen hundred homes on the 3,638-acre El Capitan Ranch, to be built on Gaviota Coast west of Santa Barbara. The Gaviota Coast consists of some thirty-five miles of mostly ranchlands and avocado and lemon orchards occupying a narrow coastal belt backed by the Santa Ynez Mountains and fronted by the Pacific Ocean. The proposed project would place a large suburban development in the heart of the untrammeled coast, some six miles beyond the nearest development. In urban-planning parlance the project was a classic example of "leapfrogging" development—skipping over a large expanse of undeveloped land and creating a rationale for future infill. The El Capitan Ranch was to be an upscale residential enclave with a "highway commercial center several times the size of Santa Barbara's largest shopping center." Fred Eissler, a locally prominent and determined conservationist, saw in this development the demise of the Gaviota

Gaviota Coast: The fight for its protection was one of the great land use battles of the early environmental movement.

Coast. As Eissler observed, "Once urban development is permitted in the agricultural region of the county, the pattern and precedent established opens the floodgate for urban sprawl across the west county from Ellwood to the Gaviota Pass and in every other rural region of the county."

What followed was one of the most contested land use battles in California's history. After the County Board of Supervisors approved the proposed project on appeal from the Planning Commission by a vote of 4–1, a powerful groundswell of opposition swept through the county. The economic and political might of a major Orange County developer, aligned with the Santa Barbara Building and Trades Council, the city's powerful newspaper, the Santa Barbara News-Press, and the Chamber of Commerce were pitted against an aroused public, incensed that it could lose its beloved Gaviota Coast after virtually losing its ocean for two years following the oil spill. A citizen's referendum was mounted to overturn the support of the County Board of Supervisors in a fiercely fought battle. So pitched was this battle that the developer influenced the local district attorney to have Selma Rubin and her elderly friend, Anna Laura Myers, who led the initiative effort, arrested for allegedly falsifying petition signatures.

This prosecution attracted national media interest and resulted in feature stories in the Los Angeles Times and the New York Times. In the end the prosecution was dropped, and the district attorney was called to task for abusing his office and was later defeated when he ran for reelection. The initiative to overturn the approval of the project by the Santa Barbara County Board of Supervisors prevailed by a near two-thirds majority, a stunning defeat for the developer and for development interests along the Gaviota Coast. El Capitan was among the first land use battles that effectively limited urban sprawl in California. To this day, though development pressures still exist, the Gaviota Coast remains much as it was in 1972, a testimonial to the durability of the environmental impulse that was set in motion following the Santa Barbara Oil Spill.

While larger environmental battles such as El Capitan were underway, our focus at work was on developing alternative visions and models for how Santa Barbara could manage its environment. We wanted to show Santa Barbara and the larger world that our environmental ideas were worthy not only of consideration but of practice. We had created the Ecology Center, a step that gave us some substance, but as we saw it, the storefront with books and organizations was only a start, not an endgame. In quick succession, a number of important extensions of our work unfolded. Some were deliberate and some came to us through serendipity.

MR. POLLOCK'S CHALLENGE

One afternoon a distinguished older gentleman, cane in hand, limped into the Ecology Center. In a crisp, almost defiant way, with his eyes blazing in his craggy old face, he said that if we wanted to do something to protect the environment, we should go and see what the Shell Ammonia and Urea Refinery was doing to the Ventura River.

He explained that the Ventura River once flowed year-round and supported large runs of steelhead, a trout that migrates to the ocean and returns to spawn and then die, salmon-like. In the 1940s the headwaters of the Ventura River were dammed. This prevented the steelhead from returning to the cool, gravel-rich spawning waters upstream. Further injury was inflicted on the river when Shell Oil built a urea refinery and began releasing effluent directly into the watercourse.

There were locals still alive in the early 1970s who could remember the abundant steelhead runs and the rich diversity of life that the Ventura River's riparian habitat supported. Mr. Pollock was among them. He wanted action taken against the refinery, and he put the question right to me, as if to say, "If you can't deliver on this, what good is your organization and what good are you?"

I was bowled over by the old man's ferocity, his unbending commitment to his cause, and his resourcefulness. He had driven some thirty miles north from Ventura to visit these young people, many long-haired, in a building with strange murals painted on the walls, to seek help in righting an offense that had clearly wounded him. After he left, I hadn't a clue as to what I could do except to at least honor him with a visit to the site of the offense and see for myself what he was talking about.

Ventura River: The Rivers and Harbors Act of 1899 was the tool used to help shut down a Shell ammonia and urea refinery that had long polluted this once supported prolific steelhead runs.

I made the drive south on a warm summer day, down the Santa Barbara coastline to where the Pacific Coast Highway crosses the Ventura River. I turned north on the highway toward the Ojai Valley, famed for its oranges, its private schools, and its history of spiritualism. A few miles into the ride toward Ojai, I saw the refinery with the river just to the west of it. I got out of my car and took a slow walk along the fence line and came across an outfall where dark fluid was pouring out. It was unquestionably going into the river. It didn't take much of a detective's mind to link cause and effect here. Simply put, the refinery was poisoning the river with apparent impunity.

It so happened that within a few days, a tall, lanky, pale- and pock-marked-faced young man in his early twenties visited our office. He introduced himself as Jim Crabtree and said that he was a graduate of Cal Tech. He was studying at UC Santa Barbara for a doctorate in chemistry, and he was interested in volunteer work. As we talked I thought of Pollock's visit and my recent trip to the refinery, and suddenly it dawned on me that Jim's skills as a chemist might be relevant in figuring out what to do about that the pollution of the river. After our meeting, he went back to the university to research recent publications on chemical pollution of waterways and came across a reference to the newly formed US Environmental Protection Agency's interest in cracking down on industrial polluters. He learned that if individuals or organizations could provide substantiated evidence that environmental harm was being done to a waterway by a company, the polluter could be prosecuted under an obscure federal law called the Rivers and Harbors Act of 1899, the oldest federal environmental law in the United States.[19] Jim Crabtree was a supremely self-confident young man. He stated emphatically, without the least hesitation or doubt, that he could devise a testing protocol that would accurately measure the pollutants flowing from the refinery into the river and thus provide convincing evidence that could stand up in a court of law. I discussed Crabtree's proposition with CEC's legal counsel, Philip Marking, a young attorney and a graduate of Boalt Hall, UC Berkeley's law school. Marking said he knew a law school classmate who had taken a position with the EPA's justice division. He would contact his friend if we could present him with a compelling case.

That was all Jim Crabtree needed. In a matter of a few days he had rigged up a flow-control device to measure effluent flows from the refinery; he'd put together a log book and gathered sample bottles and labels. Armed with all the equipment we needed for our investigation, we devised our plan of action. We would wear dark clothes, arrive at the refinery at dusk, try to slip undetected by the plant guards to the effluent pipe, gather our samples, and be gone.

Jim proved to be the quintessential scientist on a mission. He was airtight competent, meticulous in calibrating his simple measurement device accurately, and lab-perfect in gathering and preparing the samples to send off to the EPA. He wrote up one hell of a report that accompanied the samples. We presented the information to Marking, who was clearly impressed. Phil would call his EPA friend and find out where to submit Crabtree's report.

Months went by. I had forgotten all about the Shell foray, when an officious-looking letter from the EPA arrived. It stated that an investigation had been performed on the basis of our filed evidence. The EPA was filing a cease-and-desist order against Shell Ammonia and Urea from further polluting the Ventura River. Furthermore, the letter stated that the CEC was awarded a $2,500 "bounty" for submitting the report and the evidence. This was no small sum in 1972. Upon hearing the news, Crabtree breathed a sigh of satisfaction in perfect harmony with his massive sense of self-confidence, as if to say, "Why, of course, it would turn out this way. How could it be otherwise?"

I never saw Pollock again after that first encounter at the Ecology Center. I don't know if he lived long enough to read about the EPA prosecution of Shell. I don't think he gave me his contact information, and if he had I probably would have lost it. Nor for that matter did I see Jim Crabtree again.

That's how it was in those days with our work. People came in and out of the CEC's life like that—contributing much and then receding, sometimes disappearing, leaving their indelible mark. We build on the legacy of those who have come before us, those whom we meet along the way, those who mentor us, those who shake up our preconceived notions, who add a stone to the structures we are building; they make up the sum of who we are and who we aspire to be. They are our food and sustenance; they nurture, inform, and teach us. They are the soil from which we grow.

Later, Friends of the Ventura River, a nonprofit Ventura, California-based organization, would do the deep preservation work that would lead to the closure of the refinery, along with the destruction of an old and unnecessary dam upstream that impeded steelhead spawning. As I think back on the Ventura River adventure, I see it this way. I'll bet it took no more than a couple of years to build the dam and the refinery in all. Those two actions ruined a river. It took more than twenty years and countless hours of citizen initiative to unwind much of the damage. We're so quick to impose our will on the earth, to extract anything we deem necessary, and are so thoughtless in considering the future. Damage is so easy to inflict and so hard to undo. Will the steelhead that were once so plentiful in this little river ever return in large numbers?

Sustaining CEC at this time, even with its string of successes, was exceedingly challenging. To supplement what little income I could make from the CEC, I took a job with the Santa Barbara County Planning Department, where I made enough money to pay our rent and meet our modest needs. The struggle for money from the very beginning was a wrenching challenge. The situation improved somewhat when in 1972 we received a $10,000 grant from the federal government from an obscure environmental fund that was created in the aftermath of the Santa Barbara Oil Spill. This grant was made possible by the volunteer efforts of a professional grant writer from the Raytheon Corporation, a large defense contractor that had a B-1 Bomber research facility in the Santa Barbara area. Working with our inexperienced staff, he prepared a first-class proposal, no small task as anyone knows who has sought public contracts or grant awards. What motivated him to volunteer is lost to me now, including his name. But, in winning this grant, he contributed as much as anyone to giving us a chance to bring our ideas forth. His was yet another example of the many helping hands we received; like gifts out of nowhere, they seemed to come in the most extraordinary ways and at the most crucial moments.

SURVIVAL TIMES

Survival Times: *Early environmental journalism at its best.*

It has taken the world four decades to catch up with the *Survival Times*, the CEC's little but mighty magazine of the 1970s. Fueled by an idealistic crew of dedicated volunteers, the magazine featured articles focusing on recycling, alternative energy, organic gardening, transportation, and land use planning melding local with more global efforts to protect and preserve natural resources. At the time, many of the ideas presented in the *Survival Times* were considered radical, but today they are touted as necessary, called "green," and have become trendy.

Flipping through issues of the magazine, now more than forty years old, one might think it's a contemporary publication. There are articles about oil drilling off the coast, wind and solar power, hydrogen fuel for cars, and

dwindling populations of fish. Strip mining and nuclear power were debated. The topics may be the same ones we're reading or hearing about today,
but what is different is the sense of urgency. In the '70s we were talking about
"What if?" scenarios like peak oil, the exhaustion of fisheries, and the impact
of an earth population of some seven billion as it was projected to be by the
end of the twentieth century. Now these are no longer prognostications or
hypotheticals—the weight of these issues is upon us.

The *Survival Times* was the voice for our distinct brand of environmentalism. The first issue in 1970 was a simple stapled newsletter that showcased
actions that the CEC was taking to promote its ideas. It soon evolved into
an artistically designed magazine, where the developing projects and relevant topics could be discussed and illustrated. As the magazine added art by
talented CEC members, it was also enhanced with poetry and quoted wisdom on featured topics. Issues regularly included news briefs and accounts
of pending legislation at the state and federal level. Later, book reviews were
added, as well as an educational brief on the "plant of the month."

The *Survival Times* also became a forum where members of the
community could debate controversial issues like controlling population
growth, preventing urban sprawl, and saving the sea's resources. Articles
looked at the history of local planning and environmental issues, the
protection of wetlands, and offshore oil drilling.

While the focus of the magazine was regional and mostly South Coast–
oriented, sometimes statewide matters took center stage. One issue explored the question of whether Yosemite Valley was going to become too
commercial with the sale of the historic Curry Company to Universal
Studios. There was an article that lamented the loss of public transportation, the fabled Redline cable car system in Los Angeles that was driv-
en out of business in the 1960s by auto interests, and the decline of the
once-vibrant passenger rail service between Santa Barbara and San Diego.

Some of the material was prophetic. In the early '70s, writers predicted
that the Goleta Valley would one day be filled with houses—and it happened.
They explored the idea of making the Channel Islands a national park—and
it happened. Some warned that land north of El Capitan would be developed,
but it wasn't.

One of the most urgent topics of the times was the development of Santa Barbara's East Beach. What had been an ambitious 115-acre development proposal to transform the character of Santa Barbara's waterfront was drastically downsized and led to the development of a wonderful new park and other enhancements to one of America's great public waterfronts. In many ways, the *Survival Times* provided key information and articulated new directions for decision-makers to take.

The *Survival Times* also discussed wider-ranging topics: nuclear energy, population growth, timber harvesting, endangered species, agribusiness, and air and water quality. It offered an opportunity to air the expertise and opinions of members of the community, including professors, attorneys, and teachers who wrote pieces for the magazine.

All of this was done in a stylish way. Although monetary resources were slim, there was an abundance of talent in the organization. Artists like the now renowned Bud Bottoms and the talented graphic artist Judy Daniel created stunning illustrations for the magazine. Their artwork became a stylistic note of the *Survival Times*. Selecting art for the covers was a fun and creative process.

Producing a magazine at that time was much different and far more difficult than it is today. We didn't have computers—it was all typing, hand drawing, cutting, and pasting. Everything was done from scratch and then it all had to be put together for printing. Printer Dale Martin, who shared our vision and gave us a deep discount, was our benefactor. His credit said "Affectionately printed by Dale Martin."

Larry Penny was the first editor. When he moved to Oregon to take a college teaching position, Joan Crowder stepped in. She later worked as a writer and editor at the *Santa Barbara News-Press* for twenty-three years. Hal Conklin headed the production team as well as serving as a writer. He later became mayor of Santa Barbara.

We all had day jobs and many other activities, so our work was sporadic and intense and seemingly always under the threat of insufficient funds.

The *Survival Times* became an alternative voice in Santa Barbara to the News-Press, a fine newspaper with a noble tradition but very conservative when it came to matters of the environment. In a few years, an alternative weekly, the *Santa Barbara News and Review* (now *The Independent*) took over that role, and the *Survival Times* was no longer the only publication to call for environmental action in the community.

THE GARDEN AS A CENTERING FORCE

During the twentieth century, gardens for growing food and as a place for recreation were found throughout much of Europe, either within or in close proximity to cities. Called allotment gardens, they were often the work of voluntary associations, providing urban dwellers with access to land to cultivate as they wished—a pastime that would otherwise be denied them in the city. The United States had no such program, but during WWII many thousands of so-called Victory Gardens sprang up throughout the country to provide supplemental food for a country where food rationing had become prevalent.

In its earliest years, the CEC seized on the importance of emulating the European experience with gardens—providing food-growing and recreational opportunities in American towns and cities. Indeed, one of the first projects of the CEC was the development of a one-quarter-acre community garden in downtown Santa Barbara. We wanted to demonstrate to Santa Barbara that we could do more than talk about protecting or enhancing the environment. We were going to build a garden in the center of town!

The CEC secured, with the help of a local realtor, Peter Blakewell, the use of a vacant lot at the corner of Chapala and Figueroa Street for a community garden, the "Chapala Garden" as it came to be known. Peter Blakewell's generosity typified once again the many kindnesses that came our way more often than not from the most unexpected sources. Blakewell struck me as a very conservative, tough-minded man with a rather severe, even intimidating appearance. Outwardly, he was not someone who appeared likely to extend his hand to our motley crew. But appearances can indeed deceive. His outreach, like Mr. Pollock's, Mr. Crabtree's, and the grant writer from

Raytheon Corporation, taught me early on that you can never tell on the basis of externals like party affiliation, economic and social standing, and perceived self-interest where helping hands might come from. People like audacity, people like nerve, people like conviction. Our garden in the city was nothing if not bold, and that boldness prompted unexpected support.

A young Santa Barbara woman and CEC volunteer, Judy Patrick, was the force behind the garden. An accomplished horsewoman and horticulturalist, Judy was inspired by the idea of the garden, and for several years she devoted countless hours to its development and to talking to the many people who stopped by to marvel at this garden in the city. This attractive, high-octane woman was the Chapala Garden's ambassador to the community at large.

Chapala Garden: 1971, We build a garden in the center of the city.

The garden was built entirely by volunteers. A tractor was donated to clear and work the heavily compacted ground. A rail fence was erected, a water system was put in, and seed was procured from local nurseries. Many Santa Barbarans volunteered in tending the garden, which lasted only a few years until the land was sold and later transformed into what is now the Metropolitan Transit District bus hub.

The CEC garden was to carry forward the spirit of the Victory Gardens, but unlike its predecessors, this was to be an organic garden that would introduce people to growing food and flowers without depending on chemical fertilizers and pesticides. For some of the older people who were living downtown at the neighboring retirement hotels, the garden was a vivid oasis. They spoke to Judy about how they had been raised in a more rural America, a simpler time when it was common for people to grow their own food, prepare it, and eat it. The Chapala Garden dissolved the normal boundaries between people and their station in life—environmentalists, retired blue-collar workers, philanthropists, and old and young alike found in this garden a place to come together and simply enjoy the gifts that it gave forth. One of the most loyal gardeners at the Chapala Garden was "Okie Joe." Interviewed in the *Survival Times*, Okie, who lived in a retirement hotel just a block from the garden, had much to share about the garden and his life with the magazine's editors.

"Back in Oklahoma, I would ride a mule to work in the morning when I was ten years old. I'd take a team of mules and ride a cultivator all day just like a man." When asked if he minded being called "Okie," he replied, "I may be a fool, but I raise no reservations. Gee, I think it's an honor." This was one of many "Okisms"; he had a knack for capturing the essence of things and turning a colorful phrase.

"Practically everything we ate, that we served on the table, we raised on the farm and out of a big smoke house. We cured our own meat, canned lots of vegetables during the season; we had our own cotton gin, our own grist mill where we made our corn for corn bread."

"I wouldn't more think of owning a fifty-thousand-dollar home un-less I had a nice garden and fruit trees. A nice lawn is pretty, but so is a nice garden and fruit trees. I'd like to go out and pluck my own fruit. There's hardly a home in this town that couldn't have some fruit trees. You can't get a peach that tastes just like a peach. Why, we used to have Elberta Peaches on the farm there, and when you ate one of them great big things, the juice would run off your elbow. Why, these kids don't even know what a peach tastes like, or a fresh apple or fresh apricots, unless they happen to live on one of these ranches."

When asked if the Chapala Garden had a personal meaning to him, Okie replied, "For one thing, I feel a lot better physically, and it rests my mind. I don't have any worries anyway, but I won't accumulate any worries either, long as I'm over messing around that garden, because it's something I love to do. And it makes you feel like you're pretty close to nature. And when you're close to nature, you're close to God, whether you realize that or not. Because you're actually taking a personal hand in creation and making things grow."

DISPUTES AT THE URBAN-RURAL BORDER

The crisis that is rapidly building along the South Coast of Santa Barbara is part of a greater crisis facing all of America. One of its symptoms is the current sad state of the nation's great cities. We call their present condition megalopolis, and forces that have produced the megalopolis elsewhere are at work in Santa Barbara today.

ELAINE BURNELL

The explosive expansion of cities and suburbs following World War II was continuing unabated throughout much of the United States in the early 1970s. Santa Barbara, through the efforts of Pearl Chase, a grand dame in Santa Barbara history for her tireless preservation work and countless other civic endeavors, had initiated one of the first planning commissions in the United States. In 1925, a disastrous earthquake shook the city and leveled much of its downtown. In its aftermath, armed with a vision, Pearl Chase made the case for rebuilding the community to reflect its Spanish Colonial heritage, consisting of white plastered buildings and red-tile roofs. This she and her colleagues accomplished, thus creating one of the urban jewels in America.

But beyond the bounds of the city of Santa Barbara were undeveloped farms and ranches that were under the control of Santa Barbara County. Though the county had the foresight to develop a general plan for these lands, one that was considered visionary for the time, it anticipated a complete build-out of the Goleta Valley from the City of Santa Barbara boundary to Ellwood at the edge of the undeveloped Gaviota Coast.

Goleta Valley: In 1972 this was one of the nation's most rapidly urbanizing areas and was a battleground over the future of sprawl in the region.

There was very little questioning of whether growth was beneficial or even desirable; it was simply a given.

The sacrosanct role of growth and development was something that the CEC was willing to challenge when it came to the future of Santa Barbara. Just as in the aftermath of the oil spill, society was rethinking its relationship to energy development, air quality, and the protection of natural species; people were beginning to question the premise that growth and development were inevitable and necessary for a community's welfare. The CEC was soon to play a very large role in changing the way land use was thought of and practiced in the region, first by analyzing the impacts of the County General Plan, developing alternative plans for the Santa Barbara waterfront and Stearns Wharf, and participating in the landmark Impacts of Growth study that helped answer a question put to the community in 1974, "How big should Santa Barbara be?" in an unprecedented effort to preserve and protect the agricultural nature of the Carpinteria Valley. These works, among the first of their kind in the country, were remarkable for their vision, their thoroughness, and for the fact that they changed the face of the area for decades to come.

Inspired by Buckminster Fuller and Ian McHarg, the CEC, in cooperation with Santa Barbara's adult education program, offered a course in 1971 that took its name from one of Buckminster Fuller's inventions, "The World Game."[20] The World Game was an attempt by Fuller to produce a comprehensive inventory of the world's resources using the latest in information technology—the computer—as a tool to inventory and analyze vast amounts of information. Initially based at the University of Southern Illinois, where Fuller was a faculty member, the World Game spread throughout the United States and Europe.

Daniel Sisson, a political science major working on his PhD, joined me in teaching a year-long World Game course that morphed into a local comprehensive study of land use development in the Goleta Valley. While this study was inspired by the thinking of Buckminster Fuller, we found his ideas to be too abstract to apply locally and turned to the work of Ian McHarg for a practical means of translating ideas about land and natural-resource preservation and their relationship to guiding and containing development. McHarg, working with his students at the University of Pennsylvania's School of Landscape Architecture, had developed a mapping system that revealed what he called "the intrinsic suitability" of land for development, preservation, or for some other use. Working with about a dozen talented Santa Barbara adult ed students, geologists, geographers, economists, water specialists, and architects were able to make a professional quality analysis of the General Plan using the McHarg mapping system.

To put things in context, the Goleta Valley, fueled by the growing UCSB campus and a mushrooming research and development defense-based industry, was the second fastest growing metropolitan area in the United States in the early 1970s. Rapid subdivision development was underway, and it appeared that within less than a decade much of the Valley would be urbanized—an area about three miles deep and six miles in length.

Our plan, "Today's Action, Tomorrow's Profit: An Alternative for Community Development,"[21] was presented to a packed house at the Santa Barbara Planning Commission. Each of the class members contributed to preparing a three-slide-projector presentation that we considered to be the most effective way of communicating the plan to the community. While the presentation was much acclaimed, it had no immediate impact on the development process that was in progress. But it did contribute to a growing awareness that the General Plan was flawed and that there were alternatives to the accepted course of action, the complete urbanization of the Valley.

"Today's Action..." was edited by Elaine Burnell, a brilliant "student" in the class who had formerly served as the chief editor at the Center for the Study of Democratic Institutions, a landmark international think tank in Montecito. She had entered Smith College at age sixteen and was part of the US military team that broke the Japanese communication code during World War II. With students of that caliber in the class, my modest credentials and my youth were put to the severest of tests.

The World Game experience taught me what a small group of talented volunteers could contribute to important endeavors like planning the future of the community. In this case, many of these volunteers possessed skills that exceeded those of the trained professionals. They brought a rich palette of life experience, insights, and wisdom gained from their careers that could now be applied to improve the quality of life in their community. As I was to learn over and over again, it was efforts like this one where civic breakthroughs were made—not within the bureaucracies, not by the city councils and boards of supervisors. Civic insight, civic initiatives, volunteerism: this is where the best qualities of a community reside.

Interestingly enough, within just a few years, Santa Barbara County hired a planning firm to revise the General Plan, and the methodology they used to complete the work was modeled on the "intrinsic suitability" methodology of Ian McHarg. Techniques like McHarg's for identifying and mapping natural resources and scoring them for their value were seeping into the planning profession by the mid- to late 1970s.

EARTH DAY 1970

The Ecological Perspective:
All things on earth are alive and are differentiated only by their state in evolution.
Thus, all life should be treated with respect.
Man, as the highest-evolved being, has an evolutionary responsibility to all other evolving entities.
Ecology is grounded in the principles of cause-and-effect and interdependence.
Man is subject to the laws of ecology and is bound to them.

PERSONAL JOURNAL ENTRY, APRIL 22, 1972

The first Earth Day in Santa Barbara, held on April 22, 1970, was the idea of Senator Gaylord Nelson who, while on a flight home from witnessing the Santa Barbara Oil Spill, speculated, "If we could tap into the environmental concerns of the general public and influence the student anti-war energy into the environmental cause, we could generate a demonstration that would force the issue onto the national political agenda."

Nelson hired Denis Hayes to travel the nation to solicit participation in the first Earth Day event, scheduled to be held on April 22. Hayes visited Santa Barbara, where he sought our support both for a nationwide Earth Day celebration and a local one in Santa Barbara. There was no template for Earth Day, as there had never been one. Each community would decide, based on its resources and interests, what to do. In our case, we wanted the first Earth Day to emphasize practical actions that we could take in Santa Barbara to protect the resources of our area. How could we imagine that that 1970 Earth Day celebration would mush-room into the largest public event in human history, with an estimated twenty million participants around the world?

We petitioned the Santa Barbara City Council to allow us to block off one city block in front of the Ecology Center for an entire day. Volunteers built a Buckminster Fuller geodesic dome and created exhibits for organic gardening, natural foods, recycling, and alternative energy. Many commu-nity organizations developed their own booths that promoted solar energy, bicycling, zero population growth, Santa Barbara trails, marine protection, and, of course, getting oil out of the Santa Barbara Channel. Most of these endeavors, with the exception of controls on population, are now consid-ered mainstream and noncontroversial. They are supported by people of all political and philosophical persuasions. But in 1970, alternative energy, recycling, and organic gardening were considered to be fringe.

> We didn't know what kind of response we would get, but when the day came we were pleasantly surprised by a crowd that the Santa Barbara News-Press estimated at five thousand.
>
> **PERSONAL JOURNAL ENTRY, APRIL, 1970**

For forty-five years now, the Santa Barbara Earth Day has remained one of the seminal activities of the organization, and today it has become one of the most significant Earth Day celebrations in the United States, with some thirty-seven thousand participants visiting exhibits covering two square blocks in the heart of Santa Barbara—in raw numbers, nearly 20 percent of the local population.

What I find striking about Earth Day is that, unlike most festivals and celebrations, it's a knowledge-sharing event at its core. It wasn't always this way. In the earliest years it was the rock concerts at Earth Day that attracted a predominately young audience. But over the years, this has changed. Today, many more people come to Earth Day for exposure to ideas and to practical tools that can help transform their lives, their homes, their habits, their ways of thinking. There is now a very substantial component of Earth Day devoted to transportation innovations of every kind—

bicycles, motor bikes, alternative-fueled or ultra-efficient cars that are, or will soon be, available in the marketplace. We're seeing an outpouring of booths associated with neighborhood food production, vegetable and fruit growing, and food-sharing programs. There is also a mushrooming interest in the built environment, as demonstrated by a green building pavilion where building products are on exhibit that can transform the home into a more resource- efficient environment. Everything from home gray water systems, optimum home insulation materials, and more sustainable products of every sort are presented in an aesthetically refined environment. What a far cry this is from the Earth Days of decades ago, when the tools of sustainability were so embryonic; the solar collectors were primitive compared with the current systems; recycling was more of an idea than a routine practice; and there were only a handful of alternative-fueled, or fuel-efficient, vehicles. Now their numbers can't be contained on two sides of a block-long boulevard.

We should take heart in the growth in interest and commitment to education and change that Earth Day represents. It has become an increasingly prescient marker of change, at least at the individual and community levels. To a growing extent, the tools, technologies, and programs on display represent a transformative force that is incrementally moving society away from its dependency on petroleum, on food supplies that are remote and potentially vulnerable, on transportation systems that are outmoded, and on a built environment that needlessly wastes energy, water, and other resources.

I see in Earth Day an unfolding of a pattern language, a term used by UC Berkeley Professor of Architecture Christopher Alexander. He describes a "language which defines a town or community. These patterns can never be "designed or built in one fell swoop—but patient piecemeal growth designed in such a way that every individual act contributes create or generate these larger global patterns, will, slowly and surely over the years, make a community that has these global patterns in it."[22] Although *A Pattern Language* was written for architects and town planners, it set forth a design framework that I thought could help guide the choice of CEC projects. I saw the building of organic gardens accessible to community residents and school children, reclaiming discarded materials for recycling, plans to constrain urban sprawl, and green building as intrinsically interrelated activities that formed a pattern language of sustainability.

STANDING UP TO POWER

In the early years, struggles over land were the most powerful expression of the emerging environmental movement in our region. The stakes were great. Santa Barbara had not succumbed to the kind of urban sprawl and look-alike development that characterized much of Southern California. People took pride in the physical beauty, in Santa Barbara's sense of place, in its "village-like scale," its abundance of open space, and the ease of access to beaches, hillsides, and mountains along with views of the mountains and the ocean that defined the community. But the 1970s was a go-go time for development in California, and the pressures from the megalopolis to the south, the LA-San Diego conurbation, were ominous. As much as many local citizens wanted to maintain Santa Barbara's quality of life, the march of growth and progress northward seemed inevitable. The 1970s were to put the people of Santa Barbara to the severest of tests over its future—the development of its waterfront and the very size and density of the city itself.

One Sunday in February of 1972, I opened the *Santa Barbara News-Press* to a headline that screamed out at me: "Developer Set to Go." It was accompanied by a story and a front-page illustration of a proposed development. I tore through the story, learning the features of this proposed development intended for land that fronts Santa Barbara's famed East Beach[23], vacant land owned by the Southern Pacific Railroad extending north to US 101. If built, it would include a massive thousand-room hotel and two-thousand-person convention center, luxury condominiums, and a Ghirardelli Square–type shopping complex. In total the proposed project would encompass 115 acres, an area equivalent to the size of Santa Barbara's downtown.

Local elected officials, business leaders, and building and trades union officials were quoted en masse, all falling over themselves to endorse this colossus of a development. The whole power structure of the city was on board.

The following day several people from the predominantly Latino Eastside community came to the Ecology Center. They expressed a deep fear that if the project went ahead as planned, it would mean the end of their most accessible and treasured recreational resource, Palm Park. Palm Park formed a two-mile grass strip about one hundred yards wide that was used heavily for picnics, soccer, and swimming by Santa Barbara's predominately Latino community.

The Eastside is a large neighborhood of mostly wood-framed bungalow houses and is home to many of the gardeners, janitors, and restaurant, hotel, and construction workers who were and are the backbone of the local service economy, a critical part of the community fabric. If developed in the manner described in the newspaper, the people that came to the office feared they would lose their soccer fields, their picnic benches, and the beach access they had enjoyed for so long. If not lose it outright, their recreation in the future would play out in the shadow of a massive tourist enclave that would be most uninviting to them. They came to the Ecology Center to enlist our resistance to the development.

We listened and felt the depth of their concerns. We were honored that they would reach out to a fledgling environmental organization when there was historically little if any interaction between our worlds. We were just as troubled by the proposed development as they were, but for very different reasons. We decided to look into the situation. We examined the allowable land uses, the city's General Plan, and other factors and found out that a hotel was a permissible use on the site; there was no proposed violation of the existing zoning or planning standards. But the plans for the rerouting of Cabrillo Boulevard, classified as a state scenic highway, behind the hotel seemed dubious.

As we thought through the situation it was clear that stopping this project that had gathered such steam wasn't an option. But maybe we could do something to slow down the momentum and try and scale it back to something less overwhelming. I remember telling our board of directors that the likelihood of altering the trajectory of the project was less than 5 percent, making it a veritable David-versus-Goliath struggle.

Through a coincidence, another epic Santa Barbara land use issue was also in play—the proposed removal of the infamous stoplights on US 101 that created freeway gridlock, especially during the summer vacation months. For decades, the California Department of Transportation (CALTRANS) had wanted to remove the lights and establish a new section of freeway to end the snarl. The famous architectural firm of Skidmore, Owings & Merrill (SOM) had sent down two of its partners from the San Francisco office to participate in a design session sponsored by CALTRANS. I went to the session and was introduced to two individuals from SOM—Jerry Goldberg, a Harvard-trained urban planner, and John Fisher-Smith, a managing partner and Fellow of the American Institute of Architects. We had a conversation about what was being proposed and how we wanted to offer an alternative, but we lacked the skills to do so. Fisher-Smith and Goldberg told us that it was SOM's policy to loan out design time to community organizations with an interest in civic planning. Why on earth would they do that? Because it was the early 1970s, and the social foment that permeated America in those days had influenced design leaders like Nathaniel Owings, one of the firm's founders, to assume some social responsibility for the built environment. After checking back in with the firm upon their return, they told me that they could "loan" us some of Jerry and John's time to help us fashion a plan for the waterfront.

Knowing that we now had top-drawer talent to back us up, we formed an ad hoc organization that became known as the Committee for Santa Barbara, and we set up a design center in the back room of the Ecology Center. We solicited the ideas of literally hundreds of Santa Barbarans in that back room and, with the help of SOM, ideas were translated into designs. In those days I shuttled between San Francisco and Santa Barbara,

Cabrillo Boulevard:
This magnificent waterfront treasure was threatened by a massive Southern Pacific,
Hyatt development that would have changed the nature of the city.

and with the help of the CEC's new codirector, Hal Conklin, and many others in the community, we developed a "A Plan for East Beach."

The CEC persuaded the Santa Barbara *News-Press* to run another banner headline, several months after their "Developer Set to Go" one. This time it read, "An Alternative Plan for East Beach," and with it we had a toe-hold on the future. Unlike the Southern Pacific and Hyatt Plan, A Plan for East Beach tapped into Santa Barbara's rich planning legacy that had begun in the early 1920s under Pearl Chase and other prominent Santa Barbarans. These community visionaries commissioned the Olmsted Brothers, the firm of the late Frederick Law Olmsted, who with his partner Calvert Vaux designed New York's Central Park and San Francisco's Golden Gate Park, to prepare a waterfront plan for Santa Barbara. The Olmsted Plan of 1924[24] proposed that much of the area slated by Southern Pacific and Hyatt for development be developed as a park instead.

In 1924, a small but influential group of Santa Barbarans formed the East Beach Improvement Association to counter a move to commercially develop the East Beach waterfront. With their own funds, they bought up what is now Chase Palm Park south of Cabrillo Boulevard extending from Stearns Wharf to the Bird Refuge and held this land until it could be purchased from the city.

"Today, some fifty years later, another effort is being made to develop the East Beach waterfront commercially. This group, known as the Committee for Santa Barbara, has been authorized by the City Council to work with the City authorities, land owners, developers, and interested parties to develop a comprehensive plan for the "Southern Pacific Area," the 115-acre parcel lying between the freeway, Cabrillo, Milpas, and Santa Barbara Streets...Hopefully the plan will represent the best long-range interests of the Santa Barbara community—public and private, economic and aesthetic. But if the community is to reap from this effort, it must oppose any interim attempts by the developer to proceed."[25]

Reaching back to the bold vision of the 1924 Olmsted Brothers, the Committee for Santa Barbara's plan included a park of about thirty-five acres between Cabrillo Boulevard and the existing railroad tracks, mixed-income housing, a modest-sized conference center, a motel and transportation center, and a redeveloped Stearns Wharf. At the time, it was transitioning away from the working oil platform it had been up until the Santa Barbara Oil Spill. Hal Conklin took particular interest in seeing Stearns Wharf redeveloped on a Santa Barbara scale: pedestrian friendly and buildings of human scale. And not too closed in by structures that would deny people ample views of the mountains and ocean. When Hal was to go on to become a Santa Barbara City councilman and mayor, one of his first accomplishments was his work on creating a Stearns Wharf that struck the right balance between commercial development and public open space.

The Olmsted plan observed, "There are places in Europe where beautiful buildings are erected along the waterfronts, but it is impossible to point to any place in this country where it has been done. We wish to profit by the experience of Santa Monica, Santa Cruz, and other coast towns whose beach fronts are not practically spoiled by the class of buildings which have been erected, and our past experience in Santa Barbara shows we can hardly expect anything else to be put on our waterfront unless we do something to prevent it."

Our plan called for a hotel greatly reduced in size and the complete elimination of the commercial area to prevent the further diffusion of the heart of Santa Barbara. It reflected the views of many prominent businesses in town who felt that building a commercial center on the proposed scale would kill an already-struggling downtown. Other planning features included a multitransit hub, bikeways and walkways, and the creation of a Chumash Indian Village museum that would pay homage to the original inhabitants of Santa Barbara who had built some of their largest villages nearby. These components introduced sustainability concepts into the park plan, reflecting the orientation of our work. They were more a statement of intention than a presentation of ideas that we thought would get traction in the final park design.

The Plan for East Beach began what was to be a ten-year battle to preserve and protect East Beach and to expand park recreation opportunities to the north of Cabrillo Boulevard. Joining me in the battle were two of Santa Barbara's prominent citizens, James Gildea and Robert Easton, and allies from the Citizens Planning Association, a venerable planning watchdog organization founded by Pearl Chase.

At the local government level, a hometown newspaper is the vital source of information that communities rely upon to know what it going on. In the early '70s, journalism played an essential role in covering the work of the CEC. We were fortunate to have Robert Sollen, slight of build, bespectacled, mild-mannered, with an almost whimsical disposition that belied a steely and seasoned newspaperman. It was Bob Sollen who became the community's eyes and ears on all aspects of Santa Barbara's oil spill and what followed. By now he had become the paper's environmental writer, covering the many facets of Santa Barbara's burgeoning environmental movement. Although the *News-Press* editorial page was solidly in support of the proposed development, to its credit, Sollen was given great latitude to cover the stories that interested him, and one of those was the emerging battle over the pending development of the Santa Barbara waterfront. Sollen faithfully attended and covered the many meetings held by the Committee for Santa Barbara that served as a forum between the development and community interests. It was Sollen who was responsible for bringing the Committee for Santa Barbara's Plan for East Beach to the attention of the editors. And I commend the *News-Press* editors who made the bold decision to run a banner cover story about our alternative plan for the waterfront just a few months after the first story appeared.

After several years of negotiations with the Southern Pacific Railroad and Hyatt Corporation, the Committee for Santa Barbara thought it had reached an unofficial agreement over the proposed project, whereby the condominiums, the commercial center, the size of the conference center, and the size and scale of the hotel were reduced, and land was set aside for an expanded public park. Then came an unexpected turn of events that scuttled the agreement. Fess Parker, the handsome Disney actor, every American child's hero as Daniel Boone and Davy Crockett with his beguiling charm, had become a trailer-park and real-estate magnate and entered the battle for the Santa Barbara waterfront. He owned rights to a small portion of the waterfront property controlled by Hyatt and the Southern Pacific Railroad. He refused to participate in the settlement and instead leveraged his interest in this property into a controlling interest over the fate of the hotel and convention center. Thus began a new phase of the struggle.

The idea that I might now have to go head-to-head with Fess Parker, a hero figure from my childhood, was almost too much to bear. Like millions of small children in the 1950s, I had idolized Davy Crockett. I wore my coonskin cap as I whiled away hours watching Davy take on the Indians and bring justice on the frontier and die a hero at the Alamo. Now Davy had morphed into someone who, in my view, threatened the future of Santa Barbara, a wily, engaging, and powerful man seeking to impose a development that was clearly at odds with Santa Barbara's long history of preserving and protecting the waterfront.

Joining me in challenging this development were my colleagues Hal Conklin, who was now the codirector of the CEC; Robert Easton; and James Gildea. Bob and Jim proved to be two of the best allies we could ever have. Jim was a retired Union Pacific Railroad executive who began life as a poor Irish boy in Leadville, Colorado. Self-taught, he went on to become a colonel in the US Army during World War II, responsible for moving supplies through Iran and into the Soviet Union. His efforts won him the Medal of Lenin from the Soviet Union. He later was hand- picked by King Faisal to oversee the construction of the Aramco Railroad in Saudi Arabia shortly after the war.

Bob Easton was born in Santa Maria and lived a ranch life as a boy. He attended Harvard and Stanford and was an aspiring writer before volunteering for the infantry during World War II in the Italian and French campaigns. Following the war, he settled with his family in Texas, where he edited a newspaper. He later moved back to Santa Barbara with his young wife, Jane, and their three children. Jane was the daughter of the famed pulp-fiction writer who wrote under the name Max Brand. Bob had penned a well-reviewed novel about ranch life in California, *The Happy Man*[26], before he went off to war, and he would later complete an important trilogy on the history of California after writing the definitive account of the Santa Barbara Oil Spill, *Black Tide.*

Bob and Jim were indefatigable in their opposition to the proposed hotel project. Though they were approaching old age at the time, they worked ceaselessly, speaking at meetings, writing op-ed pieces, and cajoling people in the business community to support us, and in the process we forged a fast friendship that endured till the end of their lives. Their gravitas as pillars of the Santa Barbara community gave Hal and me a level of standing in the community that we could not otherwise have had at our young age.

To further our campaign against the planned development, we formed an ad hoc committee, the Committee for Santa Barbara, and established as its honorary cochairman the legendary Pearl Chase.

After many years of struggle, the Committee for Santa Barbara, aided by the Citizens Planning Association, reached an accord with Fess Parker to limit the size of the hotel to 360 rooms with Parker committing acreage west of the hotel for park purposes, which, combined with city-owned land, would create a twelve-acre park expansion. This accord became incorporated into an approved development plan for the site by the city of Santa Barbara. The nearly half-mile wall of three- and four-story buildings that was to be the hotel was reduced to mostly one- and two-story elements set way back from Cabrillo Boulevard to preserve views of the Riviera and the Santa Ynez Mountains from Palm Park and Cabrillo Boulevard. The proposed rerouting of Cabrillo Boulevard was stopped, and so was the condominium development. These concessions were consistent with what the Committee for Santa Barbara fought for. There were parties in the community who felt that not enough land was protected and that the hotel was still too big. They sponsored a referendum to scuttle the agreement, a disheartening prospect given the decade or more of work it took to reach it. The referendum created a short-lived deep rift in the environmental community. During the initiative campaign and the run-up to the vote, the Committee for Santa Barbara leadership stuck by the agreement and urged a vote of No! on principle. Fortunately, our position prevailed by a strong majority and with the vote, the deal was sealed. With an affirmative vote behind us and the deal firm, a portion of the great Olmsted Plan developed in 1924 was realized. On May 30, 1998, the City of Santa Barbara dedicated the twelve-acre Chase Palm Park north of Cabrillo Boulevard, an important addition to Santa Barbara's wonderful, publically oriented waterfront.

A FARM IN THE CITY

As Richard Merrill saw it in pursuit of his PhD in ecology, diversity was the basis of a healthy ecology, but the focus in commercial agriculture was to subvert diversity in practice. Scientists were busy in the genetics labs, the chemical factories, and in the land grant colleges masterminding schemes to obliterate diversity in agriculture. Vast tracts of monocultures were on the drawing boards along with fashioning genetic strains and the pesticides and fertilizers to sustain these "factories in the fields." There was hardly a soul in the academic community challenging this paradigm.

PERSONAL JOURNAL ENTRY, APRIL 1973

One of the boldest of our many bold experiments in the 1970s was the El Mirasol Polyculture Farm. One sunny, breezy spring afternoon I found myself, bag lunch in hand, walking to Alameda Park a few blocks from our office. As I approached the park, my eye wandered to an empty city block across the street covered with tall green grass interspersed with broken paved walkways and the remnants of foundations. This was the site of the once elegant El Mirasol Hotel, converted from a residence to, by today's standards, a boutique hotel, which had been razed many years earlier. I walked about, found a soft patch of grass, lay down, and gazed into the sky, letting my mind roam. Images appeared in my mind's eye of this site becoming a mosaic of gardens, solar collectors, compost piles, geodesic domes. These images came to me like quick lightning; I had learned by now to trust flashes of insight. They lingered with me and ideas began to congeal into a plan.

There were two people I knew at the time whom I could trust to give me perspective on what I had seen. Warren Pierce was a talented botanist, photographer, and filmmaker who had studied film at UCLA. He had been my botany teaching assistant at the university. He too had been inspired by the horticultural vision of Alan Chadwick. If anyone could speak to the possibilities of bringing my vision to life, it was Warren.

And there was Richard Merrill. Richard was a doctoral candidate in the biology department at the university. Big, burly, tough, fiercely independent, and ambitious, he had been a tight end at UC Berkeley where he did his undergraduate work. Richard was drawn to both alternative agriculture and renewable energy. He was affiliated with Dr. John Todd, founder of the New Alchemy Institute in Cape Cod. The New Alchemy Institute, through John's leadership, was to pioneer alternative municipal waste treatment systems. His colleague at New Alchemy, Dr. Bill McLarney, was among the first scientists in the country to develop aquaculture to raise the prolific freshwater fish tilapia for human consumption in the United States.

Richard and Warren had a passion for teaching. We talked about possibilities over days and weeks and gradually brought our thoughts together in a plan for the city block, an urban educational farm that would serve as a learning center, a laboratory for testing and demonstrating nonchemical means of growing food, and alternative technologies, and to teach courses offered through the community college. The University of California wasn't oriented to the kind of applied learning that we were interested in. So a traditional career path built around our ideas was not an academic possibility.

Young people throughout the country in the early 1970s were open to pursuing out-of-the-box projects and "careers," if they could be called that. We weighed the options; we were by nature risk takers fueled by visions we couldn't repress. The country was full of young people like us then, searching for answers to the questions of our time.

Of course, between the idea and the reality were formidable barriers. To start with, the CEC didn't own El Mirasol; it was owned by the Santa Barbara Museum of Art, which planned to use the property to build a new museum. The likelihood that this staid organization would make El Mirasol available to young idealists from the CEC and the university was, at best, doubtful. Even if they did allow the CEC to use it, the CEC would have to obtain a permit from the city to build the project. Why would the city allow a collection of young, "questionable" university types to bring their experimental ideas to the very center of town? After all, these were students from the campus where there had been riots against the Vietnam War, where a student had been killed the night the Bank of America was burned down. How could young people from "that place" be trusted to contribute to the quality of life in beautiful Santa Barbara? And even if these doubts could be overcome, the financial reality of our organization was that we could barely support the Ecology Center and downtown garden. How on earth could we pull this grand scheme off?

But by this time, the CEC was beginning to attract broader support from both within and without Santa Barbara. Carol Valentine, a prominent museum board member, was fascinated by the downtown community garden. She thought it a wonderful invention, and she asked her colleagues on the museum board to entertain a presentation by the CEC.

The prospect of meeting Santa Barbara's elite, its most stalwart lawyers, accountants, and socialites and patrons, was quite intimidating for Warren, Richard, and me. What chance did we have of convincing this risk-averse board to support our dreams?

How furiously we prepared for that meeting: developing a site plan, describing the teaching programs we'd offer, and explaining how we would develop the financial and staff resources to pull it off! We rehearsed our presentation again and again. This was it. We would never get a second chance.

When our moment came, Carol graciously introduced us to the museum board and we proceeded to make our case. We left the room with absolutely no idea if anyone was really listening to us, let alone agreeing with our proposition. A few days later, to our astonishment, we were informed that it was a go. An agreement was prepared. Under the agreement, the CEC would maintain the property at no cost to the museum, and that would save them thousands of dollars a year. We would be responsible for all utilities and water and carry the necessary liability insurance to protect the museum from harm.

The next challenge was obtaining a conditional use permit from the Santa Barbara City Council. With the help of influential Santa Barbarans such as Robert Easton, Selma Rubin, Carol Valentine, and Jim Gildea, who were now converts to the CEC mission, the CEC made its case to the council and the conditional use permit was granted.

Now the CEC's dream was to be tested by the fixed truth of the site— the immovable objects, the pathways and foundations, the need for water, and the immense task of building acres of gardens. How to begin?

The first efforts were directed toward breaking up and removing the foundations and walkways. A rented tractor broke up most foundations, but some were too big and were left in place. During the excavation process, an old well head was located, and with the help of an old-time well-driller (Floyd Wells), it proved to be a gusher. This gave the CEC an independent and abundant source of water. And the discovery of this free water source endeared the CEC to some of the museum board members. There seemed to be, if I must say, a bit of magic in discovering a major water source on the property.

A heavyset tractor operator working a project across the street came up to me, introducing himself as Webb Pitts. He asked if I needed help to turn the many large piles of materials being composted on site. I told him point-blank that we didn't have a dime to spend on hiring him. He said, "No problem, what I see here, I like. I've got a 'dozer, a skip loader and backhoe, my body, and I'm free one day a week. Just let me know."

Though skeptical, I called him and pressed him to make sure he was not expecting money that we didn't have. He answered, "You don't have to worry about my having an ulterior motive. It's as simple as this: You folks are doing something that has a good feel to it, and I appreciate that you're doing it. Since I'm making out okay—I mean, I can eat, pay the rent for my house and all of my equipment—shouldn't I help?"[27] True to his word, Pitts showed up the following Monday, and what a difference he made for us.

What is it that made people who probably didn't share many of our viewpoints take the initiative to lend a hand to the work? I think they were just taken by the fact that physical work wasn't beneath us. We weren't asking people to do something that we weren't prepared to do ourselves. If we were dreamers, we were practical dreamers, and practicality is a deeply held virtue, or at least it was, in America.

Within a year the center area of El Mirasol, about one and a half acres, was converted to four quadrants of raised beds, all of which were hand-dug using Alan Chadwick's refined but tortuously labor-intensive methods. To build the fertility of the ground, the CEC established a large-scale on-site composting program that included a variety of composting approaches, windrows, static piles, and an accelerated composting approach, where materials were turned at three-day intervals. Manures were brought in from horse stables and the annual horse show; food wastes were delivered from restaurants, and even grape pumice was procured from the Santa Barbara Winery.

EL MIRASOL POLYCULTURE FARM

At one time as much as several hundred tons of horse manure was being composted in the center of town. Once, during a cold spell, the heat generated by the composting manure created a vapor cloud above the piles, which prompted some neighbors to call the fire department in a state of alarm. It took some convincing to explain that what they were seeing wasn't smoke, but condensation from the warm air from the compost mingling with the cool atmosphere. After that experience, composting at the site was downsized.

The purpose of all this composting was to support the cultivation of fruits, vegetables,
herbs, and flowers. Compost
was the foundation of the CEC's
horticultural system.

Simple plastic greenhouses
were built to start seedlings, and
a large geodesic dome was erected
to serve as the nursery for raising seedlings until they were big
enough to be transplanted into
the raised beds.

Apart from the horticultural focus of the project, many
"appropriate technologies," to
borrow the term of the late

Children in the garden.

E. F. Schumacher, were demonstrated at El Mirasol, including solar water heaters, herb dryers, cookers, a manure-fed biogas unit to generate methane for cooking, and a "chicken tractor," a chicken pen that was moved down the raised beds to remove harmful insects and to fertilize the soil.

Vegetables for sale at El Mirasol.

El Mirasol was used extensively by the Santa Barbara Community College as a teaching garden and outdoor environmental education center. Students were taught by Warren and Richard the horticultural methods used by Alan Chadwick. They learned how to compost; how to companion plant to prevent garden diseases; how to create natural insectaries by cultivating certain flowering herbs and flower varieties; and they were introduced to vegetable, fruit, and flower varieties that were especially adapted to Santa Barbara's Mediterranean climate. Thousands of schoolchildren came to El Mirasol over its two-and-a-half-year life, where they had their first experience with gardening, composting, recycling, and solar energy. A German television documentary on emerging environmental consciousness in the United States featured El Mirasol, and many publications, including the LA Times and Sunset magazine, ran stories about this strange but powerful garden in the center of the city. There wasn't anything quite like it in the country.

Perhaps more than any other aspect of El Mirasol Farm, the vegetable stand developed a regular clientele consisting almost entirely of neighborhood people who became proponents of the urban farm because they were able to experience it in a most practical way. The CEC took in about $150 per week from this stand, at the time not an inconsiderable sum. Considering our budget in hindsight, this aspect of El Mirasol pointed to a future when community-supported agriculture (CSA) would come of age in America.

El Mirasol was a great laboratory experience for the CEC, full of innovation and creativity. Virtually every aspect of organic gardening, recycling, composting, the use of biological controls as an alternative to pesticides, and alternative energy were applied on a significant scale.

Solar energy became a prominent focus of the project with the arrival of Irving Thomas, a Cal Poly graduate and an electrical engineer working at that time on the B-1 Bomber under development by Raytheon Corporation, a major defense contractor in the area. Irving was conflicted by his work on stealth weaponry and longed to work on alternative technology, especially solar energy. El Mirasol gave him a place to apply this passion. Drawing on savings and an innate frugality, he cut his ties with Raytheon and became a full-time presence at El Mirasol, our resident solar engineer. He built solar-water-heating and passive-solar-space-heating demonstrations and patented a solar herb dryer as he deepened his understanding of solar applications. Soon he was marketing this newly developed skill to local architects and engineering and construction firms, who were finding a few clients here and there willing to try to heat buildings and water using this new technology.

Warren Pierce developed a wide range of compost experiments to determine which systems might work best for garden-scale development of one acre or less. He built a system of compost bins that allowed us to make fully matured compost in as little time as one month by rotating manures and vegetable wastes in a series of bins that would be turned every few days. This was the Indore method that we imported from India. It was labor-intensive, and we concluded later on that it required too much labor, so it was scuttled in favor of more passive systems such as piling manures and vegetable wastes in layers and then covering them with earth to sit for six months. Altogether six or seven composting methods were tried out and perhaps several thousand tons of compost were produced as a result, making El Mirasol an exceptional laboratory for finding the right methods to support the gardens.

South African farmer L. John Fry builds a chicken manure digester at El Mirasol.

Twenty years later, I was serving on the California Integrated Waste Management Board in Sacramento that was responsible for regulating landfills, incinerators, recycling, composting, and waste prevention. I was developing regulations and programs to try to recover and compost the ten million tons of organic materials that California was sending to landfills as solid waste from our homes and businesses. We had to find ways to promote the use of compost in California's thirty-billion-dollar agricultural industry, and as I led this effort, I was able to draw on our rich experiences at El Mirasol to help fashion our program, including developing the state regulations that were to guide compost development in the Golden State.

Like all laboratory work, El Mirasol was also full of the mundane and dreary labor and failures. The aesthetics of the project never lived up to Alan Chadwick's UC Santa Cruz garden. Not even close. Instead of dazzling the beholder, the gardens were often ragged and appeared relatively unkempt. This put off members of the community who would otherwise have been enthusiastic backers of the project. Another limiting factor to what could be accomplished was a nagging realization that whatever effort was invested, it was going to be short-lived. The museum would take the land back and then nothing would be left of all of the CEC's efforts.

El Mirasol Polyculture Farm, 1972-1974.
We built a farm in the center of Santa Barbara.

By the end of the second year, much of what the CEC set out to do was accomplished, and the project was starting to reach a point of diminishing returns. Then the museum notified the CEC that its tenancy was about to end. It had decided to sell the property instead of build on it; the end had come.

At its best, El Mirasol had become a much more serious and commanding endeavor than the little downtown garden the CEC had begun with. Whether or not one had a problem with the aesthetics, the level of experimentation was undeniably bold and visionary; large and enduring concepts of sustainability had been explored, and this portended larger things to come.

El Mirasol Polyculture Farm was the work of young people who didn't drop out of society as many were doing at the time. They were not afraid or cynical about the world as they found it. They were tough-minded visionaries who had the strength of conviction and will to explore alternative ways of living in a modern world, using their university training, including embryonic computer technology and other technical knowledge, to do so. They struggled against great odds and were subject to intense criticism. But time has shown that this work, however limited by financial constraints and time, was touching a keynote of the world that lay ahead. Those crazy-seeming compost piles, the early recycling work, the search for nonpolluting energy and more environmentally friendly ways to build, and the creation of work environments that could meet the needs of talented people who could not flourish within the university confines or as yet find opportunities in the commercial world, was of great value in and of itself.

WHEN DREAMS GET TOUGH

With the end of El Mirasol, the museum was set to sell the property; the market price was about $800,000, which by today's terms seems a paltry sum but was a princely fortune then. The property seemed destined to become a condominium complex, a depressing prospect given all that the CEC had invested in the project. If this was to happen, then at least we should try to influence what it might become. We prepared a counter-development proposal with the help of Lawrence Thompson, a Santa Barbara architect with an avid interest in solar energy. Our plan was a bold articulation of sustainable development drawing on all the elements that had been developed at the El Mirasol Polyculture Farm. It called for forty-eight condominium units at two- and three-story heights. Two intensive horticultural elements of one-half acre each were presented—one composed of vegetables and flowers and a second reserved for dwarf fruit trees and a fully containerized composting area. The condominium buildings would be off grid and facing south to optimize solar water heating and passive heat gain. The remaining land was to be used for traditional activities such as a children's play area, parking, and perimeter landscaping.

The horticultural elements would be overseen by a master gardener, one who could perhaps aspire to the level of aesthetics that Alan Chadwick achieved. We believed that, based upon its experience in intensive vegetable and fruit production, a well-managed garden could produce a good percentage of the fruits and vegetables that would be consumed by the residents and that they, in turn, could pay a good price for organically raised food that would contribute substantially to paying the salary of the horticulturalist. We thought that this food-growing system just might work financially, creating a demand for skilled horticulturalists and the training that would produce them. Vegetable wastes from the residents, along with those generated by the garden, would be composted on site in aerated bins. Residents would either bring these materials to the composting site or have them collected at the home. This system anticipated what is now referred to as green and food waste recycling. An estimate was made as to how much compost could be produced from the condominiums, and it was determined that there should be enough waste to generate enough compost to sustain the entire landscape.

We were always thinking as we went how our ideas could apply to the larger society and economy. Whether it was this idea of a sustainable urban village, recycling, composting, or green building, we realized that if our work was to make a difference, it ultimately had not only to capture people's imaginations but offer the possibility of meaningful and gainful employment.

But our design exercise proved to be a nonstarter. Although some museum trustees were sympathetic to the CEC vision for the property, the development concept was simply that; it lacked financial and technical feasibility, and it died a quiet death.

The end of El Mirasol, anticipated as it was, was a difficult time for the organization. The staff believed that the CEC should find a permanent site for continuing its pioneering work, but the reality was that the organization's resources were still meager. They included a small dump truck, tools, pipe, and construction materials; there was no money available for acquiring and developing a permanent site and dim prospects for a philanthropic windfall.

A BEACON ON THE HILL

Throughout the 1970s and early 1980s there were scattered attempts throughout the United States to create learning centers to demonstrate and teach what today we call "sustainability." In the Bay Area there was the Farallones Institute, led by Lee Swenson, initially located in Berkeley and later on a large rural site near the town of Occidental, north of San Francisco. Designed in part by Sim Van der Ryn, a professor of architecture at UC Berkeley, the institute demonstrated housing, energy, and waste system designs that suggested how communities could live more lightly on the land. In Snowmass, Colorado, there emerged the Rocky Mountain Institute, founded by Amory and Hunter Lovins. Amory Lovins, author of the landmark *Foreign Affairs* article in 1976, "Soft Energy Path," was a brilliant young physicist who articulated an energy future built around promoting energy efficiency and renewable energy. Located deep in the Ozarks in Arkansas was Meadow Creek, the creation of the Orr brothers. David, a former professor of political science at the University of North Carolina, had the idea to build a learning center deep in the Ozarks to teach sustainable living in a way he could not do at the time within the confines of the academy. Wilson Orr was a contractor who was well equipped to build the center on roughly eighty acres of land they jointly owned. To get to Meadow Creek, you flew into Little Rock. A Meadow Creek staff person would pick you up in a van, and from there it was a near three-hour drive into the Ozarks, passing through small towns like Clinton, Arkansas, where Sam Walton had founded Walmart. Along the way were the ubiquitous chicken coops that struck me as the most prevalent human marker in the Ozark mountain country.

David Orr was later to take the mantle of the Environmental Studies Department at Oberlin College and create a learning center there that has achieved international recognition. Lovins was to continue to build the Rocky Mountain Institute into a premier renewable energy think tank that influenced the automobile industry and even the Department of Defense. Brown University also developed an important learning center. Known as the Urban Environmental Laboratory, it was the creation of Dr. Harold Ward, a professor of chemistry who felt that experiential learning was a critical complement to a core curriculum of concepts and theories. Many of his students performed critical environmental studies for the state of Rhode Island and went on to distinguished careers in the sciences, business, and public policy. These were among the boldest of the sustainable learning centers at the time, all very much expressions of their leaders and their landscapes.

The Mesa Project was, in its own way, part and parcel of these efforts. We had considerable interaction with the Brown and Meadow Creek programs. David Orr and Harold Ward spent time with us at the CEC and we reciprocated. This cross-pollination of ideas and programs was one of the most exciting aspects of our work.

It was a time of extreme transition, a time of moving from projects that were conceived for the short-term to greater permanence. We began scouring the Santa Barbara coast, a search that went on for the better part of a year, assessing available farmland, ranches, and pockets of agricultural land within the urbanizing Goleta Valley. We hoped to find a site that was large enough to establish a major agricultural opportunity, housing for staff and interns, and provide a buffer between our work and our neighbors so as to minimize the conflicts that we anticipated, such as those created by composting or the use of solar collectors and wind generators. Our selection process also underscored the importance of being located in close proximity to the local population, so that visits from the public and from the local schools, the community college, and the university would be convenient.

In the end we settled for a five-and-a-half-acre hilltop site located on the Santa Barbara Mesa, some several hundred feet above the city, with spectacular views of the Santa Ynez Mountains and the heart of the down-town. The property had an old dairy building on it still—a timeworn relic of another era when dairy cows grazed on the Mesa's grasslands. One of the few large remaining expanses of open land, it had an intrinsically wild and noble air about it: almost in the city and at the same time distant and even remote. When I first saw it, I was taken aback. It didn't appear like much could be done with it; the building area was compact and maybe too limit-ed. And as for the access, it looked forbidding. There was a dirt road from below that had serviced the dairy—but making this into a bona fide access would require major grading; it would cost a fortune. A more feasible al-ternative was to bring in a road from above. There was a dedicated access and utility easement defining this connection. The easement was studied by us and presented to our attorney for review, but this review was done in haste. We purchased the property with a loan guarantee by Jim Gildea, and Warren, Irving, and I donated down payments of $3,000 each, which for us was a considerable sum of money at the time. Soon thereafter, we learned to our horror that the easement would not work. It was too steep and would require an immense amount of earth moving and even a small bridge to access the site.

The problem with the easement hit me especially hard. I agonized over my failure to be more vigilant in making sure that all aspects of this pur-chase were understood. But I wasn't adept at reading lines on a contour map showing the locations of the easement. If I had, or others had seen, it would have been clear to us that access was a formidable challenge that had, no doubt, kept others from buying the property. Now everything we had put into pulling the project off so far was in jeopardy. It didn't help that one of our mentors, on hearing the news, thought that we should pack it in, cut our losses, and shut the CEC down. I was miserable.

Fortunately, his wasn't the only voice. Jim Gildea, that wise and wry old Irishman who had walked into the bank and got us our loan based on his personal stature in the community and his string of business successes, spoke in his sage way: "We're by no means done; things will work out. There's someone out there watching over us, I know that." This expression of support in a time of personal darkness was something I badly needed, but good words could only go so far. Could we actually persevere and dig out of this mess?

Though thwarted for the time being, we decided to continue to invest in articulating what the project could mean for Santa Barbara and beyond. With our limited means we nonetheless hired Lawrence Thompson, our architect to date, to prepare a site plan. The plan that emerged came to be known as the Mesa Project. It called for the development of a horticultural center and three to five housing units for students and interns. The buildings would exemplify what we would call today "green building": the careful use of natural lighting, solar space and water heating, water recycling, and a drought-tolerant landscape at a scale that the community would have to take notice of. They would form the infrastructure for an exciting learning environment that would continue the work begun at the community garden and El Mirasol in a more permanent setting.

While planning for our future was exciting and fulfilling, there was the ever-present reality that the land we needed to gain access to the site was owned by a developer whose attorney turned out to be James Black. He had represented Southern Pacific Railroad, the company whose development plans for the Santa Barbara waterfront had been frustrated by Hal and me. What kind of karma was this? In a meeting with Black it was obvious that he enjoyed having us over a barrel. After several entreaties to win him over with a generous sum of money for the easement, it became clear that he was going to make the CEC twist in the wind over its future. He was the cat and we were the mouse.

WHEN YOU'RE BLOCKED, ADAPT

With our road access effectively blocked, what could we do with the property and with our programs as we waited for resolution of the easement conundrum? The situation was very tough. I had staff and community support ramped up for the launch of powerful new programs, but all were contingent on use of the site, or so I thought. All of us confront vexing problems, some of which seem like a Gordian knot, too difficult to untie.

In my case, I needed to gain a bigger perspective on the problem than I could generate from within. During my university days I had become acquainted with the great Chinese tome the *I Ching: The Book of Changes*, a mid-third- to fourth-century BC work that places great emphasis on the role of chance, or what we often refer to as coincidence, in determining human events, both individually and collectively.[28] For millennia, the *I Ching* has been consulted by heads of state and regular folks to shed light on problems, especially those of a seemingly intractable nature like the one I was facing.

As the preface to the *I Ching* notes, "An incalculable amount of human effort is directed to combating and restricting the nuisance or danger represented by chance." To anyone who has consulted this work for advice during times of trial and darkness, it provides a kind of clarity and insight that one associates with what we call wisdom and what the Greeks called an oracle. The wisdom of the *I Ching* is imparted through hexagrams, patterns that result from the tossing of coins or sticks that correlate to specific teachings.

In my case, the pattern that emerged was called "Ken/Keeping Still, Mountain." This hexagram signifies the end and the beginning of movement. "In exercises in meditation and concentration, one ought not to try to force results. Rather, calmness must develop naturally out of a state of inner composure." The essential lesson of this hexagram is that barriers existed both above and below us, creating a blockage that could not, by force of money or persuasion, be removed. Only time would create the conditions that would undo the blockage. So the teaching instructed me to relax, adapt, and let things take their course. This was just the perspective on our predicament that I needed. It enabled me to let go of the anxiety I felt and allowed me to turn my attention to what we could do as time sorted the easement situation out.

We decided to make temporary use of the old dairy road from below. This required approval from a family, the Wendlings, whose property this road passed through and who had once owned the dairy above. Recognizing the predicament we were in, the Wendlings graciously allowed us passage without granting an easement. In this way the CEC was able to start a horticultural program. The community could come into the site from Miramonte Drive using a path off of the easement, and supplies could be brought in from below. As inefficient and cumbersome as this arrangement was, it allowed us to do something. We weren't going to be deterred—we would move forward and make something of this land with or without a road.

With some grant support received through the US Agency for International Development (AID) grant given to the Direct Relief Foundation of Santa Barbara, an internationally recognized medical relief organization, the CEC developed a training program for intensive organic gardening. Warren Pierce, the CEC's horticulturalist, was in charge of this program that trained workers to go to Central and South American sites to teach and build community-based gardens and demonstrate composting techniques. Santa Barbara City College used the Mesa Project for horticultural education.

Warren was a superb horticulturalist with uncanny insights and capabilities. There was a steep, almost sheer cliff face above the garden that was eroding quickly, spreading a silt of sand across the garden during heavy rainstorms. To counteract the erosion, he planted a mix of native plants. Within five years, the cliff face was completely stabilized. Warren also planted a stunning herbaceous border to the vegetable beds that was in a continuous state of color throughout the year.

A renowned landscape painter, Horace Day of Alexandria, Virginia, would spend his summers painting Santa Barbara landscapes, and Warren's herbaceous border on the Mesa was one of his favorite subjects. I purchased one of his paintings of this border, and to this day it remains one of my most cherished possessions.

BUILDING COMMUNITY GARDENS

Boston's Fenway Gardens circa 1973. This early urban garden helped inspire three permanent urban gardens in our city in the mid-1970s.

In the fall of 1975, I came across an obscure book published in England about the long history of urban gardens in Europe. In England these were called "cottage gardens" or "allotments." They went by other names in Germany, France, Holland, and Scandinavia. The gardens were typically found at the edge of cities and on land that was preserved for this use. They traced their origin to medieval times where small plots were created to allow people to supplement their meager livelihoods. Even today, when you fly over almost any city in Germany, you can see these gardens, usually at the edge of town; little cottages, pathways, and garden patches are unmistakable pieces of the northern European urban fabric.

In the fall of 1974, Kathy and I made a trip to the East Coast to visit Robert Rodale, the publisher of Rodale Press in Emmaus, Pennsylvania. I had written several articles for *Organic Gardening* magazine and its editor, Jerry Goldstein, who was then a close associate of the Rodale family, had invited us to drop by, spend the night, and talk about our work in Santa Barbara. Robert's father, J. R. Rodale, was an early proponent of natural foods and had built a publishing empire communicating the virtues of organic gardening and natural health. Rodale Press was promoting the development of community gardens in cities, and this piqued my interest. We continued our trip to Cambridge, Massachusetts, then on to Vermont, and finally took the train across Canada from Montreal to Vancouver. During our trip I arranged to visit America's oldest community garden, located in the Back Bay of the Charles River in Boston. The Fenway Gardens were established in 1942 as part of a national movement to establish "Victory Gardens" to aid the war effort. After World War II, most of the thousands of Victory Gardens that blossomed throughout the country were abandoned as the lots they were located on made way for postwar development, or from neglect as Americans grew more affluent and gave up gardening for the supermarket.

The Fenway Gardens provided hundreds of individual plots of land for surrounding residents, many of very modest means, with a place to grow vegetables and flowers. As anyone who has visited a community garden knows, they are dynamic places reflecting the wide-ranging abilities of the gardeners who work them. The Fenway Gardens were no exception.

The idea of making urban land available for gardening seemed to me worthwhile, something we could focus on during our development hiatus for the Mesa Project. Gardens were popping up all over the United States by the mid-1970s, but based on what I knew, they were mostly located on land that afforded only temporary use until their inevitable development for housing or commercial use. I was drawn to the idea of making them more permanent, as in Europe.

The only way to ensure permanence was to create them on publically owned property and then designate them as part of the public parks and recreation system. And so when I returned from the East Coast, community gardens became a new focus of the CEC.

We identified our first candidate site in the Lower Eastside area of Santa Barbara, a predominantly Latino and mostly low-income area. Named after Chumash Indian Chief Yanonali, it was a publically owned parcel of about two acres earmarked for a public park but never developed as such. The Eastside community didn't have the clout that had produced many of Santa Barbara's wonderful parks in more affluent parts of the city.

Establishing a community garden on this land just might be the way of galvanizing support for converting the land to a formal public park, thus giving this high-density poor community a new recreational resource. But when we shared this idea with some of the Eastside community members who had pressed for a park over the years, we were met with deep-seated skepticism—justifiable, no doubt, given the poor history of "white folks" helping out in the Latino community.

Nonetheless, we pressed ahead. With help from board member Maryanne Mott, the Charles Stewart Mott Foundation of Flint, Michigan, granted us seed money to develop the garden and work with the community to secure the park. The idea was to develop approximately half of the land as a permanent community garden while making the other half a traditional passive public park with benches and lawns for relaxing and playing under the great old oak trees that populated the site.

The two people who played the most important role in the park's development were Joel Fithian and John Evarts. Joel came from a prominent Santa Barbara family and had earned a master's degree in agronomy from the University of Hawaii. John was an aspiring writer who attended Antioch College in Yellow Springs, Ohio. Together they had all the skills that were needed to transform the property, possessed as it was with several magnificent and ancient oak trees, into a vibrant garden. Little did they know that by bringing this first community garden to life they were sowing the seeds for future garden expansions and setting the stage for community gardens to become part of Santa Barbara's parks and recreation system a decade later.

As we moved forward with our plans, there was the predictable resistance from city bureaucracy, in this case the Parks Department, which could not see the benefits of urban gardens. Even some of the neighbors didn't take kindly to these "do-gooders" from the CEC whom they suspected could not or would not be able to deliver a public park and a community garden.

But the CEC did indeed make good on its stated intention. In 1975–76, the Yanonali Gardens had become the park that the CEC had hoped it would be. The CEC also secured very modest funding support from the Santa Barbara City Council to pay for a part-time garden coordinator to maintain the garden infrastructure and to work to allocate the private garden parcels and monitor their maintenance.

Building a community garden was one thing, but making it work was another. The idea of making space for people living mostly in apartments, many of whom were Spanish-speaking and of low income, was an altogether new activity within the community. Persuading these people to come forth and secure a parcel of land was not as easy as it might seem. Many low-income Latino people were used to keeping a very low profile and were reticent to interact with anything that involved sign-ups or having to identify themselves. The idea of a city providing land for growing at little expense was intrinsically foreign to them, and the people providing them the land were white outsiders whose Spanish language skills were limited.

Overcoming these barriers took time. Through patience and sustained effort the gardens gradually began to fill up. And then there were the inevitable conflicts between people, some substantive and others petty, but consistently a source of frustration for us. One deep conflict emerged over the use of pesticides and chemical fertilizers. Although the gardens were billed as "organic," we realized early on that we couldn't be purists if we wanted people to garden. Organic methods were not all that well known then, and some people simply didn't feel like they could garden unless they could use chemicals.

So this pitted some of the committed organic growers against those who used chemicals. And then there were the more mundane issues like the safekeeping of tools, garden aesthetics, the use of hoses, and compost. But the most trying issue of all was theft. To those inclined to theft, there is nothing more tempting than seeing fresh-ripened fruits and vegetables there for easy pickings. And there is nothing more discouraging and disheartening to a gardener than to have one's hard-earned crops picked off overnight, with plants sometimes mangled in the process.

As the old saying goes, "Good fences make for good neighbors." In the case of the community gardens, good eight-foot chain-link fences with locked gates make for good community gardens.

Two other community gardens were to follow, Rancheria and Pilgrim Terrace. The Rancheria community garden was the impetus of an older woman who lived in one of the many high-density apartments on the Lower Westside. She wanted a space to grow vegetables and flowers and identified a nearby vacant city-owned site. She pressured us to establish a garden on this site. After all, the CEC had done it once, why not again?

Although she was one of those people that you would just as soon avoid, a nasty nag of a woman, we suffered her ways for the larger purpose of developing gardens in the city. Enough muscle was applied at the political level that, together with the neighborhood support, the Rancheria Garden, unlike its predecessor, quickly developed. Although the use of the Rancheria Garden by neighboring residents came about more quickly than the Yanonali Garden, it too encountered the predictable chemical-versus-organic conflict and problems of theft.

The development of the CEC's third community garden was the result of relationships we had with Santa Barbara's Community Housing Corporation, led by Jennifer Bigelow, an enterprising and visionary woman developing the Pilgrim Terrace Housing Project for seniors on the northeast side of town. Jennifer and I got to talking about how some of the seniors who lived in Pilgrim Terrace might enjoy the opportunity to raise a garden. Jennifer pretty much made this one happen. She had the resources in her development budget to build the garden, and by this time, the CEC team knew all the elements of building the garden and developing the user base. So in 1978, the Pilgrim Terrace project was built, and this community garden designed mostly for seniors was dedicated.

In the span of three years, the CEC had built another piece of the "pattern language" within the city fabric, community gardens that together occupied about two acres of land in three distinct neighborhoods. All of the gardens were deliberately located on public land for permanence. We helped develop a strong community garden constituency that, as it turned out, was needed at times to make sure that the growing opportunity would not lose out to other park and recreation uses.

Keeping the gardens intact took extraordinary measures and talent by our garden managers who worked with a meager budget provided by the city and the limited resources that the CEC could provide given our scant financial resources.

The development of the community gardens was a small but important chapter in the CEC's work to make Santa Barbara a more sustainable community, consistent with our philosophy of creating works that endure. Today, after nearly thirty years of management by the CEC, they are part of the formal Santa Barbara Parks and Recreation System managed by the city.

By this time, a couple of years had elapsed, and the wisdom of the *I Ching*'s "Keeping Still, Mountain" hexagram came home. In 1977, after enduring a nearly three-year easement stalemate, the CEC was able to negotiate a workable easement—made possible by a $15,000 contribution by Maryanne Mott. Our nemesis, James Black, and his partners were now motivated more by money than revenge. With the easement resolved, we could move ahead with our development plans. We had used the intervening years well; we had adapted, making the best of trying circumstances. Now we could resume building our dream complex. Or so we thought. By 1977, the assumptions that we used in the design of our project had to change because Santa Barbara had adopted a bold, new land use plan, a plan that I had a hand in making.

HOW BIG SHOULD OUR CITY BE?

A pervasive attitude exists that there are and should never be limitations—self-imposed limitations for individuals or communities. Yet we know that resource constraints are real and growing. Under the circumstances efforts to limit expansion seems justified.

PERSONAL JOURNAL ENTRY, AUGUST 1974

In November of 1974, the City Planning Commission, due to growing concerns within the community about the future of the city, decided to commission a study to answer the question of how big Santa Barbara should be. A request for proposals for this study was announced by the city. At the time, I was part of an informal group that we called the Thursday Night Club, which met at the home of Dr. Richard Flacks, a professor of sociology at UCSB who had gained notoriety as one of the authors of the infamous (to some) Port Huron Statement when he was a professor at the University of Chicago. His radical nature had prompted a critic to attack him with a hammer, nearly killing him, an attack that led him to pick up and move to perhaps a safer academic setting at UC Santa Barbara. Flacks and his wife, Mickey, liked bringing people together over progressive issues, so he created the Thursday Night Club. In the course of casual conversations, the CEC's Plan for East Beach came up as an example of applying the talents within our community to the planning of the city. A provocative question was raised: If citizens had made such an impact on planning the waterfront, first under the leadership of Pearl Chase in the 1920s and then by the Committee for Santa Barbara in the early 1970s, why not form a group of local talent to respond to the city's request for proposals? And with that, the Santa Barbara Planning Task Force was born.

There were five principals in the Task Force: Professor Harvey Molotch and Assistant Professor Richard Appelbaum, both on the faculty of UC Santa Barbara; Dr. Henry Kramer, a mathematician who had a computer consulting business in town; Jennifer Bigelow, the housing specialist; and me. My involvement was made possible by the hiatus in the development of the Mesa Project. Under the leadership of Dr. Molotch, one of the youngest faculty members to receive tenure at UCSB, the Planning Task Force prepared a response to the city's request for proposals.

The Task Force proposal presented an ambitious agenda. Under the tutelage of Molotch and Appelbaum, university graduate and undergraduate students would participate in the study as research assistants, fact checkers, and gophers to handle some of the more mundane aspects of the project. The American Institute of Architects, Santa Barbara Chapter, would be involved in determining how the size of the city could impact the architectural heritage of the community. Several economists from the university were to serve as consultants to the Task Force. The proposed scope of work called for three volumes. The first would involve an assessment of five different growth scenarios, from no growth to a maximum build-out under the current city zoning. The second volume would focus on how growth would change neighborhoods, and the third volume would be a technical report containing all the data and the assumptions that were used in formulating the impact analyses.

The city council selected the Planning Task Force proposal, a risky proposition to be sure, given that the group had never formally worked together and we were not city planners in the traditional sense. But the council was swayed by the talent pool that was assembled: topflight academics, housing specialists, the coauthor of the waterfront plan, and a small army of students, both graduate and undergraduate, who, under the direction of faculty, would willingly do whatever it took to support the study.

What ensued was perhaps the most ambitious study of its time of urban growth in America. In the remarkably short time of nine months, a massive 1,100-page, three-volume study called *Impacts of Growth* was completed that shed much light on the question of how big Santa Barbara should be.[29]

Given the controversy surrounding the selection of the Planning Task Force to do the study, the group, being perceived to be university-based and liberal, if not left of liberal, and the high stakes riding on the findings of the study in terms of possible zoning changes and property value adjustments, the Task Force members realized that they had a sober responsibility to complete the very best possible study, one that was as unbiased as possible and meticulously crafted.

Creating the *Impacts of Growth* study was unquestionably the most challenging undertaking I have ever been a part of. Veterans who participated in the study look back on it in awe. The working hours were horrific and seemingly unending. The sense of responsibility was overwhelming. It was a city we loved, and its fate was partially in our hands.

The office we used to prepare the *Impacts of Growth* became like a war room that housed the students, volunteers, and core team that often worked through the night. The massive amount of statistical data we were compiling was key-punched into the computers. Students worked in every nook and cranny of the building with people coming and going at all hours of the night. All the document preparation was done with typewriters. That meant we had teams of typists and editors. Draft after draft was prepared this way, and every change meant that a new page had to be typed afresh—something that seems unimaginable today.

During the last week of the effort in early August 1974, when tourists flooded into Santa Barbara for the annual Fiesta celebrations, we were regularly pulling all-nighters. Below our sixth-story office, parties raged into the wee hours. The sounds of this revelry drove us crazy as we slogged on and on toward the finish line. By the end of August, the slog was over. The study was sent to the printers. It was the calm before the storm.

With the publishing of the *Impacts of Growth*, the moment of truth was close at hand. Anticipating a heated reception, we decided to introduce the study with some flair. We asked the famous English Shakespearean actress, Dame Judith Anderson, then retired and a resident of the neighboring wealthy enclave of Montecito, if she would consider introducing the study by a reading of the poem "Ode to San Ysidro," written by John Galsworthy in celebration of the beauty of Santa Barbara.[30] She cheerfully agreed, making the city council chambers her stage. Dame Judith delivered the poem with great aplomb. Her grand image graced the front page of the *Santa Barbara News-Press* the next day; her appearance at this event was even noted in the New York Times. A welcome bit of good cheer before the heat of battle.

The *Impacts of Growth* study's most forceful finding was that if Santa Barbara grew much beyond 85,000 people, its streets would become burdened with traffic to the point where traffic could crawl. Traffic was an especially damaging aspect of growth because Santa Barbara was a fully built-out city with mostly narrow streets laid out in the late 1800s. The city is situated on a narrow coastal shelf with the vertiginous Santa Ynez Mountains and the Pacific Ocean squeezing from north and south and only one major highway running through it, the famous US 101. The highway follows the path of the Camino Real, the "Royal Road" the Spanish had built in the late eighteenth century to link the nearly four-hundred-mile chain of California missions. Growth beyond 85,000 people would result in enough cars to force the city to widen many streets, not only an exceedingly costly proposition, but one that would change the very character of many of Santa Barbara's neighborhoods.

The study revealed that Santa Barbara's residential zoning would, at least theoretically, allow for up to 170,000 persons under the existing zoning even though Santa Barbara was thought to be almost fully built out. But, as the study pointed out, the population could increase markedly because there were still vacant lots within the city, and building densities would allow for much more intensive development than existed. Although we concluded that reaching a population of about 170,000 was highly unlikely, because cities rarely build out to their maximum allowable density, a population of between 103,000 and 117,000, a still large increase over the 1974 city population of 74,000, was probable. This lower range of growth would nonetheless force changes to the city that we thought most Santa Barbarans would find unacceptable.

Our analysis of growth included other important subjects like job availability, education quality, public safety, wastewater treatment and water supply, and the cost of urban services. Our comparison of the growth characteristics in 117 cities in America suggested that Santa Barbara growth would not benefit these key components of the city.

Perhaps the most revealing findings of the *Impacts of Growth* were those dealing with how growth would impact neighborhoods. The study's second volume, the *Neighborhood Fact Book*, began, "People live much of their daily lives in their neighborhoods, and even those whose work or recreation takes them elsewhere have social and emotional commitments to their neighborhood that make it even more important to them...Interested as we are in the effects of growth on the quality of life, a determination of how life at the neighborhood level will be affected becomes a critical factor."

An original contribution of the study was to establish, for the first time, a clear delineation of Santa Barbara's neighborhoods—identifying a total of twenty-seven. To formulate neighborhood identities and boundaries, some two hundred Santa Barbara residents were randomly telephoned and asked to indicate the names of their neighborhoods, the boundaries that they recognized, and their evaluations of the neighborhood's major assets and problems.

Building on the neighborhood identities, the study went on to ask these questions. "How, in light of what the neighborhood is like now, will growth of the city and the immediate area influence the neighborhood quality of life? What assets will be lost? What problems will be solved?"

In the *Neighborhood Fact Book*, there is a detailed analysis of how each neighborhood would be affected by the growth scenarios. For example, for the neighborhood of East Beach abutting the waterfront, the study noted, "East Beach has a problematic future. With the exception of one rather small area of complete development...development could take any of a variety of forms, leading to a variety of possible changes. In recent years the East Beach area has been the subject of intense public debate over its future development. Proposals ranging from a hotel and convention center to the extension of Palm Park have been made, but no action has as yet been taken. This neighborhood includes the Clark Estate, twenty-three acres of wooded waterfront hills, which could legally accommodate up to 128 homes under the current zoning and would probably in fact accommodate a sizeable fraction

Westside neighborhood in Santa Barbara: Preservation of the character of neighborhoods like this was at the heart of determining how big our city should be?

of that figure unless protected." In 2013, the fate of the Clark Estate was a subject of national news, a scandalous fight over the will of the eccentric Hugette Clark, heir to a railroad fortune. The estate became the property of the City of Santa Barbara and will be added to Santa Barbara's already grand public waterfront.

With the study now in the public domain, local interest groups quickly jockeyed for position as the city council deliberated the finding. Predictably, there was an outpouring of attacks from real estate and development interests that feared that the city council would down-zone properties, thus reducing property values. One of the more eloquent and frequent critics of the study was Robert Ingle Hoyt, a prominent architect, planner, and former planning commissioner, whose principal criticism of the study was its "alarmist growth scenarios." The best thing Hoyt could say about the study was that "it will serve its intended purpose of satisfying those who need it." It begs for a community reaction, adding, "I have never minded playing Peck's bad boy." Far worse words were used by some of the study's critics, and for many months fierce debate was waged in the newspapers.

But, in the end, given the public's prevailing slow-growth sentiments and the council's sympathy with this view, the council decided to pick the lowest of the growth scenarios, which translated into a population limit of about 85,000, or an increase of about 10,000 over Santa Barbara's then current population. The council "downzoned" the residential zones of the city to accommodate this population level. But the plan's proposed down-grading of the commercial land was never adopted—a proposal that drew too much flack.

Today, some forty years later, the City of Santa Barbara is estimated to have a population of about 90,000, a little more than the 85,000 population limit adopted in 1974. By setting this limit, Santa Barbara continued the trend that had begun after the oil spill, to keep Santa Barbara the small town and the relatively pristine place that it was and to try to live within its spatial boundaries and resource constraints.

Not all land use issues that were important in defining urban limits within the Santa Barbara region were the subject of large public contro-versies and battles such as El Capitan, the Santa Barbara Waterfront, and the *Impacts of Growth*. The emergence of the environmental-impact report informed the public and policy makers alike of the consequences of devel-opment and of legal protections afforded under the now enacted National Environmental Policy Act and the Clean Air and Water Acts. It also noted what obstacles project developers might face, should they bring forward projects that sparked public concerns or opposition. The Santa Barbara City Council and the County Board of Supervisors proposed land use initiatives of their own. One example of a planning effort by one county supervisor was to prepare a local plan under the newly enacted Coastal Protection Act of 1972. Among the many facets of this plan was a focus on a small agricultural valley just south of Santa Barbara that was in the path of urban development pressures.

IN DEFENSE OF AGRICULTURE

The spirit of place is a great reality, different places on the face
of the earth have different effluences, different vibration, different
chemical exhalation, different polarity, with different stars.

D. H. LAWRENCE[31]

In 1972, the California electorate, frustrated by what it perceived to be the
out-of-control development of coastal resources, approved a bold initiative
to create the California Coastal Commission and six regional commissions
whose authority would supersede local government control. This became
known as the Coastal Act. The premise of the act was that local governments
lacked the vision and the fortitude to preserve and protect coastal resources
such as estuaries, farm land, view corridors, and, most importantly, public
access to the coast. It gave final authority for preserving and protecting these
resources to the Coastal Commission. The commission in turn directed local
governments to prepare land use plans for the coastal zone of California, a
strip of land of varying depth for the length of California's coastline, 1,100
miles as the crow flies.

In 1976, Santa Barbara County applied for and received support from the
State of California to hire a planning team to prepare what would be the first
local coastal plan under the new law.

I was asked to head this effort by the county's assistant planning director,
Paul Wack, now a professor of urban planning at Cal Poly, San Luis Obispo,
and a lecturer at UC Santa Barbara. I agreed to become part of the team but
not lead it, as I wanted to keep one foot in the door of the CEC, and I didn't
want to be in another management position.

One of the most interesting challenges of this new project was to find a way to protect the Carpinteria Valley as an agricultural resource. The Valley was in the path of urban development pressure from the south. It included two coveted coastal resources, a large estuary, and prime agricultural soils, making it some of the best farmland to be found anywhere in California. The estuary was threatened by urban and agricultural runoff; the agricultural lands were targeted for urbanization.

The Carpinteria Valley is about four miles long and two miles deep, backed by the rugged Santa Ynez Mountains. It boasts some of the greatest growing conditions in the world with three growing seasons and a mild climate that varies barely twenty degrees between summer and winter. In the 1950s, Dutch flower growers who had grown restive under the increasing urban pressures and regulations in Holland[32], searched the world for the best climatic conditions to grow and prosper. They found it in the Carpinteria Valley. Within twenty years they transformed a hundred acres or more of the valley lands into greenhouses, where they raised cymbidium orchids, carnations, poinsettias, roses, and other in-demand flora.

Greenhouses presented a perplexing challenge for our preservation efforts. They required large areas of paved surfaces for roads and loading docks, night lighting, and large applications of pesticides creating runoff that would find its way to the wetlands. Furthermore, the growing environment didn't involve plants in the ground. These were grown in container environments. Given these impacts, how could continued greenhouse development be reconciled with the Coastal Act mandate that required the protection of prime agricultural land within the coastal zone?

If we were to make the decision that greenhouses were industry, and not an allowable use in the Valley given that the Coastal Act called for the preservation of prime agricultural lands, what would replace these greenhouses? This question had important economic implications for land preservation. The cost of land in the valley was very high, too high for most forms of agriculture to survive, given the expense of water and the assessed tax evaluation that reflected the potential for the land's conversion to residences. Greenhouse flower production was profitable enough to pay the freight for this high-cost growing environment—perhaps the only type of agriculture

Carpinteria Valley: Preserving agriculture in coastal California in the path of urbanization

that could pay the water and tax bills and still produce a profit. If there was to be a way to preserve agriculture, we had to understand the dynamics of cultivating flowers, and the only way to do that was to learn what we could from the masters of floraculture, the Dutch growers themselves, now only one generation removed from Holland.

The lead family in this business was the VanWingerdens. They had left Holland, where the family had been grocers since the 1600s, to come to the Carpinteria Valley in 1967, where they assumed that they would be free from what they considered to be oppressive regulations in Holland. It was understandable that the VanWingerdens were none too pleased when we contacted them and asked them to share some of their knowledge and their perspective about floraculture. They tried to be as civil as they could be to us, but we could feel a kind of seething contempt for the complexities that we were bringing into their lives.

They grudgingly told us what they could about their growing practices and that, combined with what we learned from our research about the economics of floraculture (a global business where producers from

Venezuela were becoming an ever-bigger influence on the American flower market), gained us a reasonable perspective on the world of flower growing.

We wrestled with the seeming incongruities between the goal of preserving farmland and the industrial nature of flower growing. In the end, we concluded that, in spite of the paved surfaces and the artificial growing conditions under greenhouses and artificial light, the preservation of the greenhouse industry was necessary for preserving the land as an agricultural resource. Instead of eliminating greenhouses, we chose to limit their development footprint in the Valley. To that end, we sought to designate the smallest remaining parcels of land for greenhouse development, thus concentrating them where they were, and then designating larger land parcels for nongreenhouse land use such as for avocados, lemons, and nursery stock. These were high-value agricultural uses that we thought might be sustainable in the high-cost growing environment of the Carpinteria Valley. Naturally, the compromise that we reached was one that neither the growers nor the surrounding urban dwellers much liked. The greenhouse growers could continue to grow but not expand by much, and the urban dwellers would have to coexist with the growers, endure the trucks coming and going, and have the darkness of their nights spoiled somewhat by the glow from the greenhouses.

While the rest of the Carpinteria Valley was going to be spared more greenhouses, there was the vexing question of how to preserve this valley when there were so many parcels, some as small as a few acres. While the land was rich and the climate perfect for growing everything from open-field flowers to strawberries, kiwis, lemons, and avocados, earning a living or at least enough to pay the property taxes on a few acres was next to impossible.

Although we had a resource economist in our group, we lacked expertise in open-field agriculture, and for this we called upon the University of California's trusted Agricultural Extension Service for advice. With headquarters at UC Davis in the heart of the San Joaquin Valley halfway between the Sierras and the San Francisco Bay, the UC Extension was famed for expertise in growing virtually all the principal crops raised in California and respected for the advice offered to everyone from backyard orchardists to captains of industrial agriculture.

Knowing this, I was ready to be wowed, expecting to gain the insights that would secure this jewel of a resource for posterity.

The UC agent assigned to us was Jack Bivens, a tall, surly, rail-thin man. I remember well his glassy, bloodshot blue eyes, deeply recessed under his furrowed brow, staring me down with a cold and vicious contempt. He was like a rattlesnake always coiled and ready to strike when he was in our presence. We asked Bivens to suggest the minimum parcel size that could sustain agriculture in this valley. He answered testily with two words that left little room for interpretation: "One acre." In disbelief, I gasped, "One acre! You've got to be kidding!" But kidding he wasn't, and he held his ground not just then but throughout the planning process, even testifying before the County Board of Supervisors that had to approve the plan.

I had faced my share of controversy, people with whom I didn't see eye-to-eye, but never had I run into such an unbending individual. Bivens was determined to counter us from his position as an agricultural expert. At first I was flummoxed and then, I must admit, became unbending too— unbending in my contempt for someone who could use his trusted position to take such an obviously absurd position.

Later, I learned that Bivens had assembled some considerable real estate holdings, including an apartment complex that housed my father-in-law in neighboring Santa Barbara. And then it dawned on me that he was a landholder and developer and that his allegiances were perhaps tied more with development than agricultural preservation. Long deceased, Jack Bivens still makes my blood boil!

Since we couldn't get any worthwhile information from the UC Extension Service, we were forced to construct a zoning framework based on what information we could gather and interpret about the per-acre value of the prevalent crops versus the cost of land, the tax load per acre, labor, and other expenses and profit. We made extensive studies of the parcel sizes in the valley and learned as much as we could about the economics of commercial flower, avocado, and strawberry growing, the most value-rich crops grown in the valley at that time. We sifted this information and a picture began to emerge about the minimal parcel sizes needed to maintain the Valley in agricultural use. Based on what we learned, the minimum parcel sizes were five and ten acres, respectively. We found that most of the parcels that were closest to the residential uses in the Valley were larger than five acres and fewer than ten. If five-acre zoning was adopted, the effect of this would mean that any parcels of between five and ten acres could not be subdivided. In the more rural part of the Valley the prevailing parcel sizes were between ten and twenty acres. That meant that if we proposed a ten-parcel size minimum, no properties of between ten and twenty acres could be subdivided. This was the best framework we could devise given the agricultural protection mandate of the California Coastal Act and economic realities of sustaining agriculture within the Carpinteria Valley.

By conventional agricultural measures, five- and ten-acre zoning for an agricultural area would seem too small to be economically viable. But in the Carpinteria Valley, rich and deep alluvial soil and the temperate climate made growing up to three crops per year possible. This, coupled with tax reductions under California's Williamson Act that allowed farmers with prime agricultural lands to be taxed at their agricultural value and not their speculative value for other land uses, made it possible to maintain agriculture on holdings as small as the five- and ten-acre limits we proposed in our plan.

Upon completion of the plan in 1976, the time had come for it to go through the public review and comment period followed by a public hearing before the County Board of Supervisors and an up or down vote. The public-hearing process was predictably testy; the greenhouse growers were firm in their opposition to the restrictions we were imposing on greenhouse development. They cited a growing encroachment by government on their way of life and their livelihoods, hearkening back to the conditions that drove them out of Holland. Many Carpinteria residents were strongly opposed to our plan's limited accommodation of greenhouses. They argued that the impacts of greenhouses exceeded those of in-field agriculture in terms of noise from the trucks servicing the greenhouses, ugly structures, and the high use of fertilizers and pesticides that produced runoff to the downstream estuary.

Regarding the proposed parcel sizes for the remaining lands, we faced the property owners who wanted to subdivide their five- and ten-acre parcels and were understandably upset. As anyone knows who has served on a county commission, a city council, or any other public body that makes irrevocable decisions over land use, these are among the most stressful and antagonistic environments short of open conflict and war.

As we looked ahead to the vote over the future of the Valley, a clear divide was evident. There were two solid votes for the plan and two against. The fifth and deciding voting member was undecided, although we felt that based on his voting record, he was likely to go against us. His name was Robert Kallman, a political conservative and a strong private property rights advocate, as well as a pillar of the Santa Barbara community. It was at Kallman's initiative that Santa Barbara was selected to be the first of the counties in California to prepare a coastal plan. And his was the decisive vote in a three-to-two roll call that resulted in the Carpinteria Valley remaining the agricultural gem that it is today. His vote attracted little media attention at the time, but it was a mighty vote indeed. And it instilled in me a perspective that has never left me: you should never assume that people are hard and fixed in their positions; that they won't rise to take a position, argue a point, or cast a vote that seems contrary to their past. Bob Kallman's vote taught me that!

As with the *Impacts of Growth* study and the subsequent council vote to downzone the residential densities of Santa Barbara, the vote to downzone the Carpinteria Valley to conform to the policies of the California Coastal Act was a milestone for the Santa Barbara region. In both cases, the community made decisions that were starkly different from the prevailing growth-through-urbanization paradigm that has characterized what has been the hallmark of progress in our country for the past seventy-five years.

Decisions to reverse the perceived natural order of development are not, of course, without their own consequences. The *Impacts of Growth* study predicted that restraining growth in Santa Barbara but not regionally to include the urban center in Ventura, twenty-five miles to the south of the city, and the cities of Lompoc and Santa Maria, fifty miles and sixty miles, respectively, to the north, would result in people commuting long distances to Santa Barbara, which was the employment hub for the region. That, in fact, has occurred and has contributed to massive traffic jams during the rush hours north and south. Avoiding these transportation impacts would have required zoning to limit job growth in Santa Barbara, an act that would have been politically over the top given the resistance that was mounted against the residential downzoning action that the council took in 1975.

With respect to the downzoning of the Carpinteria Valley, I'm sure there were many private disappointments and joys that followed the plan's passage. For some it meant that the prosperity that they counted on from the sale of their land to developers wasn't to be, and that would be stinging in its impact. For others it was a relief; it removed the fear that the Valley would be suburbanized, bringing an end to more than several hundred years of an agrarian-based life.

From the vantage point of more than nearly forty years, I think it's fair to say that these land use decisions have preserved qualities that have become ever more rare in our landscape, values of community, scale, aesthetics, local enterprises, smaller-scale employment not subject to the massive employment dislocations that result from major companies moving in and out of an area, and, in the case of Santa Barbara, the successful preservation of a visitor-serving resource that people prize coming from Los Angeles, about one hundred miles to the south, and from literally everywhere around the world. To an increasing degree, it is the specialness of place, not sameness, that draws people, talent, and capital. This is an essential lesson in thinking and acting in the future—how to use the essential values of place, or, in the language of Ian McHarg, its "intrinsic suitability."

Some will regard this assessment as smug and elitist, the position of privileged people living in a privileged place remote from the challenges and realities of much of the modern world. There is no doubt that the area has attracted wealth and accompanying privilege. But it wasn't wealth that drew most of us here, and what privileges existed by no means assured that the place we had grown to love would remain the place it has. Its preservation has required the dedication of hundreds of citizens working over decades, creating an intergenerational tradition of selfless actions on behalf of land and place.

By the time the *Impacts of Growth* study and the Coastal Plan for protecting the Carpinteria Valley were completed, I was able to resume plans for the development of our Mesa Project. The nearly three-year standstill that resulted from the lack of a viable easement to the property was now resolved. Working with our architect, Lawrence Thompson, and our staff, we developed a comprehensive plan for the property, calling for the construction of the access road and then a garden building to be followed by the development of a large combined office and meeting room for seminars and residential quarters. These were grand plans considering that we had little or next to nothing in the bank to start, just faith and the determination that the money and the resources would come.

The access road was our first big hurdle to overcome. The road, about one hundred yards in length, would traverse a steep thirty-plus-degree slope necessitating retaining walls both above and below the road. But first we had to raise money. Were it not for Maryanne Mott and her ties to the Charles Stewart Mott Foundation, the Mesa Project might never have happened. She arranged to have the executive officer from the foundation come out for a site visit. I had met him several years earlier when Maryanne had invited me to visit the Mott Foundation in Flint, Michigan, where she introduced me to the foundation officers, the mayor of Flint, and others. I remember this trip vividly. I flew into Detroit; it was a grim time indeed for the auto industry.

Detroit was an altogether strange and forbidding city on the gray-cool day of my arrival. Prominently featured in Detroit then (I don't know if it still is there today) was a brilliantly lit sign that displayed the number of cars manufactured by the auto industry so far that year; if I recall correctly, the production count was down by several million vehicles. This was the first of a wave of recessionary cycles that were to hit and ultimately, along with serious corruption, take down this manufacturing center in America. At this time, the Big Three auto makers were beginning to feel the inroads Japan was to make in car manufacturing. Together with the recession, Japan's ascendancy was hollowing out Detroit and other auto manufacturing centers.

On the drive north to Flint, I passed under that sign and cringed as I thought about what those numbers meant in terms of human misery for Detroit and all of the other industrial cities in the region who owed their life to the making of automobiles.

I was met by Maryanne and graciously put up in Applewood, the estate of Charles Stewart (C. S.) Mott, who had died many years earlier and where his widow, Ruth Mott, lived. I stayed in Applewood two nights, in the very room where C. S. had slept. Next to his bed was a journal that contained accounts of many of the business transactions that led to the General Motors of his day.This is the very same Applewood described in Michael Moore's 1989 movie *Roger & Me*. I wandered about this impressive, but by today's standards of ostentatiousness relatively modest, estate. It contained an expansive basement that housed a picture gallery of the many university and other public buildings that C. S. Mott and the Mott Foundation funded with the vast wealth he had accumulated as an original partner in the creation of General Motors.[33] "Thanks, C. S." was the common expression on letter after letter, for this or that building at the University of Michigan and the University of Chicago. For an impressionable young man, it was abundantly clear what wealth could buy.

I met with Bill White, the Mott Foundation's executive officer, and the other key staff of the foundation and explained to them what the Community Environmental Council was trying to accomplish. The foundation environment was stiff and strained, made all the more so by the clash between two distinctly different cultures: the conservative Midwest industrial world that was in a trajectory toward decay and that of a California dreamer, talking about ideas and projects that were a world apart from Flint. But there was one fellow, a senior consultant to the foundation, Dr. Herman Warsh, who was a different breed altogether. He spoke a language that was familiar, savvy by my book, accessible, and warm. He was later to become Maryanne's husband and to move to Santa Barbara.

Three years later, I was standing with Bill White, still the executive officer of the Charles Stewart Mott Foundation, pointing out the location of the easement that was to connect the Mesa Project with Santa Barbara. He was there only because he had been prodded by Maryanne to consider funding us; his body language said that he wasn't a bit happy to be there on the hilltop with a young man who might as well have been speaking a foreign language. The easement that I saw as the critical bridge to our future was no doubt, in his mind, a bridge to nowhere. Fortunately for us, it was Maryanne, not Bill White, who controlled the foundation's purse strings. Shortly after this visit we received word that $15,000 was coming our way to purchase the easement, ending the deadlock.

Building the road on that easement was a task that at times seemed overwhelming for such a crew of novice builders, most of whom were volunteers. Among them was Arnette Zerbe, a local artist married to the fine character actor, Anthony Zerbe. Arnette, in her early forties at the time, spent countless hours toiling away with the other volunteers, always cheerful and resourceful. She was an inspiration who lifted all of our spirits when they were flagging. She was a dynamo, focused, resourceful, and full of fun. I can hear her laughing to this day. In time the building of the road was finished, and in more than a symbolic sense it meant that the long-sought-for "bridge" between the landlocked property and the community was realized.

The first project we undertook after the road was the destruction of the remains of the old dairy building remnant. The work force for this project was a small group of students who were involved in the training program at the Mesa Project, supported by the grant to the Direct Relief Foundation through the US Agency of International Development (AID). The purpose of the program was to train young Americans in intensive organic vegetable growing methods so that they in turn could teach these methods to peasant women in Central and South America, where much of the Direct Relief Foundation's assistance was going. I remember weighing how to demolish the structure: bring in a tractor and have done with it, or take the funds that we would pay to have it demolished and pay the students to do it? When presented with the choice, they wanted to do it, and in about a week's time they had taken it apart, and the remnants of steel and concrete were trucked away. On reflection, the choice was the right one. It meant much less damage to an important part of the site and it forged a "can-do" spirit in the students that would serve them well on their difficult assignments.

BUILDING OUR DREAM

I see a future where "buildings" are no longer buildings, considered as inert containers for people to inhabit, but rather more living environments that are life-giving and self-managing, that like plants adapt between day and night, heat and cold, dryness and moist times. When buildings become managed biological systems that produce their own energy they will no longer be called "buildings."

PERSONAL JOURNAL ENTRY, OCTOBER 18, 1981

In 1976, there were very few "green buildings" in the United States, or for that matter anywhere in the world, and of these, almost all were residences. Indeed, there was no term for "green building." But there were early attempts scattered about the West and East Coasts that the CEC was aware of. The *Whole Earth Catalog*, published in the Bay Area, was always a source of insight into new ideas about building with less environmental impact.

The CEC was inspired by this thinking. Irving Thomas, the talented engineer who had built the solar collectors and patented a "solar herb dry-er" at El Mirasol, collaborated with Lawrence E. Thompson to design what would be the CEC's Garden Building. The task of creating a simple struc-ture soon morphed into a complex, hybridized building that included a solar greenhouse, a basement composting toilet, a demonstration of passive solar heating using water tubes, an earthen cover to "blend the building in with the garden" with a small amphitheatre built into the earth berm, and a patio-veranda.

At that time, there was little experience with solar architecture and building techniques. There were essentially two solar building paths that were thought to be promising. One was to use fixed technologies like solar water heaters and pipes and ducts with complex controls to collect solar heat and distribute it through a building mechanically. The other was to exploit "passive" solar design, the kind that had been incorporated over millennia, using building orientation to capture sunlight and sky-lights and eaves to shade buildings in the hot summer months and allow the sunlight in during the winter. An example of the latter passive-design method is found at Thomas Jefferson's home, Monticello. Jefferson inge-niously designed an "earth tube"—essentially a duct some five feet deep in the earth—to capture the ambient temperature of the earth at that depth to cool the home.

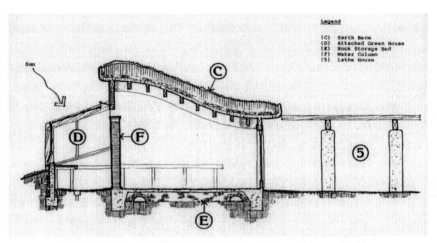

The Mesa Project Garden Center Design: 1978, Early green building.

Among the most successful community-based programs at the Mesa Project were workshops devoted to building solar collectors for water heating. Irving developed a simple solar water heater design, procured the parts, and provided the on-site expertise to help people build their own solar water heaters. Over a period of about one year, several hundred solar collectors were built. If people wanted help with their installation, Irving would hire himself out, and later his colleague, Cydney Miller, who was to go on and collaborate with Irving in the writing of one of the first solar textbooks in the United States. Irving became the go-to guy in Santa Barbara if you wanted a solar water or heating system, and increasingly his higher-level knowledge of the field led to several major collaborations with architects and engineers in the region.

Another significant environmental design feature to be incorporated at the Mesa Project was a still unproven system to compost human waste, a Clivus Multrum composting toilet, invented by Swedish inventor Rikard Lindstrom in 1939 to prevent pollution in the Baltic Sea.[34] Sweden is replete with lakeside homes that rely on septic tanks to hold and treat human waste. Lindstrom knew that septic systems were polluting the Baltic Sea, and he wanted to stop the pollution. Lindstrom conceived a device, a large-chambered structure that could be installed in a basement. Within the chamber the waste would move very slowly, decomposing as it went. By the time it would reach the other end of the chamber, it would be completely "composted" and rendered into a soil product, both sanitary and odorless. The liquid waste would be sent into a leach field, much smaller than those in conventional septic systems, and thus less likely to reach the lakes.

I was introduced to the technology by the son of the inventor, Carl Lindstrom, and his then wife, Abby Rockefeller, the daughter of David Rockefeller. The two visited Santa Barbara in 1976 and stayed with Kathy and me in our newly constructed solar home in Mission Canyon. We had a great time together, and in the course of their visit they connected with the CEC Mesa Project mission, agreeing to contribute a Clivus Multrum unit to the project. This had implications for the design and construction of the Garden Building that went well beyond my understanding at the time.

Indeed, as we went on, the building design became more and more complex, a catchall of environmental technologies—a sure prescription for trouble given the primitive state of environmental technologies in the mid-1970s and our lack of experience with building and design. The final design included a sod roof, the Clivus Multrum in a basement structure about eight feet below the building, earth tubes, and water-filled water columns to passively capture and hold heat for the building. In addition, a tile floor provided thermal mass to retain the warmth of the winter sun.

A solar greenhouse and a solar water heater were additional elements in the strategy to have the building harness energy from the sun. The greenhouse had rotating doors that could hold composts and soil amendments that could be filled from the exterior of the building. The water-efficient landscape was one of the first to incorporate the Catalina ironwood, a native species found on the Channel Islands of California. In keeping with an adherence to passive solar design principles, the building was oriented east–west to optimize solar gain.

The CEC began the project with an anticipated budget of about $70,000, an amount that proved to be woefully inadequate given the complexities of the structure. The earth structure and the Clivus Multrum required special features that were costly and difficult to execute. To carry a sod roof and to have the garden flow onto the roof in an organic way, the architect specified custom, compound-curved laminated beams. The Clivus Multrum needed a basement to house it and mechanical controls. To drain the basement area demanded that a trench with a drain pipe be installed to a depth of up to twelve feet, a costly and dangerous construct. The desire to have an organic, curving structure to conform to the soft lines of a garden and our decision to incorporate a parallelogram-shaped greenhouse requiring specially cut glass and highly custom wood framing and bats to anchor the glass were serious design errors.

As construction proceeded, the cost estimates were soon a mess. Technical difficulties were taxing the building effort. We had overloaded the Garden Center with complex technologies. We were in over our heads but too far along to turn back or to turn it off. It was on-the-job learning at its worst. The cost overruns were an enormous drag on the organization's finances, and the technical challenges of executing such a complex building exceeded our skill sets. At one point, it didn't look like we could financially complete the project, and only an unanticipated contribution by a young philanthropist gave us the funds to finish it off. The experience was humbling and searing. It taught me never to undertake a building project in the future that I didn't completely understand, and to shun complexity wherever it could be avoided. In the end, the Garden Center was an expensive and impractical experiment. It was the gift that kept giving with chronic maintenance problems and marginally working systems.

It wasn't the only building failure of its kind. Through the network of similar endeavors, I realized that there were many problems in these early sustainable development projects that were compounded by inexperience, untested technologies, unrealistic building expectations, and limited financial resources. While the Garden Center project was personally exhausting and professionally disappointing, the experience prepared me for the next time we built. When that time came, I was determined that the design would be comparatively simple, carefully planned, and that it would come in on budget.

BETWEEN THE IDEA AND THE REALITY:
EARLY SUSTAINABILITY METRICS

The CEC's gardens always worked very well educationally. Warren's talents as a teacher had produced a loyal following in the Santa Barbara community based on his extensive knowledge of ecosystem horticulture. The herbaceous border that separated the Mesa Garden from the adjacent chaparral was a remarkable achievement. Warren had calibrated the plantings so that the border would be in bloom all year and so that it would be a magnet for beneficial insects to inhibit plant disease and optimize pollination throughout the garden. But, from an aesthetic perspective, the gardens continued to fall short. They lacked the "wow factor" that I associated with Chadwick's gardens. As great a horticulturalist as he was, Warren couldn't command an army of volunteers as Chadwick could, and we certainly didn't have the money to hire the number of workers it would take to achieve that standard.

Our garden challenge was compounded by the intrinsic lack of fertility of the garden site, about half an acre in size. There was very little topsoil. It was mostly yellow sand that was mined half a mile away for many years for roadbed and as a base for foundations. We had to build up the fertility by applying large amounts of compost, most of which had to be imported. This process of building fertility was a never-ending challenge and a lesson in appreciating just how valuable fertile land is and why it should be preserved to the greatest extent possible. Ian McHarg's principle of intrinsic suitability couldn't be illustrated more clearly than by building a garden on an intrinsically unsuitable site! In hindsight, it would have made more sense to containerize all the growing areas, importing soil and composting to sustain it once it was placed in containers.

But even with our garden shortcomings, the horticultural knowledge and vision that was embodied in these early organic gardening efforts were groundbreaking and a source of inspiration for many in Santa Barbara. I run into people all the time whose lives intersected with our gardens as long ago as forty years, and they often recall with delight their experiences with Warren Pierce and our gardens.

A comprehensive postscript was written about the Mesa Project by Emilie Barton, a graduate student at the UC Santa Barbara, who provided a masterful account of the Mesa Project in her thesis, "The Mesa Project Phase I: A Resource Conserving Systems Catalogue." She begins her remarkably clear and effective analysis of all the technologies employed by the CEC as follows:

"In 1975 the Council decided to purchase and develop a permanent facility to be known as the 'Mesa Project' for testing and demonstrating solar heating, cooling, and electrical generating technologies, water and waste recycling systems, water conserving technologies, and agricultural systems which can be applied throughout the Southwest." She observed that while much was written about the so-called "soft technologies,"[35] there were "still comparatively few works which treat a whole complex of renewable energy and conservation measures which can be applied to the home as well as larger scales of development. Most works are theoretical, describing projects that never got off the ground, or those which are remotely located and rarely subjected to rigorous planning, zoning, and architectural standards that many people face when they want to apply these technologies in and about the home."

Barton's work, in retrospect, is compelling because of its completeness; it is a detailed account of each technology, design specifics, and most important of all, the strengths and weaknesses of each technology. Her eye for detail was exquisite, as the following paragraph demonstrates:

"Regarding the earth tubes [closed columns of water that when warmed by the sunlight provided interior heat], the surfaces of the tubes are easily nicked and scratched producing a cloudy appearance over time. The round tanks can trap insects and cobwebs. Oil which is added to the top of the water columns to prevent evaporation can filter down into the tanks, spotting the inside surfaces. New presealed 'water storage' furniture is available as a possible solution to these problems."

With respect to the "naturally convected ventilation system" consisting of clerestory windows, skylights, and upper venting windows that induce ventilation by drawing rising air out of the building, she observes, "the building remains remarkably comfortable during our warmest summer days which may run in the high 90s in August and September."

Barton's work underscored the CEC's commitment to gaining a practical understanding of what works and what doesn't, a process that contributed to the CEC becoming a knowledge-based organization that informed its policy-making work with a rigor and impartiality that was uncommon in the environmental movement. It underscored the CEC's basic iconoclastic working hypothesis that no one person or organization had a fundamental working grasp of sustainable systems that could be counted on for wide and successful application. The technologies were mostly embryonic and in a state of flux. They were pioneering ventures requiring much trial and error. We understood this implicitly. It made us humble, and I think this gave our work some ballast in a field where there was more exuberance than capable delivery. Our experience-based philosophy suggested that forging renewable energy, effective conservation, and a new architecture were going to take more than years; they would take decades, maybe many decades. How could it be otherwise? After all, our fossil fuel world is the product of more than a century's work, investment in the trillions of dollars, and the working lives of tens of millions of people.

As I saw it, the environmental movement as a whole suffered from an inflated sense of possibility, understandable perhaps, but essentially naïve. It was natural to hope, as was common in the '70s, that through a combination of vision, idealism, and determination, environmentalism would be widely embraced, and the pollution of air, water, and land could be greatly reduced, and renewable energy could substitute for petroleum. But though grand expectations may motivate, they don't sustain work beyond a point. Grand expectations may have little relationship to knowledge.

Take solar energy, a technology we initially thought could be swiftly implemented in the early 1970s. After building the Garden Center, we knew that our own solar projects were beset by a host of problems, poor technology, a limited contractor infrastructure to ensure that installations were done right, and most of all, limited capital in the solar field. All of these problems could be overcome but would require a mature solar industry, and a solar industry could only mature in an environment of sustained financial incentives backed by consistent public policy. Lacking those, this industry would be stillborn. Indeed, by the '80s, much of it had atrophied or died out. It had been built on tax and rate subsidies, and when the politics changed along with the subsidies, the entire industry—the manufacturers, the installation contractors, and the repair and maintenance infrastructure—just dried up.

Since the initial renewable energy impulse of the 1970s, the story of renewable energy development has been one of ebb and flow. In a flowing cycle, the United States would implement bold renewable energy standards, research and development programs, and incentives. This would be followed by a conservative backlash against rich subsidies, born in part from an innate conservative distaste for environmentalism. When conservatives came back into power, they quickly severed the subsidies and tried, as much as they could, to render renewable energy obsolete and unnecessary. This would have a crippling impact on every aspect of the renewable energy industry, including the financial community, which is particularly allergic to ebb-and-flow economics. Investors lose confidence, companies lose money, and the momentum is lost. Over the years there have been at least three renewable energy cycles initiated at the federal level and each has been short lived.

MAKING USE OF THE LULLS

Between 1975 and 1976, coinciding with the tortured construction of the Mesa Project's Garden Building, I built our family home. I wanted it to be as environmentally sound as possible and draw on my ideals. I wanted it to contribute to our knowledge base at the CEC and to serve as a stepping stone in the evolution of the CEC's thinking and doing. In that vein, it was natural that I would hire the CEC team to help me: Lawrence as the architect, Irving as the solar designer, and Larry Tower—who worked at El Mirasol—as our carpenter. Irving and Lawrence collaborated on the design of a passive and active solar heating design. Because the building site was constrained, it had to be a two-story structure, and for this Irving designed a two-story south-facing block wall nearly a foot thick. The south-facing blocks were painted black and covered with mylar (a heavy polymer film plastic material) to create a heat space between the black concrete wall and the mylar. Air was to be drawn mechanically off the wall's surface into ducts and distributed into the house by small fans that were to be turned on and off by heat sensors. The building contractor was Dennis Allen, a former scholar at the Woodrow Wilson School at Princeton, who had recently resigned as an assistant dean at the University of California, Santa Barbara campus. Like many young professionals at the time, Dennis wanted to make a contribution to society beyond academia; he was drawn to becoming a contractor as way of giving practical expression to his ideals.

My home was the first construction project for Dennis, who was to become one of Santa Barbara and California's most prominent green builders; it served as the CEC's de facto second building to incorporate conservation and renewable energy features that deepened our combined experience and better prepared us for the next stage. While I would like to relate that the experience of building the Garden Building had inoculated me from taking on unnecessary complexity, I was only partially successful in doing so. The solar system that Irving designed for the house was mechanically complex and unable to handle the wide heat variation in a two-story structure. The Trombe wall was massive and ugly with its mylar face. (It later came down.) But many aspects of the building worked very well; the large eave on the south-facing side kept the summer sun off the wall, and the skylights flooded the interior with natural light. And I was proud of the fact that we were able to bring the project in near budget.

PAY DAY

The years 1982–84 were very powerful years for the CEC. The board and staff had decided to develop what would be the second and final building at the Mesa Project site. Having absorbed the lessons of the Garden Center, the CEC was buoyed a remarkable, singular contribution by one of its board members, Jim Tremaine. A graduate of Cal Poly, San Luis Obispo—California's renowned architectural school—Jim specialized in institutional architecture, in particular, school design.

With several years of building trial and error now behind us, the paramount importance of project planning was in our organizational DNA. Jim volunteered his time and talents to aid this phase of work. He prepared a detailed design program, specifying every feature of the building in advance of the final design. With this detailed framework available to us, we decided that rather than commissioning through the selection of an architect, we would go the route of a public design competition, challenging the architects in Santa Barbara to come forth and offer their best ideas. The local chapter of the American Institute of Architects was enlisted to assist the competition. The CEC and the AIA would select a jury to review the designs and select a winner.

The competition required that the architects evaluate the materials that the building would be built from in terms of their total energy impact, from mining through fabrication. Architects were tasked to provide a building that would achieve a minimum of 75 percent energy self-sufficiency and to create a building design that would be relatively simple to construct, so that we had a good prospect for completing the construction on budget.

We realized that the design program was extremely demanding. It would involve much research and considerable originality. We figured that few well-established firms would submit; that the submittals would mostly come from young architects committed to our values and/or intent on building a name for themselves in the community.

In early 1982, the widow of the late James Gildea made a $200,000 bequest to the organization for the development of the "Gildea Resource Center." This was the sum we needed on top of other contributions and pledges we had received to allow the building of the Gildea Center to proceed. Marie Antoinette Gildea, the widow of our beloved Jim, deserves more than a mention in our story.

Born in Bordeaux, France, in the late 1800s, Madame Gildea, or "Ninette" as she was affectionately known, was the stuff of European novels. As a child she was a musical prodigy. She was to go on to become an actress in Berlin and a race car driver. She held salons at her Parisian home that attracted the likes of Andre Gide, Pablo Picasso, and many other great artists and intellectuals of her time.

She was later married to a prominent German industrialist. In the late 1930s, she was told personally by Joseph Goebbels to flee Germany because her husband was Jewish. Fortunately, Ninette and her husband took heed of the warning and got out of Germany just in time, settling in New York City.

After her husband's death and following the war, Ninette returned to Paris, where she met and married Colonel Gildea. After the war and Jim's retirement from Union Pacific Railroad, they came to Santa Barbara, where they purchased the West Beach Motor Lodge, a somewhat rundown waterfront hotel that they soon transformed into one of the better visitor-serving establishments, in keeping with their keen business and aesthetic acumen. They kept a beautiful, large apartment on the top floor of the complex, overlooking the Santa Barbara Harbor. Here they held salons where my colleagues and I were regulars and where we shared and discussed our environmental ideas and explored what we thought best for the future of our community. In this grand and enchanting room, filled with treasured Arabian rugs and pictures of Jim and Ninette with King Faisal in Saudi Arabia, we talked about the future and laughed and took in the incredible stories that Madame Gildea shared with us about her most extraordinary life. What an irony it was to be in this setting, surrounded by the oil riches from Saudi Arabia. Jim, who had built the Aramco Railroad that was to deliver the riches of the Saudi oil fields to the world, was part of our quest for a postoil world!

Unlike her husband, Ninette Gildea had no intrinsic interest in environmental issues. Hers was a world of culture inhabited by the literary and artistic giants of the twentieth century. But she was gracious, witty, and extremely intelligent, and she was dedicated to contributing to the work of the CEC because it was, in part, her husband's legacy, what he called the "college education he never had."

Having assimilated the lessons of the Garden Building fiasco, and with the aid of architect Jim Tremain's thoughtful and visionary building criteria, the CEC set about two courses of action: the design of the Gildea Resource Center and the design of the educational programs that it would house.

In 1982, there were only a handful of green buildings in the United States and little or no framework for building green. One exception was Village Homes, a subdivision of 225 homes and twenty apartments in Davis, California.[36] They incorporated passive solar design, a project that in its historical context is remarkable in many ways. It incorporated a free-ranging variety of passive and active solar systems, many customized by the owner; it had narrow driveways to calm traffic and minimize the amount of paved surface; it utilized natural swales to contain and drain runoff water; it reserved a generous amount of land for community gardens, orchards, and even a small vineyard. It was so far ahead of its time that it is still ahead of its time. Its homes are among the most prized in Davis today, where they have sustained their value better than other subdivisions in this university town. From my perspective, Village Homes was an unprecedented accomplishment. I understood how hard it was just to create a green building let alone a green subdivision, when the entire built environment bureaucracy didn't understand it and certainly wasn't inclined to accommodate it.

By 1982, I became a more fervent believer in the importance of design for our work. Design is unique among the disciplines in its comprehensiveness, unifying light, materials, and environmental conditions in both physical and psychological ways, embracing complexity in a unified way, as nature does. Design is an essential means of embodying ecological thinking and function in every facet of urban life—workplaces, factories, governmental institutions, schools, and child-care centers. Good design, like clear thinking, just makes life better, by bringing beauty and elegance into our urban surroundings. I wanted the development of the Gildea Center to serve as an opportunity for our design community—architects, landscape architects, and artists—to clothe our ideas in the most fitting way.

A DESIGN COMPETITION

The design competition we sponsored involved the local American Institute of Architects (AIA) chapter who would select a jury of five to review and choose a winner. We would exploit Jim Tremaine's ability to communicate our intentions to the architectural community such as passive and active solar systems and energy efficiency, features that are so hardwired in good design today. More important, we wanted the architects to be challenged to think in ways they hadn't thought till then, to consider the source of the building materials they were to use, both individually and in combination, and to think about where and how these materials were extracted, whether they were renewable or finite, what the environmental costs would be for transporting these materials where they came from, and what their energy impacts would be in the construction process. We charged them to present to the jury a comprehensive analysis of the embodied energy and environmental impacts, from their cradle to the completed building. I think this was quite unique in 1982, certainly a rare assignment then in the design community, and I think it could only have been done with the kind of dedication that Jim Tremaine gave to it.

Recognizing the amount of work required to respond to the design competition, we reserved a modest sum to help offset some of the costs for the second and third runner-ups.

Six submissions were received, mostly from younger architectural firms who were eager to help establish themselves with this commission. Several of the designs had great appeal to the jury and there was much discussion and debate over them, but in the end the selection was unanimous. The winning design was submitted by the firm Design Works led by Brian

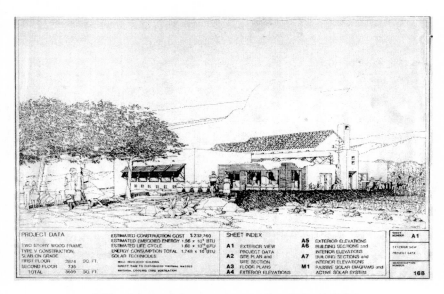

Gildea Center: A design competition long before LEEDS.

Cearnal, who, like Jim Tremaine, was a graduate of the California State Polytechnic University's (CalPoly) School of Architecture. Cearnal had assembled a young and motivated team that included other architects, a landscape architect, and an interior designer. Winning this competition did exactly what Brian had hoped it would. It helped launch his practice, and in time, Design Works became one of Santa Barbara's most successful architectural firms.

It would be fair to say, I think, that the design competition was an important event in the transformation of the design profession in Santa Barbara; it tasked the young architects, who were to mature and become the profession's mainstays, to think outside of the norms established in their education and in so doing helped prepare them for the future when clients were ready to commission more and more projects with a green bent.

As conceived, the Gildea Resource Center was to emphasize passive solar design, with simple lines and limited reliance on mechanical devices. By this time, I was adamant that the building should reflect simple elegance. Anything that was unnecessarily complex, such as difficult angles,

The completed Gildea Center.

untested materials, or exposed wood surfaces that would require much maintenance, was to be avoided.

The building was to utilize newly developed solar photovoltaic technology for generating electricity. Complementing this active solar energy technology was its massive and passive solar wall, a so-called thermal mass that would provide heat for the main meeting room that was to be made of reinforced adobe block. Above the adobe wall were automated retractable awnings to shade the wall during the summer months, to open when the thermal temperatures of the wall exceeded 75 degrees Fahrenheit. Lighting in this room was created by reflective light fixtures that would bounce light off white surfaces to illuminate the conference room and indirect natural light that came in through an east-facing door and west-facing recessed window sculpture. A small gas heater was installed to provide supplemental heat during long periods of coastal fog or overcast weather or during sustained storms.

Other building features included a long hallway of saltillo tile, under which there was a rock bed to store and distribute solar heat and clerestory windows to naturally illuminate the hallway during daylight hours. A rainwater cistern was called for over an east-facing deck and a large, paved patio area with a trellis to highlight the entrance to the building and to act as a cooling influence.

The location for the building was almost precisely over the old dairy building that had occupied this portion of the site for nearly half a century. We observed that there were only a few hairline fractures in the foundation, indicating excellent site stability given the soil factors, the steep surrounding topography, and our proximity to a major earthquake fault line just a few hundred yards down at the foot of the hill. These stable features contrasted sharply with unstable soils that marked the southern boundary of the hilltop site prone, as they were, to threatening levels of erosion.

Since the Gildea Center was all about green design and education, we were not shy about soliciting support for technologies that we felt should be incorporated in the building. At the time, ARCO, the oil giant, owned a subsidiary. ARCO Solar built solar photovoltaics at its production facility in Chatsworth, California. Underscoring how times have changed and opportunities have been squandered in the United States, ARCO was the world's largest manufacturer of solar photovoltaics through the mid-1980s. ARCO had built one of the largest installations of photovoltaic panels in the world at that time in the Carrizzo Plains north of San Luis Obispo—about one hundred miles north of Santa Barbara. We badly wanted to use this technology at the center, but the cost of a system sized for our building was about $35,000—in today's dollars over $100,000—and well beyond our financial reach. With persistence and some luck, we convinced the officers in Arco Solar to donate an entire system, enabling the CEC to be among the first larger-scale users of the technology in Santa Barbara County.

In the mid-1980s, ARCO's CEO was Robert O. Anderson, an oil man with a strong and progressive philanthropic vision and a believer in renewable energy. He supported many conservation programs during his tenure at Arco and after his retirement. Unfortunately, his successor quickly dispensed with ARCO's solar division after becoming CEO, and that signaled the decline of US leadership in the PV industry, a decline from which we are just beginning to recover.

William Norris was another corporate sponsor of the CEC. Norris, an ex-navy officer, became head of Control Data Corporation, based in Minneapolis, Minnesota. Control Data built mainframe computers. In the mid-1980s, it was one of the largest computer firms anywhere, employing some seventy thousand people. Our connection with Control Data began as a correspondence. I had read about Norris being interested in alternative technology. Norris believed that Control Data could tap emerging renewable energy and other environmental technologies, tie them to an education delivery system that the company had developed, called PLATO, and provide both technology and information systems to clients that he believed would be cities.

I felt we knew a thing or two about what Norris believed would be a major new business development opportunity for the company and told him so in a letter I sent him. Thus began a correspondence that resulted in my being invited to the Control Data headquarters, where I had a private meeting with him. I remember entering the lobby entrance to Norris's office, the inner sanctum of Control Data Corporation. There was an ominous shark sculpture in attack mode, circling in the waters. I was a bit taken aback by the ferocity of this piece of corporate art. I guessed that Norris might have a bite to him.

He did indeed. He was opinionated and iron-willed. I discovered that he had a tin ear when it came to listening, especially to criticism. He brought in one of his senior executives to take notes, and after an hour or so our meeting was over. I wasn't clear on what, if anything, had been accomplished. I can't say I felt I had learned anything; it was one of those experiences preceded by a big buildup and then the sense of, "is that all there is?"

The next day I decompressed by experiencing the beautiful Upper Mississippi cities of Minneapolis and St. Paul. Minneapolis seemed so clean, so vibrant, and it was full of parks and lakes. And there was a distinct corporate philanthropic presence, strong but not overpowering, and seemingly much more engaged in civic life than the Southern California cities I was most familiar with, such as Los Angeles, Long Beach, and San Diego.

A few months later, Norris and a small support group decided to visit the CEC in Santa Barbara to talk things over. I met him with the CEC's lawyer, Phil Marking, when Norris's corporate jet arrived at the Santa Barbara Executive Terminal. We drove up to the Gildea Center, which consisted of a framed-in shell of a building and not much more. I had set up a simple few chairs and a wooden table with refreshments in the center of what would become our seminar room. After the briefest of introductions we began to talk. I thought of the meeting as a negotiation over what Control Data would contribute to our work and what we might provide them. Norris agreed to provide the PLATO computer-based education system to us without charge, but he would not provide us with any direct financial assistance.

Our meeting did, however, give me insight into the man and the corporation. The senior vice president of the company that accompanied Norris, along with a whip-smart young woman executive, gave away much with their body language. It told me that there was a disconnect between the boss and his underlings over the direction of the company. Norris's interest in steering company assets into urban ventures like solar and wind energy, hydroponic rooftop gardens, and tapping urban redevelopment funds was a misguided adventure with at best limited revenue-generating prospects. Norris didn't seem to appreciate how difficult it would be to generate corporate rates of return from building greenhouses and rooftop gardens in the inner city. Without massive subsidies, this business prospect was astonishingly delusional. Equally and perhaps more problematic for any prospect for success was the obvious lack of a shared business vision with his corporate officers. From my conversations with them, I realized that they didn't buy into his vision one bit. I could only imagine the kind of talks they had about the boss behind his back about his losing focus and sending them to pursue ventures that were far afield and far more suited to nonprofit organizations, like ours, than to a high-tech giant competing in the relentlessly driven computer world that moved lightning quick.

This experience of interacting with a Fortune 500 company taught me one important lesson. The heads of multibillion-dollar companies can and sometimes do get it all wrong. Control Data made two grave mistakes. The company bet part of the farm on a social venture scheme that was utopian in nature, a vision that could have easily been corrected if they had listened to the likes of the CEC and others who had worked for more than a decade in areas that they were interested in. The second mistake was to seek to centralize their information system, betting the company's future on supermainframe computers collecting and distributing information that they thought they could sell to local governments. They failed to perceive that the information world was moving rapidly to the personal computer and thus unshackling itself from the centralized computing and information systems that had built Control Data.

Within just a few years of that visit, Control Data was in a catastrophic free fall, and within a few more years it was essentially gone—along with its seventy thousand employees, its gleaming corporate complex, and the god-awful shark that I encountered on my way to meet with Norris. And here we were, the little old CEC with its patchwork of projects, still moving forward and growing. The thought was sobering.

INVITING ART IN

Shortly after the completion of the Gildea Center, the CEC initiated another competition for a mural that would hang in the building. Art was at the heart of the CEC when we launched the downtown Ecology Center fifteen years earlier. We had an outpouring of art on the walls of the Ecology Center and in our magazine. Environmental work and programs largely neglected art and aesthetics. What is more inspiring to the psyche and the soul than beauty, whether in a garden, a building, or a painting? I was committed to embedding art into our work as far as possible, even with our very limited financial resources.

The winning mural design was by Cheryl Bowers, who at that time was a professor of painting at UCSB. This former psychiatric nurse, who changed her life course in midcareer to pursue painting and teaching, presented us with a mural that incorporated our mission. It began in the murk of a misty abstract scene of muted color next to a totem that she constructed that was made with lead, not to be touched. The painting was bridged by a wire mesh fabric that carried the viewer to a more promising abstract landscape of brilliant color and vibrancy, followed in turn by another totem, this one white-tipped and light in nature—healthy and touchable.

The response to this mural was mixed: some liked it in its entirety; others were confused and even put off by the totems and the grimness of the first images. The controversy over the piece pleased me. It provoked a response.

The core rationale for building the Gildea Resource Center was to further the educational mission of the organization, advancing environmental theory through practical means. With the help of Robert Fitzgerald, a retired corporate attorney for the entertainment industry who joined the CEC Board in 1981, and Dr. Eugene Bazan, a former systems professor from Pennsylvania State University, the CEC developed what we termed a "triad" strategy. The strategy called for three basic educational functions: an intern program, policy seminars, and publications. The Gildea Center would house a small intern program offered to four recent university graduates each semester. The interns would work with staff on environmental policy development. They would be responsible for research and contributing to the writing of policy papers that would form the backbone for seminars that the CEC would offer.

Fitzgerald and Bazan believed that the three activities of the center would seamlessly reinforce each other and result in a small but powerful means of advancing environmental policy from a setting far distant from the corridors of power in Sacramento and Washington, DC. In the larger scheme of things, we were a tiny organization trying to influence a very big ship indeed—the state of California. But we were optimistic, given our track record and our allegiance to our tried-and-true theory/practice approach to prompting change.

GARBAGE

It would be a blessing if it were possible to study garbage in the abstract, to study garbage without having to handle it physically. But that is not possible. Garbage is not mathematics. To understand garbage you have to touch it, to feel it, to sort it, to smell it. You have to pick through hundreds of tons of it, counting and weighing all the daily newspapers, the telephone books, the soiled diapers, the foam clamshells that once briefly held hamburgers, the lipstick cylinders coated with grease, the medicine vials still encasing brightly colored pills, the empty bottles of scotch, the half-full cans of paint and muddy turpentine, the forsaken toys, the cigarette butts.

WILLIAM RATHJE [37]

The problem of waste was becoming apparent by the early 1980s. Several large urban landfills were filling up, creating the prospect that garbage could hit the streets, a politician's worst nightmare. Per capita waste generation was on the rise, along with proliferation of new and more complex waste materials entering the environment from the electronics revolution. These developments presaged the growing enormity of the waste problem in both developed and undeveloped countries.

Fundamentally speaking, pollution is waste from the cars we drive, the oil or fracking wells we drill, the machines we operate, the homes we heat, and the products we make. Waste contaminates the air we breathe, the land we grow our food in, and the water we drink. Even outer space is no longer immune from the waste problem, where the discards of our satellite programs and space explorations clutter the band of outer space where our launched operations reside. The manifold dimensions to the problem were still in their nascent phase when the CEC targeted the waste problem as the focus of its next endeavor.

By the mid-1980s, there had been much advocacy behind the idea of increasing the role of recycling in managing our wastes and nearly twenty years' worth of advocacy behind the phrase "reduce, reuse, and recycle." But little concrete progress had been made in translating this important perspective into the body politic; recycling languished and remained the domain of small nonprofit operations like the CEC and its counterparts in Berkeley, Santa Monica, Modesto, and Solano in California, as well as enterprises such as the Institute for Local Self Reliance in Washington, DC, and Eco-Cycle, a nonprofit recycling organization in Boulder, Colorado. We decided that the time was ripe for a concentrated, multiyear policy development effort that would build on the knowledge gained from operating programs, coupled with applied research into waste system economics, consumer interest and trends, and changes within industries like the paper industry, steel industry, and other manufacturers. By this time, our recycling operations had linked us to many of the key companies and people in these industries. Reflecting back on those times, I think that some of the representatives of the companies we were interacting with appreciated our willingness to try to understand their operating realities, even if they didn't subscribe to our environmentalist bent. Some deep relationships were forged that were to carry forward to my role in Sacramento and later in the business world.

As we developed a program agenda, we recruited our first interns who would assist us in carrying our mission forward. I was keen on bringing energetic, talented, and open-minded young people into the fold because I knew, from my own experience, that young people in their early twenties can make important contributions to the kind of work we were dedicated to. I was now in my midthirties, and some of the most significant work that I and my colleagues had undertaken was behind me already. I knew in my heart that we had to tap the talents of the young, who were intellectually developed, full of energy, and freer from the cynicism that comes with too much worldly experience. Such a collaboration, focused on topics within our ken, would likely result in fresh approaches to addressing the waste challenge.

Among the topics that we thought needed attention were the future of markets for recyclable materials, both domestic and foreign; the development of more of a systems approach to the development of recycling; the possibilities of minimizing waste generation; and the potential for composting. Once we identified these topics, we assigned our interns to the subject areas, developing background papers that could be used to focus meeting discussions. These proverbial "white papers" are common to think tanks. Extending these white papers to formal policy papers that would take the information from the meetings and translate them into working policy agendas is how theory is translated into practice. Once again, Schumacher's admonition to me years before to create a linkage between the governmental, industry, academic, and public sectors became our focus as we sought to bring ideas to fruition.

One of the first forays into the intern program work was an assignment we gave Jon Clark, a promising graduate student enrolled in the University of Southern California's joint MBA Urban Planning programs. Jon, a Santa Barbara resident, was one of the first four interns to reside in the Gildea Resource Center. His task was to test the attitude of the waste industry toward the role recycling could play in managing the nation's solid wastes. We had been exposed enough to the waste industry to know that it was generally uninterested in, and even antagonistic to, recycling. The waste industry's business model was about as simplistic as it could be: collect trash, put it into a hole in the ground, and make a lot of money. In many communities, it had a tradition of making stunning profits performing this one-dimensional ritual, and since it didn't consider the system broken, it wasn't about to embrace recycling.

Overseeing the Gildea Center program was Dr. Anthony Dominski, affectionately known as Tony. Tony had won a full scholarship to Rutgers University and upon graduation received another to pursue his doctorate at Yale University's School of Forestry. Brilliant, brainy, affable and self-effacing, this practicing Buddhist was the ideal choice to steward the intern program during its first few years. Tony was among the warmest, most dedicated, and most collegial colleagues one could have in every undertaking, from the writing of policy papers, to the care and nurturing of the interns, to his manifold interests in environmental technology. Tony gave his all with grace, warmth, and humility.

Jon Clark was tapped to go on an investigative trip to the headquarters of the nation's second largest waste management company, Browning Ferris Industries (BFI, now Republic), based in Houston, Texas. His assignment was to meet with the company's top officials and ask them where they thought recycling might be headed and why. In arranging the trip, Jon contacted BFI, not as a Gildea Center intern but as an MBA student at USC. This was done on purpose so that he would not be perceived to be part of an environmental organization that could bias the corporation's response to Jon's questions.

Jon was warmly received by several senior executives at BFI, who openly shared with him their view of recycling. Bluntly put, they told him that recycling was for "Boy and Girl Scouts" to raise a little money. This take on recycling was pretty much what I expected, given my interactions with the solid waste industry.

What they were missing, of course, was the growing public interest in parts of the country—especially on the West Coast and in New England—in recycling. The extent of this interest was to reveal itself in only a few more years, when an event happened on the East Coast that illuminated the waste problem in the United States. A barge with an innocuous name, the Mobro 4000, was loaded with solid waste from New York City and destined for Belize. The barge was chartered by an entrepreneur and a mob boss. Setting sail on March 22, 1987, from Islip, New York, with three thousand tons of garbage to be converted to energy in Morehead City, North Carolina, officials representing that state halted the unloading of the waste, directing the barge to go somewhere else. It made it as far south as Belize, where it was again rejected. The Mexican Navy forbade the barge from entering Mexican waters before returning to New York, where, after a protracted legal battle, the waste was unloaded and incinerated in Brooklyn. The garbage barge ignited public opinion behind the need for an alternative to managing the mountains of waste generated in our cities. Once it caught the attention of the national media, its chaotic journey was chronicled on the nightly news, and with this exposure, solid waste entered the nation's psyche and prompted growing efforts to recycle waste materials.

As Jon found out, BFI executives seemed clueless about a changing attitude toward the waste problem and a heightened interest in recycling. And they paid a heavy price for their inattention. Within a year they lost a major municipal contract for the City of San Jose. San Jose officials found that BFI was tone-deaf when it came to listening to the interests of its citizens, so the BFI contract was discontinued and put out to bid. BFI lost out to another service provider that made recycling central to their bid response. This was a contract worth tens of millions of dollars per year.

AT THE GROUND FLOOR OF RECYCLING

Until the late 1980s, recycling was a limited enterprise, the domain of junk dealers who made a living recovering discarded paper and metals and a few nonprofits like the CEC. When world markets for these commodities were strong enough to make collection worthwhile, scrap collectors jumped into the marketplace, and when commodity prices fell during times of recession, they pulled out. As such, recycling was a feast-and-famine, bottom-feeding business, and so it remained until the 1980s.

With a heightened concern about the future of natural resources following the birth of the modern environmental movement, the subject of consumption and the lack of recycling of resources began to grow legs. Images of bulldozers shoving massive quantities of waste into landfills were now commonplace in the media, and environmental organizations were beginning to create a drumbeat for recycling as an alternative to the sense that we had become a nation that profligately wasted resources. But even as public attitudes about waste shifted, next to nothing was being done to translate this change into practice.

The CEC's work in recycling preceded its think tank role, which began with the development of the Gildea Center and its intern program. It started when into our then downtown office came a tall, casually well-dressed man in his early fifties by the name of Robert (Bob) Klausner. He introduced himself as a just-retired businessman who had settled with his wife and young children in Montecito, the exclusive residential enclave just south of Santa Barbara. We had a long and provocative conversation that revealed that Bob's wife, Betty, was a patron of the arts. Yale-educated and a veteran entrepreneur who had built a successful garment business in New York City, Bob had had enough of the Big Apple; he wanted to decompress and enjoy life in our small coastal city but not live the life of a retiree. He was looking for a way to apply his protean energies and his business acumen to a civic-oriented enterprise.

We hadn't seen or met anyone quite like him, but then again, I hadn't spent much time in New York City, where there were undoubtedly many Klausners who operated with razor-sharp clarity, clipped speech, and an impatience that impatiently sought the proverbial "bottom line." Here we were, Hal Conklin and I, products of California and the counterculture, engaging this hard-driving New Yorker looking for common ground— New York hardwired meeting California unplugged. After our conversation we were sure of one thing: this guy was a catch, and we didn't want him to get away. How could we hook him?

As Hal and I spent more time with Bob, the idea of creating a recycling center emerged. We had always wanted to get a recycling program going, but this was 1974—a time when recycling was limited to the margins of society, poor scrap dealers, and collectors. There were no publically funded recycling programs of any kind. And as Bob thought about it, his entrepreneurial mind spinning away, he came up with a very creative idea. The CEC could design a recycling program that would be built around the idea of people dropping materials off at a designated recycling center—in other words, a philanthropic enterprise to its very core. Those who wished could contribute the value of their materials to the not-for-profit organization of their choice. Since there were no public subsidies to collect recyclables and the value of scrap commodities was typically quite low, sending a truck out to collect recyclables was out of the question. People would have to bring their recyclables to us.

It seemed that in no time, Bob, working with Hal, put forth a plan to approach the Santa Barbara City Council to develop a recycling center at an old warehouse and vacant lot owned by the city a few blocks off of Santa Barbara's main drag, State Street. They convinced the council that this site should be provided to the CEC for one dollar a year. The CEC would develop and operate the recycling facility without any further resources from the city, and any building improvements that the CEC made would become the city's property.

Bob's no-nonsense, can-do business approach was influential in getting the council's winning nod, and on a 7–0 vote, the site was secured and a multiyear lease was awarded to the CEC. Ever the consummate businessman, Klausner proceeded to find a market for the key commodity that the CEC would collect: old newspapers. Yes, at that time newspapers were at the heart of the recycling business because people read newspapers then. Bob made contact with Richard Scudder, President of the Garden State Paper Company based in New Jersey, which had one of the few paper mills in the United States that could convert old newspapers into new newsprint. The mill was in Pomona, California, about 130 miles from Santa Barbara. Interestingly, we learned from Bob's interaction with Garden State Paper Company that one of their engineers, Scudder, had developed paper recycling technology, the first of its kind in the United States. We were going to tap into the technology as an outlet for Santa Barbara's old newspapers.

Bob negotiated with Garden State Paper to establish a floor price for old newspapers of forty dollars per ton. It was the minimum dollar value needed to support the CEC's ability to pay the public and thus maintain some incentive for people to go to the effort of bringing materials to the recycling center. This floor price would also be enough to cover salaries, equipment, and overhead. This level of business analysis, with a focus on securing markets before launching the enterprise, characterized the CEC's entry into recycling. We didn't have these skills in-house, but at least we knew enough to know what we needed. By this time, we had a pretty good record of identifying and attracting those who could help us take our work to a new level. With the floor-price agreement in place with Garden State Paper Company, the conditions were set for the CEC to launch its recycling program in the fall of 1974.

On a parallel track, led by Hal, the CEC and the newly founded California Resource Recovery Association (formed as a grassroots recycling advocacy organization in the early 1970s that has grown into one of California's leading advocacy groups for advancing recycling and the idea of zero waste) were lobbying the state legislature to provide a grant fund to enable organizations and communities to receive funds and to

Santa Barbara Recycling Center, 1976: Pioneering recycling in the U.S.

purchase recycling equipment, such as forklifts, trucks, and machinery, to process and bale recycled goods. A fund was established, and the CEC was one of the earliest beneficiaries of this program. We received enough money to purchase a paper baler, a used forklift, scales, tools, and small machinery needed to operate a facility. Separately, the CEC obtained a grant from the Santa Barbara Foundation to remodel an existing building on city property and to erect a new one that would be used to store bales of newsprint, cardboard, aluminum, and office paper for shipment to end users. This was a big breakthrough for us.

Staff was hired, accounting methods were developed, and in 1976 the Santa Barbara Recycling Center was opened. For nearly thirty years, it was a vital part of the Santa Barbara community, providing some $200,000 per year in donations (the equivalent of more than one million dollars per year in today's value) to participating organizations and creating about a dozen jobs in the management and operation of the center and income, at least intermittently, for the sustenance of the CEC for nearly twenty years. Another nonprofit recycling program (SUNRAE) developed in nearby Goleta that was eventually bought out by the CEC.

The CEC's recycling programs exemplified its commitment to developing practical and entrepreneurial environmental programs in the context of our larger worldview of environmentalism that involved integrating programs into the fabric of a community and the larger state and national context. Our approach was to gain on-the-ground experience, and once acquired, be able to move small, pioneering endeavors into mainstream society and the economy. From this early enterprise, the CEC learned about recycling health and safety issues, markets for recycling, contract negotiations, transportation, and, most of all, understanding the costs and benefits of recycling. Recycling became a hook to the larger economy of paper and steel mills, aluminum manufacturing, and plastics production. Understanding these industries and their relationship to recycling enabled me, and eventually other staff, to earn a seat at the table at public policy discussions and ultimately a role in key efforts to develop and pass legislation that would in time embed recycling into society.

An example of the kinds of links to business that recycling fostered was the CEC's connection to a recycling company based in Stanton, California, in Orange County. In 1976, Hal, who oversaw our recycling programs, decided to leave the CEC to pursue a political career by becoming one of the youngest councilmen in Santa Barbara's history and then its mayor. When he announced that he was leaving, I realized that I would have to take on recycling, a task that I was none too thrilled to assume. From my perspective, recycling was a dirty enterprise that reeked of stale beer, sweat, and diesel fumes. But once I stepped into the world of materials handling and marketing, a new and interesting domain opened up to me, with characters the likes of whom I had not met before and challenges that I enjoyed meeting.

I began spending time with Gary Petersen. Gary was a contemporary of mine and a friend of Hal Conklin. In 1970 he started EcoloHaul, a recycling business in Pacific Palisades, a wealthy enclave near Santa Monica. Gary was a born entrepreneur who came of age in the early environmental movement. Irrepressible, affable, and a salesman extraordinaire, he was determined (unlike most of us, as most of us were not) to make money doing good. Working initially out of a VW bus, he learned the ins and outs of collection, processing, and marketing and seemed to be making a living at it, which in itself was impressive. Gary became a fixture in the business in Southern California as he came to know all the traditional players handling scrap metals and paper and then expanded his horizons to do business with aluminum companies such as Alcoa and paper-makers such as Garden State and Weyerhauser. Gary would eventually sell his operation to the world's largest waste company, Waste Management Inc. As part of the sale, he was kept on as an employee to help them adapt to a new business climate where recycling programs were integral to the business. He would go on to be appointed by Governor Schwarzenegger to the California Integrated Waste Management Board in Sacramento, where he influenced waste policies on high.

Gary introduced me to Cliff Ronnenberg, the CEO of CR&R Incorporated, a fledgling recycling company that within two decades had become one of the largest privately held waste and recycling companies in the country. Gary thought that Cliff could help me figure out how to improve our operations. We initially had a phone conversation with Cliff. He was interested enough by what he heard to drive the 120 miles to Santa Barbara to meet in person and look things over. Cliff was the complete opposite of Gary. Standing about six feet five, powerfully built, Cliff was a strong, silent type, a kind of John Wayne of recycling. He had grown up in the 1950s on a dairy farm in the then agricultural village of Stanton in Northern Orange County. After doing a stint in the construction business, he and his brother took over a one-truck trash service for Stanton after Stanton City officials pleaded with the family to take it over and make it work. The thought of collecting waste was abhorrent to him, but within a few months he realized there was money to be made, and for three years he and his brother woke up in the predawn dairy-farm hours and did the job. I don't think he had touched a trash can for more than a decade when we met, but he sure knew the business. We visited the downtown recycling center and in no time at all he saw what we needed most to improve efficiency. It was a device called a rotating head, which installed on a forklift would enable us to load buckets of loose newsprint, thus avoiding the high costs of baling paper with wire and the high labor costs we incurred with our current practice. This single change saved us tens of thousands of dollars per year in operating expenses while making the Santa Barbara Recycling Center a safer place to work.

As my relationship with Cliff developed, he assisted in other ways. At his machine shop he had built for us a mobile recycling center that we could transport to neighboring communities who were further afield and had no recycling opportunities. He devised a trailer that we could tow that had compartments for the various recyclable materials—paper, cardboard, glass, aluminum, and other metals.

We established a collection schedule and would place the mobile unit for a day at a time at various locations and then haul it back to the recycling center for unloading and processing. Cliff paid for the trailer and all the engineering and customized fabrications. He just gave it to us! Later, Cliff became the CEC's largest contributor.

His relationship to the CEC was a symbiotic one. He gained a window through our think tank efforts on the future of his business, while we gained a knowledgeable business partner who not only made our operation more successful but contributed mightily to the big-picture work of canvassing the future of recycling.

Cliff appreciated that smart young people with vision had taken a strong interest in his life's work in an industry that society shunned. And he wasn't the only one in the industry to become interested in our work. They were moved to generosity in helping this group of young environmentalists learn the ins and outs of their business. They were by no means environmentalists and, more often than not, far from it. But they overlooked the different value system we represented. Ours was a symbiotic relationship.

It became clear to me as we developed these relationships that there would be skeptics and critics within the environmental movement who would consider any partnerships with business to be suspect, if not a sign of a sell-out. Although we had proved ourselves to be fierce opponents of business practices that threatened the Santa Barbara environment, it never made any sense to me that business itself was something to be diminished or shunned. As Schumacher had said, to be effective, the environmental movement had to engage business and learn from business in order to better understand and develop policies and programs that could win broad-based support and thus make a difference for the long term.

As our skills in collecting materials increased and the reach of our programs grew, so did our interest, understanding, and commitment to attacking the much larger question of managing the growing waste problem. Our consumer society was generating ever more goods and services that were delivered in one-way containers, or containers within containers that were ending up in landfills. New products were proliferating that were delivered in multimaterial containers: plastic combined with paper combined with aluminum that defied recycling altogether. And we were beginning to see the emergence of the electronic waste problem—all the gadgets and innovations that consumers were buying up and then discarding within a few years, gadgets that essentially had no place to go.

Our on-the-ground exposure to the problem, combined with our growing curiosity and interest in the public policy dimensions of waste, resulted in an almost perfectly timed nexus for the launch of the Gildea Resource Center in 1984. We decided that we would tap our near decade of operating experience with a long-range look at what the possibilities might be for recycling in American society.

Within two years, our triad strategy at the Gildea Center proved effective as the CEC published important policy papers on the proposed California Bottle Bill, Recycling Markets in California and the Pacific Rim, Composting, Waste-to-Energy, Waste Reduction, and a policy paper that presaged landmark recycling legislation, AB 939, which transformed recycling in California over the next two decades.[38]

Our first policy push was the result of a meeting we held at the Gildea Center in 1984 on the question of legislation aimed at capturing bottles and cans for recycling. For more than fifteen years, environmentalists and recycling advocates had wanted legislation that would mandate container manufacturers to take back their glass, plastic, and aluminum beverage containers. Organizations like Californians Against Waste, based in Sacramento, and the California Recycling Association had sponsored so-called take-back legislation, but the big beverage companies like Anheuser

Bush, Coors, Miller, and grocers like Vons and Ralphs would stave off legislation year after year, spending millions of dollars in the process. But by the mid-1980s, several of the companies were getting tired of supporting what were seemingly endless campaigns to defeat pending legislation. We thought it was the right time to exploit this division in the ranks.

The concept behind bottle bill legislation was to place a redemption value on each aluminum, plastic, and glass beverage container sold in the state and allow the public to take back their containers and recover the container redemption value, either at a supermarket or at a neighborhood recycling center. The grocers were aghast at the prospect of the public inundating their stores with filthy old glass bottles, smelly beer cans, and foul plastic bottles. And they most certainly did not want their checkers having to "redeem" these containers in the checkout lines. Apart from the logistics of the transactions, the grocers would have to store the recovered containers in their warehouses until they could be hauled off in economically sized loads. They argued that their stores were not designed for a take-back function; they would lose valuable inventory space and be exposed to public health scrutiny. And the fact is, they were not.

The states of Maine and Oregon had managed to pass simple redemption laws placing a five-cent deposit on containers. The beverage and grocery industry was especially concerned that this type of measure would pass in California and that if it did, it would likely spread to the rest of the country. In those days at least, anything passed in California carried with it the assumption that as California goes, "so goes the nation."

In this environment, against a backdrop of pending bottle bill legislation, the CEC held a two-day meeting in 1984. For the first time, the CEC was to sit down with industry and business to find out if there was any common ground, and if so, what kind of law could be fashioned that industry could live with as California increased its recycling efforts. This meeting was at times very contentious, with some representatives from the grocery and beverage industry coming down hard on their peers in the room who were open to accepting some kind of legislation. I recall the representative from Ralph's supermarkets barking out, "We'll fight any and all legislation and spend whatever it takes to defeat it, year after year if necessary." I found their intransigence remarkable given the momentum in favor of a legislative initiative.

We didn't resolve a bottle bill in that session, but the outlines of the legislation that was to be enacted within a few years emerged. A redemption value would be placed on beverage containers sold in the state (excluding wine and liquor, since their lobby was effective in keeping them out of the proposed system). Collection centers would be established throughout California where containers could be redeemed for money, without requiring grocery stores to take the containers back, avoiding their most dreaded concern.

With the seminar and sometimes brutal exchanges, our interns, staff, and editor had plunged into the policy world of waste. Despite the testiness in the room during this first foray, we liked the policy platform we had created and felt confident we could contribute to reforming the waste system in California and beyond.

By the mid-1980s, our experience operating recycling programs and selling into the marketplace in times of strong demand and recessions led us to believe market development had to go hand-in-hand with policies aimed at increasing the collection of recyclables.

We relied on the public to bring recyclables to our downtown facility and paid what prices we could for the materials. At times, demand for recyclable materials was low (and this was most of the time) and the operations generated little or no profitable revenues, while every few years scarcities would cause prices for commodities to balloon and operations like ours would prosper.

But if recycling was to move into a mainstream waste management practice, the CEC knew that it would be necessary to subsidize the development of a collection infrastructure to allow waste companies or others to be adequately compensated for collecting and processing recyclables. The revenues from materials alone would not be nearly enough to pay for the trucks and the other heavy equipment needed to handle the materials.

Today recycling is a multibillion-dollar industry and a still-growing one, employing thousands of people alone in California. According to

CalRecyle, the agency that oversees recycling in the state, it generates about the same amount of gross revenue as the movie industry.[39]

While the focus of our initial work in waste management was the promotion of recycling, we learned that there was a much deeper side to the waste problem. One-way disposable containers for beverages and fast foods and a rapidly expanding use of complex packaging materials were creating perceived, if not real, capacity problems for some landfills, consuming large amounts of energy and depleting natural resources such as forests. If we were to retain our role as a leading light for contending with the waste problem in our town, in California, and throughout America, we needed to dig into these issues. And so we did, first by articulating the core problems facing recycling and then by suggesting solutions that the government, the public, and industry could consider. Our recommendations were based on intense interaction with industry experts, our own research, and the practical knowledge we gained from the full sweep of building and operating our recycling businesses.

THE POWER OF THE WORD

Two of the CEC's public policy papers were to prove to be particularly influential. In 1986 the CEC published "Beyond the Crisis; Integrated Waste Management." This paper described the current waste management system—essentially a two-dimensional one consisting of landfill and waste incineration—along with a futuristic, much more diversified approach that gave increased emphasis to waste prevention, recycling, and composting. In the mid-1980s, landfills received most of the more than two hundred million tons of solid waste that the United States generated annually. Landfills were cheap, efficient, and convenient. The low cost and ease of disposal went hand in hand with the "out of sight, out of mind" attitude that characterized our consumer society.

"Source Reduction, the Next Frontier," the CEC's next policy paper, was written in large part by a former Brown University intern, Karen Hurst. This paper put forth the thesis that recycling efforts alone weren't enough to address the manifold problems of a consumer society bent on throwing things away or recycling them. Preventing the generation of waste in the first place should be emphasized in national and state policies by creating products that use less materials, by designing products to be recyclable, and by reducing the toxicity of materials used in the manufacture of products.

By 1986, the CEC's work had built a knowledge base that was in demand and financially valuable to the organization. I realized that we could take on consulting work for local governments, undertaking studies, preparing plans, and providing timely advice. We would be paid handsomely for this type of work, and the income would be put to use supporting the larger purposes of the CEC. The key to building this consulting income in a compatible way with our educational mission was to be highly selective about the projects we undertook—choosing only those that could provide important feedback for our educational/policy-making mission.

Income from our recycling operations and consulting accounted for nearly 75 percent of our operating budget, more than $2 million per year, something that I was very proud of. I detested having to grovel at times for foundation support. The fact that we had developed marketable knowledge reinforced my belief that we had built intellectual capital, that our ideas and practical insights were deemed worth paying for and implementing. To this day, I believe that NGOs must strive to develop levels of knowledge, insight, and expertise that are of economic as well as social value, and if they do, their work will become ever more influential.

INTO BERKELEY WE DARED TO TREAD

Can a city recycle 50% of its waste? Berkeley on the environmental front in 1986.

The 1980s were a decade that tested the scale and durability of recycling. Large waste incinerator projects were proposed in the Bay Area, in Los Angeles, and San Diego. Proponents of these projects were typically the public works sector, project developers, and waste incinerator technology companies. The projects that they proposed called for tens of thousands of tons of waste per day to be burned in facilities that they claimed met and exceeded air-quality standards. The burned waste would generate electricity that would be fed into the electricity grid and the residual from incineration, called ash, would be put into landfills if it wasn't deemed toxic.

Early in the decade, in the wake of the 1980–81 energy crisis, the federal government passed the Public Utility Regulatory Policy Act (PURPA), a law to encourage domestic energy production, including waste incineration. The law provided generous electric rate subsidies to waste incinerator projects—sometimes as much as five or six cents per kilowatt hour. These electricity subsidies provided one of the financial legs for the incinerator industry. The other was what are called "put or pay" agreements that require the delivery of a prescribed amount of waste daily, no matter what external conditions might affect delivery, such as recessions when waste volumes fall.

Environmentalists were alarmed by the "put or pay" provisions of proposed projects, believing that the development of incineration as a primary waste option would deal a death blow to the growth of recycling. Environmentalists fought these projects tooth and nail. Also, since a number of the projects were proposed in inner city areas where the poor resided, they were joined by community activists—so-called people of color. Politically, the combination proved overwhelming and one project after another was politically rejected, thus opening up the prospects for recycling.

In 1986, the city of Berkeley was in a funk over what direction to take in managing its solid waste. In 1982, a hotly contested election campaign had been waged to build a waste incinerator on the Berkeley waterfront,[40] a prospect hard to imagine today. The incinerator project was prompted by Berkeley's Public Works Department and had advocates on the city council. Not surprisingly, the proposal drew vehement opposition and it was soundly defeated. In the aftermath of the defeat, the city committed itself to seeing just how far recycling could contribute to its waste management future. A 50 percent recycling goal was adopted by the city council. In characteristic Berkeley fashion, the city wanted to be the first community in the country to forge a bold recycling path. Berkeley issued a request for proposals seeking a firm that could assist the city in charting a path toward a 50 percent recycling rate. When it came to my attention that the proposal was on the street, I thought that we should compete for the contract; if we were selected, it would tap all that we learned about recycling and force our work to another level.

There was an inside favorite firm for the consultancy within the Berkeley bureaucracy, but our work had gained the attention of a young Berkeley councilwoman, Nancy Skinner, who championed us in what proved to be a fairly bruising battle for the job, which we ultimately won. Nancy is today a leading assemblywoman in the California legislature.

The CEC went into this project with some trepidation. Berkeley was a notoriously difficult city to work for. The council had two factions, liberal and radical by any measure. The two factions didn't like each other. In between the council factions stood the Public Works Department that was distrusted by Berkeley's influential nonprofit organizations, the Berkeley Ecology Center and Urban Ore, because it had advocated the discredited waste incinerator proposal. I was warned by some who had ventured into Berkeley's territory that these turbulent cross-currents ended up in legal battles with the city over contract issues. Doing business with the City of Berkeley, especially in the aftermath of its waste wars, was not for the faint of heart.

With assistance from William O'Toole, a private recycling consultant who had majored in systems design at UC San Diego, we and our interns took a deep breath as we approached the precipice of what was to be one of the most ambitious recycling studies in the 1980s, a study with the innocuous title of *A Solid Waste Plan for the City of Berkeley*.

Next to the landmark *Impacts of Growth*, this was the most challenging study I had worked on. To begin with, there were few precedents for demonstrating how a city could recycle 50 percent of its waste, only work done by the Washington-based Institute for Local Self Reliance and a recycling assessment study conducted by the well-known scientist, Dr. Barry Commoner. Our work preceded by several years any significant policy support to build recycling infrastructure such as the curbside commingled and green separation systems so prevalent in California today.

The recycling system in Berkeley was much like the CEC's and others run by nonprofit organizations. There were several drop-off centers around town, a curbside collection program that utilized multiple colored containers, small boxes for newspaper, others for metals and glass and plastics.[41] An old truck would come by, staffed by Berkeley Ecology Center employees, from the very same organization that had inspired the CEC's earliest work. The amount of physical labor used to lift the boxes into the basic stake-sided trucks was painstaking, and the processing equipment used to prepare the materials was labor-intensive, inefficient, and not the best practice for worker safety.

Now in our Gildea Center think tank mode, we were venturing far and wide throughout the world for information—looking for approaches and systems that were well beyond our ken and the capacities of our home-grown recycling operations. With O'Toole's connections, we were able to tap into consulting engineers and industry people who had access to information that was completely new to us.

In 1986, the level of understanding of collection and processing systems was limited. There were few operating curbside programs in the United States and but a handful of material recovery facilities (MRFs), essentially factories that employed material sorters and sorting equipment to segregate and prepare materials for marketing. We combed the literature worldwide and realized that Europe was generally way ahead of us in the design and implementation of recycling equipment and processing know-how.

After mulling through volumes of European studies and considering the current recycling operations in Berkeley, we concluded that with an improved curbside collection program, stronger buy-back centers, and the addition of a processing facility, Berkeley could achieve a recovery rate of about 46 percent, very close to its 50 percent goal. In order to attain this rate of recovery, Berkeley would have to invest in improved materials processing and develop a more sophisticated material recovery facility, essentially a small factory where collected materials could be hand- and mechanically sorted. We developed scenarios for two approaches: a lower-tech, more labor-intensive sorting system and a higher-tech, more mechanical one, the latter based on European technology.

When we unveiled our conclusions, I took in the response with some amusement and exasperation. Berkeley's leadership tended toward all-knowingness when it came to just about everything, and it was no different when it came to recycling. Berkeley-centric, it was—if it's not invented in Berkeley, it couldn't be very good. Our higher-tech version of a material processing facility drawn from the European experience was greeted with derision by the nonprofits and by their advocates on the city council. What I found most disturbing was how little curiosity there was, except for Nancy Skinner amid the body politic or the recycling community, about the possibilities for something radically new that could improve working conditions for the people doing the collection while contributing to improved system economics. At the public hearings before the city council, there was essentially no public discussion of the options and their merits or weaknesses. Ours was a study destined for the shelves—depressing, considering the enormous amount of work we had put into it.

But I had been forewarned. At least we were not embroiled in a lawsuit with the City of Berkeley!

Putting these frustrations and disappointments aside, we knew that the opportunity to conduct such a far-reaching study at such a pivotal time more than served its purpose. We had stretched ourselves mightily to understand and articulate all facets of the means to collect and process recyclables. It was this knowledge, coupled with our on-the-ground recycling experience, that greatly enriched our theory/practice approach to environmentalism and that deepened our influence in shaping what was to come in California.

In the end, Berkeley took the low-tech approach to its recycling future, a position supported by the influential Berkeley Ecology Center. The community decided that this option would best maintain the local nonprofit recycling organization running the program. At the time, I found this perspective limiting, though I thought well of the Ecology Center. Berkeley has always had a mind of its own. It revels in its quirks, its idiosyncratic nature that resists outside influences, and its downsides are more than counterbalanced by the caliber of the leaders Berkeley has produced over the years, leaders like Nancy Skinner who have proven to be such an important environmental force in California. Not to mention Alice Waters, David Brower, and a host of other environmental luminaries.

RECYCLING GOES MAINSTREAM

As the CEC's work branched out into publishing, lead seminars, and think tank studies, we continued to expand our recycling programs within Santa Barbara. In 1985, we initiated the first rollout of what was to become Santa Barbara's curbside recycling program. With seed funds from the county of Santa Barbara, we developed a pilot neighborhood program, distributing blue containers to participating residences, collecting and processing the recyclables, and monitoring the program's effectiveness over a period of one year. Another recycling innovation that the CEC initiated during the early to late 1980s was a Material Recovery Facility (MRF), essentially a factory where workers separate recyclable materials from waste that moves on a conveyor belt. Today's MRFs are altogether different animals from our simple hand-separation factory; they now use a wide range of equipment, including magnetic separators, eddy machines, optical sorting equipment, and complex screens, to do much of the work previously done by hand. We built a second MRF at the county's transfer station (a place to consolidate loads of waste to ship to the distant landfill), along with a demonstration composting facility. These facilities were undertaken with a combination of the CEC's own money, contracts, and grant funds.

The MRF at the County Transfer Station received and processed the curbside collected materials, prepared them for shipment to markets, and arranged for the transportation of these commodities to paper mills, glass factories, steel mills, and aluminum smelters. The CEC developed and managed the entire program until the county of Santa Barbara, as it began to grow a recycling and waste management bureaucracy, could ease the

CEC out of its operating position as it realized that recycling could further boost government.

The MRF was set up as a buy-back center for the community, taking in all types of recyclables, including glass, metals, office, newspaper, cardboard, and plastics. It also processed office paper that the CEC collected from programs it set up at the University of California, Santa Barbara, and commercial establishments throughout the community, including banks, research and development facilities, and offices of all types and sizes.

This MRF was run entirely by the CEC with limited support from the county from the revenues received from the recyclable material. It became the centerpiece of our recycling enterprise, which now included two buy-back recycling centers, a small truck fleet, and a mobile recycling collection program that collectively employed some thirty staff members.

As we continued to develop our recycling business, we deepened our reach into the recycling policy arena in Sacramento. California's waste stream, amounting to some forty million tons annually, contained materials that were about 65 percent recyclable, yet only about 10 percent of what was recoverable was being recovered. Of these forty million tons, about ten million tons could be composted, yielding as much as five million tons of finished compost. The potential of composting at least a portion of these ten million tons of organic materials was intriguing to us. After all, we had begun our work pioneering composting projects in our garden projects. Composting was part of our organizational DNA.

By the late 1980s, as the result of our recycling work and our growing think tank reputation, we had developed numerous relationships with experts in academia and industry covering all facets of recycling, including composting. One of our relationships was with Phil Legge, who had spent his career with Proctor and Gamble. Since diapers were a key product of P&G, Phil had been asked by the company to identify possible solutions to handling diaper waste, something that had attracted the ire of environmentalists throughout the country. Indeed, diapers had become synonymous with the waste problem; they were allegedly filling up landfills, according to many activists and the media.

Dr. William Rathje was a Harvard-trained Mayan archaeologist who became the world's first person to research the diaper issue in depth, along with many other facets of municipal solid waste. Beginning in 1973 and continuing for some twenty years, he worked in cooperation with the city of Tuscon's solid waste department. Rathje looked at "the streaming detritus of daily existence with the same quiet excitement displayed by Howard Carter and George Herbert, Earl of Carnarvon at the unpillaged, unopened tomb of Tutankhamun. Landfills represent valuable lodes of information that may, when mined and interpreted, produce valuable insights—insights not into the nature of some past society, but into the nature of our own. Garbage is among humanity's most prodigious physical legacies to those who have yet to be born, if we can come to understand our discards."[42]

Into the breach of the diaper wars waded Rathje, armed with the tools of an archaeologist, heightened powers of observation, and the ability to scientifically measure the evidence before him. What did he find? Again, in *Rubbish!: The Archaeology of Garbage*, regarding the popular view that diapers were filling up landfills throughout America, he found that disposable diapers in fact "constitute no more than one percent of the contents of landfills by volume. These findings have been confirmed in excavation after excavation. Disposable diapers may be a big-ticket item in landfills compared with toothpicks and check stubs, but they are simply not in the same league as paper of various kinds. Given all the other, larger targets of opportunity, it may be misguided to draw a bead on disposable diapers. It is certainly an illusion to believe that eliminating disposable diapers would have anything but an imperceptible effect on the larger garbage picture."

Although concern about disposable diapers may have been misplaced, the perception of diapers as a problem was real and a deeper consideration over what might be done with them was of interest to us. Legge, Dominski, and I explored the possibilities of compost as a solution to a wide range of organic waste problems including diapers. P&G was involved in a number of exploratory ventures to show that it was taking the waste problem seriously. Among its most far-reaching endeavors was the introduction of concentrated laundry detergents in a single plastic bag instead of the usual large cardboard package that included a large amount of "filler" to make the consumer believe that he or she was buying more product than he or she thought. To its credit, P&G made a serious run at selling concentrates, more so than any of the other consumer product companies at that time.

Our discussions with Legge and the Santa Barbara County Public Works Department led to a grant to the CEC that allowed us to undertake a three-year compost development program. Legge had introduced us to an agricultural scientist, Dr. Assiz Shalarapour, at the time a dean at the University of Florida in Tallahassee, to head a compost demonstration project that would include disposable diapers as one of its inputs.

The prospect of receiving funding from a company with an economic interest in the findings of a grant project involved a CEC board decision informed by a thorough discussion of the pros and cons, in a similar vein to what we had done when we had the opportunity to receive grant support from ARCO Solar. By this time, we had developed a board policy that established that any funding from the private sector could not be tied to a hoped-for outcome by the funding party, and that the CEC alone would remain in control of the project and its findings. The CEC was scrupulous in vetting any conflicts of interest or possibilities of having its work become a front for what was to become known as "greenwashing." There were numerous occasions when possible private funding was rejected by the staff and board for such reasons.

Of course, to some in the environmental movement, any funding by the private sector was seen by some as an anathema. We just didn't subscribe to that, given the mission we had set out for the organization—as theory/practice oriented, with a commitment to develop practical solutions and practical policies. In certain situations, such as employing the most promising solar, waste, or other renewable energy or conservation systems, our interests and that of some of the companies who gave us technology were aligned. We were unapologetic in such cases, and when criticisms were leveled at us we faced them and went on. In the case of taking funding from Proctor and Gamble, we felt that the investigative path of building a composting demonstration project that included diaper waste, in conjunction with the county of Santa Barbara, was a worthy one.

In a policy paper we wrote in 1987, "Composting California's Ten Million Tons," the CEC advocated that a strong education program was needed to communicate the safety and ecological value of compost products; that the question of whether compost derived from mixed waste was safe and able to meet end-use markets and that home and institutional composting should be encouraged by local and state government. The CEC also recommended that health and safety standards for compost and mulch products needed to be developed as well as product testing procedures and technical training for operators and state regulators. Little did I realize that within four years of publishing "California's Ten Million Tons" I would be in a position to help lead the state's efforts to educate, inform, and utilize compost generated from our towns and cities, and that by 1996, most of the goals set forth at the CEC would be institutionalized.

Ever since I saw compost piles made by Alan Chadwick's apprentices at the UC Santa Cruz campus, I have been enchanted by what composting can accomplish. From death comes birth and regeneration. From the wastes of cities, resulting from food processing, from dairies and rendering plants, the compost process is a path to convert waste into products that can replenish our soils and our damaged landscapes, nourishing nature and man alike. It would be no easy challenge to begin to transform ten million tons of organic materials into compost, but what could be more than important than composting to help move us out of the wasteland of our own creation?

The CEC's long experience running a recycling program based on the wild up-and-down swings of the commodities marketplace was proof that without policy intervention, recycling would remain a small, cyclical enterprise. That's why, with the inception of the Gildea Center, the CEC began to focus its work on advancing a policy impetus to make recycling a centerpiece of a new waste management paradigm.

The CEC's experience running recycling facilities had underscored how key markets were for the success of recycling. Indeed, there could be no recycling unless there were markets for the collected materials. This fact became fixed in the CEC's mindset because of the economic recessions in the 1970s and 1980s. Recessionary economic conditions meant low demand, if any, for recycled materials such as old newspapers and steel.

Prior to the growing interest in recycling in the late 1980s, recycling was a purely economically driven enterprise, subject to the laws of supply and demand. When paper prices were high, and the demand for paper strong, old paper became valuable, and its value supported an informal but nonetheless effective sub-economy of what we then called "scavengers." When prices waned, this collection network would break down and, during the most severe downturns, people just stopped collecting because it simply wasn't worth the time and effort. Conversely, during periods of strong demand for recyclables, the informal network of scavengers would grow, sometimes very rapidly.

As interest perked in recycling and it became apparent that there would be a policy intervention in the marketplace that would subsidize the collection and processing of recyclables, the CEC quickly seized on the importance of understanding the capacity of the recycling marketplace to absorb the new quantities of materials that public policy would generate. Without elasticity on the demand side, simply collecting recyclables wouldn't ensure adequate demand. If oversupplies resulted from increased collection, there could be price collapses, effectively undermining the growth of the policy-driven collection programs.

The market dimension of recycling fascinated me. The condition of that marketplace determined the financial base that the CEC depended on, the payroll that I had to meet as its executive director, and the profits that I could use to pay for staff and research that were essential to our think tank function. I met with many market experts in all of the main industries—paper, glass, plastics, and metals—and read the market journals and studied both domestic and foreign market trends. As I deepened my understanding of the recycling marketplace, it became apparent to me that Asia held the key to the supply-demand equation in the future. Domestic growth in recycling would depend on growth in demand from Asian countries.

A JOURNEY TO THE FAR EAST

In 1987, I requested and received support from my board of directors to make a major trip to the Far East, accompanied by my wife and young children, to investigate the emergence of Asia as a market for the anticipated growth in the supply of recyclables from California. Preparations for this trip were many months in the making, involving several of our staff and outreach to high-level people in industry and the US government. In setting up key meetings in Asia, no one was more helpful to me than Senator John Melcher of Montana, the father of Joan Melcher, the editor of the Gildea Center's quarterly publication, the Gildea Review. Joan arranged a meeting for me with Senator Melcher at his office in Washington, DC. I found Senator Melcher had a wealth of contacts that were indispensable to me. He was close friends with Mike Mansfield, the former senator of Montana who was then the US ambassador to Japan. Melcher prevailed on Mansfield to arrange meetings for me in Japan and China. Melcher himself was close to the Philippine government, and he arranged meetings for me while I was in Manila.

In the late 1980s, Japan was among the largest buyers of scrap materials from the United States. Japan had been the largest buyer of US-generated scrap steel in the run-up to World War II, and as Japan rebuilt its economy during the postwar years, it once again resumed robust purchases of secondary commodities from the United States.

Japan was our first stop on the trip. It was considered then to have the world's leading industry—indeed, all eyes and ears were on Japan. At the height of its spectacular rise, one block of Tokyo real estate was worth all of Manhattan Island.

My first meeting in Tokyo was with Ambassador Mansfield, who was much revered by Japanese officials and citizens alike. Fluent in Japanese and an ardent admirer of Japanese culture, Mansfield was the archetypal ambassador. Although he passed on many years ago, he remains a legendary figure in the history of American diplomacy, a proverbial wise man in the world of geo-politics. The ambassadorship to Japan was one of the most important diplomatic posts for the United States in the late 1980s, given Japan's ascendancy in the world economy. It was the preeminent manufacturer of sophisticated electronics, and its "just in time" manufacturing system was admired throughout the world.

Mansfield could not have been kinder and more helpful. Although he had seen and done almost everything at this stage of his life, he exuded warmth, care, and empathy. No wonder he was so revered in a country where finesse and sensitivity were of paramount importance.

Mansfield wired ahead to China when our plans were still formative. China at that time was like a black hole when it came to setting up meetings and logistics for a family visiting that country. Without his call, our trip to China would have been a bust.

Before we arrived in Japan, Mansfield's office had contacted Japan's Ministry of International Trade and Industry (MITI), the famed governmental institution responsible for identifying and assisting in the development of Japanese technology. This contact led to a full itinerary and a luncheon meeting with MITI officials in the plush Okura Hotel where visitors of state, including US presidents, would stay when in Japan, and a dinner for Kathy and me with one of MITI's rising young stars, Kensuki Kobayashi, and his wife—a meal that cost a small fortune (fortunately, not ours).

Accompanied by Kobayashi, I visited a Styrofoam recycling plant next to Tokyo Bay. Japan's huge fishing fleets used large quantities of Styrofoam to insulate the fish caught by their fishing fleets that plied the world's seas. The fishing industry, with MITI's help, was trying to develop technologies that could use the discarded Styrofoam to produce energy or other products. Visiting this plant gave me a window on the enormity of Japan's seafood enterprise.

The most interesting and memorable part of my site visits was a tour I was given of a waste incinerator operated by the Tokyo Municipal Government. Waste incineration has been heavily relied upon in Japan for many decades as a primary means of managing solid wastes because of the country's great population density and mountainous terrain that left little room for landfills.

The incinerator in Tokyo that I visited was built next to an elementary school.

The incinerator consisted of an immense building housing the waste-receiving area, the combustor, and the control room, where temperatures were regulated and air emissions monitored. Rising out of the building was a vertical stack at least forty stories in height. The stack towered over the densely packed city below of mostly two- and three-story buildings. I winced when an elementary school was pointed out in the shadow of the stack. Next to the school was a large swimming pool, a community center, and a Japanese garden. What to make of this?

Tokyo officials explained to me, through an interpreter, that a social compact of sorts was struck between the neighborhood where the incinerator was located and the municipal government. In return for hosting the incinerator, the neighborhood received amenities including an Olympic-sized swimming pool heated by the waste heat from the incinerator, a community center, a hotel where people visiting residents of the neighborhood could stay, and a Japanese garden.

While I was familiar with the practice of land use exactions, where in return for accepting the environmental burdens of a project, such as traffic and pollution, a community receives either cash payments to support public services or specific amenities like parks or recreational facilities, I had never seen anything like this. In my mind the "compact" meant either one of two things: the Japanese public trusted its government to do what was right and was willing to make sacrifices for the larger good, or the Japanese public was much more docile in exercising its rights, and the power of government was just too strong to be bucked. As an outsider, I wasn't likely to learn which interpretation was the correct one; it was probably a bit of both.

In addition to waste incineration, recycling is a key means of managing solid waste in Japan. The country has a very sophisticated system of separating recyclable materials from nonrecyclables or burnables. Residences must separate their recyclable items into roughly eight different components and set these out on the days prescribed for their collection. I was once privileged to have a Japanese student in my class at UCSB who gave the class a presentation of how the Japanese go about their intricate separation of materials. She explained that each material was collected separately on a given day—and if you didn't abide by the separation techniques, collection would be denied to you. She also gave a breathtakingly beautiful demonstration of how Japanese women use a scarf-like material as a shopping bag, which becomes capable of holding a wide range of product sizes and shapes.

Experiencing a society that by and large trusted its government and acquiesced to expert opinion was new to me. I was of a generation that rebelled against authority, questioned experts, and wasn't good at discriminating between larger and lesser societal goods. On one hand, I was appalled by a Japanese society that would allow an incinerator to be built over a school with possibly serious environmental consequences for the children that played below it. On the other, I was intrigued that Japan was able to build projects that it deemed necessary, and that Japanese society was willing to make the sacrifices that needed to be made for the larger society to function and prosper.

It struck me then, as it does today, that in looking to our future, American society will have to face many hard trade-offs in the coming years and decades. The choices are sometimes stark, pitting the protection of the environment and the preservation of natural resources against very immediate and real human needs for jobs and energy. Consider several examples where hard trade-offs must be made. Solar energy development requires large tracts of land and the development of new electrical transmission systems to carry solar energy–derived electricity to users. Natural habitats will be disturbed or even destroyed in building solar energy–generating systems, and transmitting the electricity requires rights-of-way purchases and unsightly transmission lines. Similar impacts accompany the development of wind farms with their huge windmills often three hundred feet or more in height: noise, bird deaths from the rotating blades, and the construction of transmission lines to carry the wind-generated electricity to customers.

I grew up with the pervasive smell of petroleum in the air; the loud sounds of power boats racing in the waterways every weekend; highway lights casting a harsh glow on our once quiet and dark neighborhood street. I am certain that constructing a renewable energy future won't have the degree of negative impacts in terms of public health that building our industrial infrastructure and our fossil fuel–dependent way of life has had. But we'd be foolish to think that a renewable energy future will come without a price.

TAIWAN: A GLIMPSE INTO THE WORLD'S ELECTRONIC WASTELAND

After our visit to Japan, we went to Taiwan, where I was the guest of Taiwan's Industrial Technology Research Institute (ITRI). We spent a day in Taipei, which in 1987 seemed raw and dirty—understandable, given that it was barely forty years since mainland Chinese had fled to Taiwan to escape the Chinese Revolution. A new country was being built on the quick.

While in Taiwan, I visited several paper mills that were consuming used fiber from the United States, and I made the long trip from Taipei down to the southern port city of Kaohsiung, where one of the first electronic disassembly and recycling facilities in the world had been developed by the ITRI engineer who drove me there. The paper plant was unremarkable, a small facility that would process old fiber into container board used for packaging. But the trip to Kaohsiung was a revelation.

Kaohsiung is a port city and Taiwan's second largest metropolis, located on the southern extremity of the country, some 250 miles from Taipei. On the long drive south, we passed through the agricultural heart of Taiwan, a landscape riddled with small freshwater ponds. Fish ponds were everywhere, and they gave the landscape a plundered and battered look. There were many abandoned ponds where possibly the pond environment was no longer suitable for the fish—perhaps too toxic from the application of heavy amounts of pesticides to control insects and from accumulated fish food and fish wastes in the water?

Also along the way I observed workers with little protective gear, save for masks, spraying their crops with pesticide by hand. I couldn't help wondering what the human price would be in terms of cancers and other diseases for this seemingly indiscriminate and intimate use of pesticides.

174

We didn't arrive in Kaohsiung until nightfall, when after a quick dinner, we awoke in the morning to a bustling, humid port city with the worst-quality air I had ever experienced. Visibility was, at best, a few hundred yards; my eyes screamed with pain as we drove toward our destination, a port-side complex of mostly mom-and-pop businesses that dismantled and recovered precious metals such as cadmium, silver, copper and gold found in some of the electrical appliances and devices.

Next to this recycling industrial zone was the port of Kaohsiung. It was filled with ships unloading the developed world's electronic and mechanical discards, used utility cables, transformers, household appliances—including air conditioners, televisions, refrigerators, and stoves—old computers, auto mufflers, and catalytic convertors. For each of these products and devices, there were one or more businesses that specialized in dismantling these creations to extract precious, semiprecious, or just plain metals with value.

We walked from one dismantler to the next. Men wielding sledgehammers were breaking apart catalytic converters; men and women without masks or any other kind of protective gear were working in the open air, using torches to extract the precious metals found in the catalytic convertors. Toxic smoke and dust were everywhere. This scene was repeated in other mom-and- pop enterprises throughout the several blocks of the zone, creating a landscape the likes of which I had never seen. What I remember most clearly were the sounds: the light and sporadic pounding of hammers, the hiss of the acetylene torches, the roar of trucks coming and going in this shadowland of our consumer society.

Yet, as appalling as the conditions were, when it comes to the handling of wastes it was all relative. At least this complex was in a designated industrial area where the activities were conducted on paved, impervious surfaces and firefighting equipment was available, along with hospitals in the event of accidents. At least it was a project by design and not accident.

As we left, T. E. Lung, the industrial engineer who had designed the hazardous waste industrial zone, informed me that the facility was going to be shut down within a few years. But why? I asked. It seemed to me to be such an accomplishment. He explained that the Taiwanese government was increasingly uncomfortable with the idea of being a dumping ground and a recycling center for Europe and the United States. Taiwan was on a rapid development trajectory, and these recycling activities were a source of embarrassment to the leadership. Also, labor rates in Taiwan were rising to the point where this kind of work could be accomplished for much less in places like mainland China, India, and Bangladesh.

As I reflect back on the trip, some twenty-five years distant now, I wonder what it would be like to make that same trip today. Taipei is now a very prosperous, modern, and, I'm told, clean city. Central Taiwan, with its rich agriculture, is probably a far cry from the pockmarked, scary landscape that I witnessed then, raw and dirty. And what about Kaohsiung? I would imagine that its air quality is much improved, as Taiwan has been able to invest in environmental management.

I know one thing: the flow of electronic waste that was ceaseless then is probably only a memory to a very few Taiwanese. The industrial zone that I visited is long gone—as is the electronic waste of the world found in new homes in China, Bangladesh, and Africa. And there is an important story in this. It illustrates how quickly, armed with the resources to do what it takes to clean up the environment, it can be done. And we should take heart in this. We have the knowledge, the tools, and the resources to positively impact our environment. A one-generation effort to change the course of man's impact on nature can result in immense benefits that, once established, will likely be sustained.

CHINA: A RECYCLING DRAGON AWAKENS

From Taiwan we flew to Beijing. China in 1987 was still climbing out
of the nightmare that was the Cultural Revolution; there were few automobiles—the city was a sea of bicycles, people, and hand carts. Construction
sites were defined by their ubiquitous bamboo scaffolding. People were clad
in old Chairman Mao coats, and with the exception of the rich and vibrant
colors of the Forbidden City and the bright red flags of China that flutter in
Tiananmen Square, Beijing was a drab and somber place.

Our four-day stay in Beijing was headquartered in an old Chinese-style
hotel, not by choice but by necessity. It turned out that our travel agent had
booked us into a hotel that didn't exist. As we scratched our heads in front
of a vacant lot that marked the address we were given on our itinerary, we
realized we were going to have to improvise, and do it fast.

I don't recall how we found it, but taking a cab going east on Chang'an
Jie, the main boulevard that fronts the Forbidden City and Tiananmen
Square, we found our way to a hotel that had a vacant room. The room was
large, with shabby furniture and stained rugs that made you want to walk
lightly and sit that way as well. The hotel lobby was a scene of some in-
trigue, with lots of young Chinese men hanging about, looking scruffy and
sinister. Fortunately, it was in that lobby that a young man of twenty years
introduced himself to us in halting but understandable English as "John."

At first suspicious, we warmed to him, and during the course of our
four days there, he became our constant companion, negotiating cab fares,
going to the local store to buy us stuff that would cost twice as much in
the hotel, and later telling us his story and how he learned English through
The Voice of America.

He had been an oil worker in a far-off region in China and made his way to Beijing, hoping to find a way out of China through contacts that he would make in the capital. Later, he did make his way to the United States through a woman in Florida who sponsored him. He soon married, qualified as a mechanical engineer, and, last I heard from him, was living the American Dream in Houston, Texas. He was a rebel at heart befriending an American family, and when getting close to any foreigners, especially Americans, he could attract the interest of the local ubiquitous spy force. He beat off many taunts that came his way. John was steadfast in defending our interests and accompanied us on our obligatory visit to the Great Wall, where throngs of people gathered around my seven-year-old daughter, drawn to her by her wavy light brown hair—a type of hair that they had not seen before. And some of those who cast their attention upon her actually reached out and touched her hair, making the experience for her all the more "hair-raising." It was all in good humor and innocent, but for her this was an unnerving experience that presaged a truly harrowing one that was to come our way a week later in Shanghai.

As we walked through cobbled Tiananmen Square at sunset in the soft smoggy light, we stopped to watch the color guard perform its evening ritual, the lowering of the flag in front of the Forbidden City where the image of Chairman Mao watches over the motherland. As we focused on the color guard's precision in this calm and empty sacred center of China, we could hardly have known that in less than a year the square would be filled with young Chinese celebrating what they hoped would be a new dawn in Chinese history—a celebration that was to end in the tragedy that the world now knows as the Tiananmen Square Massacre.

The Chinese section of our trip was thrown together, as diplomatic efforts within the United States had yielded no official response. But thanks to Ambassador Mansfield's proddings from Tokyo, a number of visits with government officials and tours were hastily arranged. We were taken to a recycling facility that processed some of the millions of bicycle tires generated within Beijing each year. We also visited a plastics recycling plant. Plastics were not in widespread use in China then and one rarely saw plastic bags being carried around, discarded in the streets, or strewn about the countryside, but the plastics that were in use were being collected and used to make products such as vials for medicines or flooring products.

After Beijing we flew to Shanghai, where I met with American consul officials. No facility tours were arranged, so we experienced Shanghai as tourists, going about the city on our own. We were fortunate to have at our service, courtesy of the US Consulate, a fine interpreter, a graduate of the prestigious Fudan University in Shanghai, who befriended us. He honored our family by inviting us to his family's autumn festival meal, an invitation I was told was rarely extended to visitors and especially not foreigners. We eagerly anticipated our visit the next evening.

It was dark when we took off in a taxi from our hotel to the family home, an apartment deep within the vast metropolis. Upon arrival, we were greeted at the curb by our interpreter's family. A young girl of my daughter Sarita's age approached us, dressed in the most beautiful golden costume with intelligence and beauty to match. We learned that she was a member of the Shanghai Ballet and was dressed in her performance regalia.

Sadly, what began so wonderfully turned quickly into an ordeal. During dinner, Sarita started to complain about pain in her stomach, which under the circumstances we tried to suppress. But the pain didn't go away, and soon she couldn't sit up. Our interpreter's father was a doctor. He took her into another room, where he examined her. He returned and spoke to his son, who in turn told us that she was suffering from appendicitis. His son called a taxi and we were taken to the diplomats' hospital, where he thought we could get the medical attention she needed. Medical facilities in China were very basic in even very large cities like Shanghai in the 1980s. I could barely make out that the building we had been taken to was indeed a hospital. There were no people at the door, no wheelchairs, nothing. I had to carry Sarita into the building, only to find that they did not accept children at the hospital—and we were shooed away!

What happened next became a nightmare. Alone in the depths of Shanghai, unable to speak Chinese, we were taken to one hospital after another. Finally, early in the morning we made our way into a children's hospital. Our introduction to this hospital couldn't have been more un-nerving. At the front desk, a child was wailing and writhing with pain, his head deformed by some terrible accident. Holding Sarita in my arms, we were shuttled to a room filled with cribs, and I was directed to put Sarita in one of the cribs. A nurse brought an IV to the crib and hung it from a coat hanger. A chair was brought over, and there I sat holding Sarita's hand, the poor child in pain and terrified by her surroundings. Adding to her misery were mosquitoes and flies everywhere.

A young male physician attended to us. He was very attentive and friendly, but spoke only a few words of English. We labored to communicate. Thinking back to the circumstances for our Chinese hosts, it probably was not a good situation for them to be associated with foreigners and dealing with a medical emergency. While I was trying to cope with my distraught daughter in a difficult setting, Kathy was frantically calling the US Consulate for help. Although communication with the doctor was minimal, the message that came through was that Sarita needed to be operated on by the following morning. Her appendicitis was acute and her life was at risk. The prospect of surgery under these circumstances was frightening, because Sarita had been found at birth to have a weak immunological system and had had several near-fatal hospitalizations. The possibility of her getting an infection in the aftermath of surgery was terrifying.

With each hour that passed, our situation became more complicated and desperate. Kathy had made contact with a US Consulate nurse, whose every word of advice we came to hang on. She urged us to take Sarita out of the hospital unless there was no alternative but an operation. She stated that the likelihood of infection would be high if we went ahead with surgery. Based on my wife's description of her medical condition, the nurse wasn't convinced that Sarita's condition was acute. But the doctors kept insisting that surgery was imperative. Then the stakes of our situation were raised when the head of the hospital showed up in our room, a tall, commanding woman of maybe fifty, who spoke decent English and said that she knew then US Surgeon General C. Everett Koop, an association that she no doubt thought would reassure us.

Kathy and I had been talking to each other throughout the early morning hours, trying to figure out the best course of action. These talks were agonizing because the situation was so dreadful and we couldn't be sure what to do. But clarity came with the dawn. As light began to penetrate the hospital room, it came alive with the movement of children. Those who could walk found the presence of foreigners fascinating. Soon there was a throng of children around Sarita's crib. At first, I encouraged the children to be there with us, but then they began to get aggressive, some reaching into the crib to touch Sarita's hair. Some were wounded, others deformed, and poor Sarita, vulnerable as she was, was subject to yet another terrifying situation. It was then that we decided that we had to risk it and try to make our way to Hong Kong as the consulate nurse had suggested that we do.

Our decision to leave the hospital was made more agonizing by the kindness that was shown us by the young doctor and the hospital director, insisting as they did to the very last breath before we left that a decision to leave was to put our daughter's life at grave risk.

Once our decision was made, Kathy went into high gear. She dressed Sarita in her best outfit, braided her hair and made sure she looked picture-perfect by applying make up to cover her drawn and pale appearance. We knew that in order to get onto our flight that morning, Sarita had to look healthy. Kathy did a masterful job, and Sarita played her part to a T; we made it onto the flight and pretended everything was well with the family.

Kathy had prearranged with the US Consulate nurse to call ahead to Hong Kong and make plans for Sarita to be operated on shortly after our arrival there. Just after midway through the flight, the point where we knew the airplane couldn't turn back to Shanghai, we got the attention of the stewardess and told her that our daughter was ill and that we would need medical assistance in Hong Kong. When we arrived, Sarita was rushed to the Hong Kong Adventist Hospital, where she was operated on. Our harrowing ordeal was over. The consulate nurse's assessment of Sarita's condition was right. The appendicitis was not acute.

Following her operation, Sarita could not travel for ten days by plane. She and Kathy ended up staying at the Peninsula Hotel, one of the most elegant in the world. It so happened that we had the good fortune of obtaining travel insurance for the family. All the hotels in Hong Kong were full, and by default, the Peninsula was the only one with an available room. The insurance company had to book it for us. Kathy and Sarita were picked up at the hospital and taken to the hotel by a Rolls Royce and spent a week in the lap of luxury.

As we put our all-too-interesting trip to China behind us, there was nothing I had seen that could predict that within twenty years China would become the world's recycling dragon. Starting around the mid-1990s, China's fast-growing economy, built on exports and nurtured by both foreign direct investment and a shortage of commodities like paper, began to build recycling industries that helped feed the country's expanding need for raw materials. As demand for packaging to ship goods abroad increased, China made large new investments in paper and board manufacturing, and within a matter of years it became the largest importer of recovered paper, the largest consumer of packaging, and today, the largest paper and board manufacturer in the world.

SMOKEY MOUNTAIN, MANILA

Smokey Mountain, Manila, 1988.
The notorious landfill in the heart of Manila that typified
"recycling" in the developing world cities in the 1980s.

What he knew about mainly was trash. For nearly all the waking hours of nearly all the years he could remember, he'd been buying and selling to recyclers the things that richer people threw away.

KATHERINE BOO
BEHIND THE BEAUTIFUL FOREVERS:
LIFE, DEATH, AND HOPE IN A MUMBAI UNDERCITY [43]

Now in Manila, I was the beneficiary of Senator Melcher's very special relationship with the Philippine government. He arranged for me to be met by the secretary of commerce, who introduced me to leading recycling companies in Metro Manila. He also arranged with the mayor of Manila to have me taken, along with my son, Andre, to visit Smokey Mountain, Manila's landfill located at the edge of Manila Bay. Smokey Mountain owed its name to a continuously burning fire deep within the landfill that was the source of a constant smoke plume. Like most landfills in poorer countries throughout the world, it supported a large population of people who scavenged whatever valuables could be recovered from the deposited waste. According to reports that I had read, thousands of people lived at the edges of the landfill in shanties built from materials scavenged from the landfill.

My contacts in Manila were aghast that I would want to visit a place like that. But I was determined to go if possible. It took some maneuvering from the higher-ups in the Philippine government to arrange the tour. The government was sensitive about a foreigner visiting so unseemly a place as Smokey Mountain. I probably would never have been granted permission to go there had the request not come from a sitting US senator who was highly thought of within the Philippine government.

In the end, the mayor of Manila's office arranged for and supervised the tour. My entourage consisted of an official within the mayor's office; my son, Andre; and two trucks—the first for me and my son, and the second a military vehicle with two soldiers carrying rifles.

The drive into the area was surreal. Our truck creaked and rattled as we hit one pothole after another. We passed by a vast landscape of shanties where thousands of people lived under unfathomable conditions. On the long approach, the sound of rock music seemed to come from everywhere, amplifying the surreality of the approach to Smokey Mountain.

Nothing could prepare us for the sights and sounds we experienced when we reached the summit of the landfill. In the mountains of trash all about us there were people everywhere. Many were carrying sticks with nails at the end that they used to pick up a bit of cardboard, a plastic container—anything of value they could find. As they picked through the waste, one truck after another came lumbering in, extremely loud, belching fumes, and creating extra danger in an already dangerous environment.

As disturbing as it was to see and smell what was before us, what really silenced Andre and me was the presence of children, some so small that you weren't really aware of them until they were right up next to you. I shall never forget the images of those children, dressed in shorts, wearing rubber boots, their faces full of soot, their eyes alert to any little treasure they might find, walking all about that fetid, ghastly place. And to think that their homes, just a few hundred yards away, were built from the very trash they were picking through. And that their fate was to live out their lives in such an environment.

If you go to a less developed country like the Philippines, you soon realize that recycling is a well-honed and pervasive part of a mostly underground economy. If there is a formal waste collection system or not, before the discards reach the collection truck the material has been picked through for valuables. What remains is picked through again as the trucks transport the waste to a landfill, and then when it arrives at the landfill, there is a hierarchy of scavengers who have rights to the most valuable materials, sweeping through it before the second-tier scavengers get their turn. You learn that we have little, really, to teach people in these parts of the world about recycling, unless a city develops to the point where the scavenging economy is not allowed to continue. It is then, and only then, that the recycling systems we have developed in the West will have relevance.

I took extensive video footage of our trip to Smokey Mountain. I have often shown it to my University of California environmental studies students, some of whom are from the very countries that have such landfills. Most of these students don't have a clue that such places exist and act almost appalled that their professor would go to a place like Smokey Mountain. Yet I don't see how one can penetrate the problems and come up with workable solutions without experiencing firsthand the human and environmental impacts of our creations.

Apart from the many insights I gained from the Asian trip—insights into Third World waste problems and the emerging nightmare of electronic waste proliferation and the nascent recycling industry in China—I made other trips that contributed to a wider perspective on ways to reduce, reuse, recycle, and convert waste into energy. In 1987, I was invited to Rome to visit and meet with executives and to observe facilities developed by Sorain Cecchini, the largest waste company in Italy. It operated the huge Rome landfill, but more important, it had developed new technologies to separate waste streams into recyclable components and produce compost on a very large scale. Earlier I had met Pietro Carrera, their chief engineer, who was charming and brilliant.

A graduate of the University of Milan in civil engineering, Pietro spent years designing food processing systems. Now he was applying his food processing know-how to the solid waste challenge. He took me to Sorain Cecchini plants in Perugia and near Monte Cassino, the likes of which I had never seen. The plants were enormous. They contained a maze of equipment, conveyors going every which way, machines that would break plastic bags, and air jets that could separate heavier materials from lighter ones such as plastics and sheets of paper. Carrera and Sorain wanted to sell their waste technology in the United States, and they were eager to convince me that their systems were the best in the world.

I must say I had a terrific time in Italy. Visiting a composting plant admid olive groves with the beautiful hilltop town of Perugia in the distance was a far cry from the wastelands I experienced in Asia. And the plant near Monte Cassino appeared to be a technological marvel, except that it wasn't operating. Why not?

As sophisticated and impressive as these plants seemed to be, I began to have reservations about their applicability in the United States. For one thing, they were extremely expensive—so expensive that I never could quite figure out how Sorain was able to build them, let alone operate them, even in Italy, where cost-plus operations seemed to flourish. Sorain must have been subsidized, but I never did get a satisfactory explanation of how this happened. They were far too expensive for the US market, where we had few subsidies for recycling and where landfill costs were a small fraction of those in Europe. When I would press Carrera about the quality of the compost produced from mixed waste–sourced material, the answer that came back was not reassuring. He said it was being used for "land reclamation," whatever that meant.

I dug for more, asking if I could visit one of the farms where Carrera claimed that some of the compost was being applied. That never happened. There was simply no transparency when it came to divulging the markets for the product. And to borrow the cliché, where there is smoke there is fire. It turned out the reassuring claims made by Sorain regarding the marketability of its product proved to be false. The fact is that the old adage "dirty in, dirty out" holds true with compost. Repeated attempts by Sorain and other technology providers to make viable composts from mixed waste were largely failures.

The Sorain experience was nonetheless helpful. As with my dealings with Control Data Corporation, I learned that the technology marketplace is replete with smoke and mirrors. Exaggerated performance claims are commonplace. With enough money and marketing dollars, a company can put on quite a show. It can manufacture a convincing case that it has a product that is worth the investment of millions of dollars. Sometimes it scores a success—sadly, more often with public rather than private clients, and frequently because of political pressures. But more often than not, unsubstantiated claims don't hold up; they are found out, and when they are, the technology vendor is doomed.

USING LESS STUFF

Using fewer materials to make products and deliver them isn't something new in the manufacturing sector. Less waste translates into less energy consumed, lower costs for raw materials, and the cost avoidance of having to get rid of less stuff; making the most efficient use of materials has always been a focus in wastes. Generating less waste was at the heart of the CEC's policy development and its organizational ethos. But as with the objective of achieving higher rates of energy conservation in the built environment, what makes the most sense rationally is countered by the force of inertia and short-term economic thinking.

Fifty years of rampant prosperity in America seemed to have obliterated the basic tenets of a conservative and frugal America up to and through World War II. For the Depression-era generation it was natural to reuse things when possible, to recycle, to garden, and to generally conserve.

Beginning in the late 1950s, Madison Avenue tapped a pent-up demand for goods and services, supported by brilliant and unceasing marketing. After the Great Depression and World War II, material and psychological scarcity and the prospects for upward mobility in a postwar economy set the stage for vigorous consumer spending. Consumerism was coming of age in America, and with it emerged a growing sophistication, rooted in the social sciences, that proved to be brilliantly adept at motivating people to buy things that they might not intrinsically need or want. The American journalist Vance Packard coined terms like *planned obsolescence*, *functional obsolescence*, and *style obsolescence*[44] to describe the nature of the new goods and services coming into the marketplace.

Planned obsolescence was attributed to products that were designed to fall apart and be replaced within a prescribed time frame; functional obsolescence referred to products that would likely have a short life, not from a working standpoint but because newer products would prove better and more desirable; while style obsolescence described changes in fashion and other material expectations motivating people to replace their wardrobes, their cars, and even their homes. Underlying the consumer society was a powerful set of social and psychological drivers that at the very least needed to be understood and weighed when it came to encouraging something like reducing waste.[45]

In 1987, the CEC published a paper, "Source Reduction: The Next Frontier," written by Karen Hurst.[46] This publication attempted to lay out a framework for how our society might begin to put a check on some of our most wasteful practices, offering both practical and policy suggestions. We pointed out that "[s]olid waste programs across the country have failed to seriously pursue this front-end approach that addresses key contributors to the solid waste management problem, excessive volume, and growing toxicity. The focus has been on designing systems to handle whatever waste is generated, rather than decreasing the need for such systems by minimizing both the volume and toxicity of the solid waste stream."

As we struggled to advance source reduction as a waste management objective, we realized that there was another type of waste being generated that was being neglected: what we now call "household hazardous waste." Household hazardous waste includes myriad products ranging from motor oil to pesticides to cleaners, solvents, and paints—the kinds of products one accumulates over a lifetime to make home repairs and maintain one's household. According to the US EPA,[47] household hazardous waste makes up about 3 to 5 percent of all solid waste. That doesn't sound like much, but considering that we were disposing of more than 40 million tons of solid waste in California and more than 200 million tons in the United States, this translates to between 900,000 and 1,500,000 million tons of household hazardous waste deposited in California landfills each year and 6–10 million tons nationwide. They contribute to producing a nasty brew of what is called toxic leachate—landfill liquids that can and will eventually leak into our underground water supplies. Our government determined that most of these products are hazardous in nature and that they should not be thrown out with household trash. Unfortunately, there was no organized means of collecting or processing this stuff, so most of it was going into landfills. The CEC decided to do something about this, first to raise awareness of the issue, but then, in characteristic CEC fashion, to design a program that would enable people to collect and dispose of these materials in a more environmentally safe way.

Working with county officials, we proposed that a household hazardous waste collection day be held at our local fairgrounds. We contracted with a hazardous waste service provider to take the collected waste for proper disposal or treatment; in other words, to a special hazardous waste landfill designed to entomb the materials in places where the liquids could not get into the ground or groundwater, or where they could be burned in a high-temperature incinerator.

The CEC organized and implemented its first household hazardous waste collection program, where a few hundred people participated, driving their wastes to the fairgrounds to be met by workers suited up in hazardous waste gear, wearing goggles, hoods, and gloves to receive the materials and segregate them safely. This first event led to many more. The CEC was given a contract to continue the program, which ended up lasting more than a decade. Participation grew with each event to the point where the scale of the operation became too big to continue as it was.

After several years, the CEC proposed that what was really needed to reduce the amount of toxic materials going to landfills was a permanent program available to consumers on a daily or at least weekly basis. We thought that the program should also provide an outlet for small businesses to manage their hazardous waste in a cost-efficient way, since arranging for hazardous waste pick-ups from vendors providing collection services could be cost-prohibitive for many small businesses. We proposed that such a facility be built at the County Transfer Station, where South Coast residents were accustomed to bringing their discards. But what made sense logically didn't fly with the residential community near the transfer station. When our proposal went forward in public, there was an outpouring of opposition from the neighboring residents who had recently been traumatized by a forest fire, called the Painted Cave Fire, that raced through the area of the landfill, burning some 450 homes in its path as it nearly reached the ocean on its fearsome advance down the Santa Ynez Mountains and the foothills below them. Some residents were incensed that the county would consider the storage of household hazardous wastes nearby. The political atmosphere became charged enough to erode political support for the project, causing us to withdraw from seeking a permit. It seemed as if locating a household hazardous waste facility to manage a growing environmental problem was going to be an impossibility. The proverbial "Not in My Backyard" had become a reality for the CEC.

But, ever determined and resourceful, we didn't give up. Sometimes just around the corner is an insight, a person, or an opportunity that reveals itself and is better than the one you just watched slip through your fingers. And it turned out to be just so for us. As one door slammed in our face, another one opened.

Attending the volatile public meetings with the neighbors of the proposed facility was Ross Grayson, the manager of the local University of California's campus hazardous waste program that collected hazardous materials from the large assortment of laboratories and research facilities on campus. He sympathized with our plight and informed us that the university was planning to build a new hazardous waste facility and suggested that there might be an opportunity to make the facility available as a hazardous waste drop-off center for the Santa Barbara public.

Over the next year, this idea was developed between university staff and Karen Feeney, a graduate of UC Santa Barbara's Environmental Studies Program and an astute program manager for us. The concept of making the university's facility available to the public sailed through the approval process. Within a year, the facility became a reality. This linkage between the resources of the university and a public need developed into one of the most successful collaborations between "town and gown" in the area's history. At the time of its development, it was among the very first programs in the United States to combine household and small business hazardous waste disposal. Operating for more than twenty years now, it has become a permanent piece of the sustainability infrastructure of Santa Barbara, another piece in the pattern language, and another experiment in the Santa Barbara laboratory that had justified its existence.

OUT OF THE COMFORT ZONE

By 1990, I had been executive director of the CEC for twenty years. The organization was in the best shape it had ever been in; we had some forty employees and we were self-generating, by our wits, about 75 percent of our budget from our recycling operations and waste management expertise. Jon Clark, one of our first interns who was blessed with better management skills than I, was being groomed as my understudy. Although I was still young—in my late thirties—I thought an organization like ours needed a continuous infusion of young leadership. What an inspiring life it was to be working on the leading edge of environmentalism, from a hilltop green office building that we had designed and built, with a magnificent view of one of the most beautiful small cities in the world! On top of that, I was making a real living, enough to support a young family, and my colleagues had steady incomes as well—very modest ones to be sure, but steady nonetheless. What more could I want?

But I was growing restless. My travels to Asia and my frequent trips to Sacramento, Washington, and many other cities in America had opened me up to a larger world. As much as I appreciated what the CEC was able to contribute to forging a sustainable future, I was seeking a more challenging situation, one that would test and stretch my abilities.

Over the years, people in Santa Barbara had urged me to run for public office such as county supervisor and, if successful, to go on to the state legislature. It was flattering, but I was never interested in a political career. I liked being involved in planning, design, and environmental innovations such as gardens and the green buildings. I was Janus-like, part policy wonk and part environmental entrepreneur. I loved the creativity of formulating an alternative plan for the Santa Barbara Waterfront, a plan to preserve the Carpinteria Valley as an agricultural resource. I loved helping to build the recycling operations and dispersing our knowledge to other communities in California. At the same time, the idea of crafting policies on a larger stage that could change the way waste management operated, and press industry to take on recycling and composting as primary rather than incidental practices, appealed to me. I was open to making a change, and the opportunity came in the summer of 1991.

The California Integrated Waste Management Act of 1989, legislation that I and my colleagues at the CEC had had a hand in shaping, created the California Integrated Waste Management Board, a new full-time regulatory board to oversee California's ambitious recycling legislation and its solid waste system consisting mostly of landfills and a few waste incinerators. This new board would have six board members representing the governor, the assembly and Senate, the industry, and the environment.

In early 1990, I received a call from the owner of one of the companies that had purchased the CEC's recycling commodities. He asked if I would consider seeking an appointment to this new board as its environmental member. The new legislation specifically stated that the environmental member needed to have expertise in recycling and experience with a nonprofit environmental organization. These qualifications fit me to a T. I mulled the idea over—it would certainly be in line with my expertise and my broadening interests, but the process of being appointed to such a position was completely foreign to me. The appointment would be made by the governor, and at that time this was George Deukmejian, a very conservative Republican. Why on earth would a Republican governor consider appointing a Santa Barbara environmentalist with a background like mine, who was a registered Democrat to boot? My initial take on the matter was that there wasn't a chance in hell that this governor was going to give me the job.

A few months later I received another call, this time from a very conservative lobbyist for the waste industry, Z. Harry Astor, whom I had met when I served on a Senate task force to help shape what would become

AB 939. He was a confidante of Governor Deukmejian; Harry encouraged me to put my hat in the ring and get in the hunt.

Getting into the hunt meant making calls and talking strategy with people inside the recycling industry, in the environmental community, in local government, and, yes, even lobbyists. This was all new to me; in a sense, it was like running for public office, though there was no official campaign and the voting was done in private by one individual, the governor of California. Looking back on it, I guess I was ready for this new challenge. Frankly, I found the campaigning and competing for the position exhilarating.

For several months, I engaged the field. In spite of what seemed to be long odds, within a few months' time, I felt I had a real chance at winning the appointment. But, as it turned out, my initial instincts were right. I was a virtual unknown to the governor. I had no Republican bonafides; I was far too liberal. In the end, he appointed someone to the position who was much better connected to the powers that be. That was lesson one in my political education. Don't assume that qualifications and experience make the critical difference in an appointment process like this. It was political connections, fundraising experience, and other factors that were paramount. I was upset; after that decision, I felt the position was completely outside of my grasp.

As it turned out, all was not lost. The appointment required Senate confirmation. The Democrats held sway in the confirmation process. Key environmental organizations like Californians Against Waste, the lead nonprofit on matters of recycling and waste management, along with the Sierra Club and the Natural Resources Defense Council, had a great deal of influence on the votes by the five-member Senate Rules Committee. They did not believe that the candidate put forth by Governor Deukmejian had the qualifications for the appointment, and they opposed the nomination. The candidate, facing certain defeat, bowed out rather bringing the appointment to a vote. This opened the door once again for me.

By this time, Governor Deukmejian had completed his two-term governorship and was soon succeeded by a more moderate Republican, Pete Wilson, a former US senator and mayor of San Diego. He came to office with a credible environmental record, having established a reputation for managing growth when he was San Diego's mayor. It's worth noting that in the early 1990s there were still quite a few moderate Republicans who genuinely believed in the importance of preserving and protecting the environment. Their means to that end differed from that of the Democrats in some important respects, but there wasn't the cleavage in viewpoints that has grown so sharp between Republicans and Democrats today.

When Wilson assumed office, he appointed Huey Johnson, a highly regarded environmental leader in California, to lead the state's Resources Agency. He appointed Richard Wilson (unrelated to Governor Wilson), who had led the battle to stop a dam in Northern California, to head the state's huge Department of Forestry, and James Strock, who served as chief of enforcement of the US Environmental Protection Agency under the able leadership of William Ruckleshaus, a former Indiana congressman and deputy attorney general in the Justice Department under President Nixon. These were seasoned and competent people who had vision and exercised a degree of independent thinking that has become an increasingly rare attribute in modern political life. Unfortunately for me, I had no standing with Governor Wilson. I was an unknown. I wasn't a contributor or a player in his election. I had no ties whatsoever to the Republican Party. But I did have a few things going for me. The environmental community knew of my work with the Community Environmental Council and respected the accomplishments of the CEC, particularly for its pioneering work building recycling programs and developing waste management and recycling policies. From the industry perspective, I was a known quantity, with a long record serving on key national and state committees developing recycling policy and with in-depth knowledge of the waste and recycling industries. Also, I had by this time developed many ties with local government officials throughout the state, and they provided letters of support.

The appointment process dragged on for weeks and then for months. Though I thought my chances were improving, the appointment process was far from transparent. There was a group of people in the mix, some real, some rumored to be contenders, and I had no idea how I stacked up against them. But in the end, I received a call from the governor's appointments secretary, Charles Poochigian, saying that if I wanted the job it was mine to have, and that if I was to take it I needed to report to Sacramento by August 1, 1991. It turned out that, as unknown as I was to Governor Wilson, his advisors knew that I was confirmable, unlike my predecessor. Secondly, William Ruckelshaus had read a paper that Dr. Anthony Dominski and I had cowritten that he liked and said so in a letter of support for my appointment to Cal EPA Secretary James Strock. A Ruckelshaus recommendation was golden.

With my appointment, my life in the safe world of Santa Barbara and the Community Environmental Council was about to change in a very big way. I was suddenly, almost overnight, in Sacramento, sitting on a politically charged board that reflected all of the cross currents and tensions between the Democratically controlled assembly and Senate and a Republican governor.

Among my first political awakenings in Sacramento was my passage through the Senate confirmation process. No one I knew well had ever gone through a Senate confirmation. Anyone who has gone through a confirmation at this level knows full well that it can be a politically charged experience that is fraught with personal dangers. Should you find yourself coming up for confirmation during a budget crisis that pits the party of the governor against a majority from the opposite party in the legislature, you can become a political Ping-Pong ball in a fierce match between competing interests. If you have managed to alienate an interest group, whether public, private, government, or academic, this is the moment when others can exact their revenge and try to hold up your confirmation.

During my time on the board, I went through three Senate confirmations; two were a cakewalk and one was an ordeal, thanks to a petty power struggle. Confirmations can transport you into a no man's land where colleagues can fall away, where rules seem to evaporate, and where your fate lies in the hands of the five rules members—a majority of whom you must win over. I've never felt my life more outside my control than during that one troubled confirmation in which the governor and legislature battled over a dismal state budget. I was a pawn in their game.

In my case, things turned out fine in the end. I was unanimously confirmed. But the experience was searing and clarifying. As I was going through my drama, I could understand why so many qualified people refuse to subject themselves to the possible humiliation of being in the wrong place at the wrong time when the political game is going down.

As a neophyte to political life, my new role as a regulator and policy maker took getting used to. Of our board of six, four were political pros—a former chief of staff to the governor; the state treasurer; a multiterm county supervisor; and a close personal friend of the legendary Willie Brown, one of the most powerful politicians in the history of California. They knew the ins and outs of Sacramento, how power was wielded and how to watch one's back. It took me several years before I began to understand this world, how to navigate its land mines, and how to define and accomplish the things that were important to me.

Experienced politicos with a commitment to accomplishment know that in the exceedingly complex and convoluted world of state government, you can effectively focus on only a few issues. Taking on too many things will dilute your abilities and more likely than not leave you, at the end of your time in government, feeling bereft. I was determined to stay focused and leave with a sense that I had made a difference.

POLITICS

State Capitol, Sacramento, California.
Regulations and policy on recycling, renewable energy and sustainability.

Politics are scorned, thought to be nasty and corrupt. Politics are end-lessly derided by pundits and readily dismissed by many who consider themselves to be above the fray. Yet politics are as fundamental to the human condition as a pod of orcas coursing the waterways of the San Juan Island, a flock of Canadian geese making their winter migration south, or the pattern of water charging down a stream. Politics are the business of human beings interacting.

Scorn politics, heap insult after insult upon the political institutions and their players and demean them all you will, but politics undeniably affect our lives personally and collectively in the most fundamental ways. Like it or not, politics determine to no small extent the safety of the products we buy, how we design and build our communities, our access to and the quality of the health care we receive, how many of us will fare in our retirement years, and how we protect ourselves from threats foreign and domestic.

In my own case, it was politics that produced the law that created the funds to buy equipment for our recycling center. It was politics that established our first community gardens. It was politics that limited the size of Santa Barbara. It was politics that protected agriculture in the Carpinteria Valley. It was politics that determined what the Santa Barbara waterfront was to become and whether or not the Gaviota Coast was to be covered with homes. And it was politics that set California on a course to recycle 50 percent of its waste by the year 2000.

While these outcomes were initiated by a small group of informed and motivated individuals, the political process was the delivery mechanism. To illustrate my point, I'll offer the following example. For twenty years, recycling in California remained within the domain of nonprofits, the motivated, so-called do-gooders operating on society's fringes. But it wasn't until the California Integrated Waste Management Act of 1989 was passed by the legislature, and signed into law by the governor, that cities and counties throughout the state were compelled, upon penalties of fines and public humiliation, to institute recycling programs in earnest. It wasn't until local governments were compelled to initiate recycling programs that private companies could accumulate the capital needed to build the infrastructure to collect and process millions of tons of recyclables and deliver them to the world marketplace. And it wasn't until it was apparent that millions of tons of recyclable commodities were coming into the commodities marketplace that industries like the paper industry began to undergo a technological transformation to utilize these resources.

As I gained my political chops during my Sacramento years, it became clear to me that any success I was to realize in advancing my objectives depended on maintaining focus and building support within and outside of the institution. What was important to me in my new role was to make sure that there were sufficient markets to utilize the millions of tons of recyclables that we were now going to generate, and to increase the recycling of organic materials through composting and other means, so that our farmlands and our home and institutional landscapes could be enriched with little or no adverse environmental impacts. This had been the center of my work building the Community Environmental Council; these were the subjects that were at the heart of my work then and that were just as important to me now, but now I was operating in a much larger arena, overseeing a staff of more than four hundred civil servants with a budget exceeding $120 million a year.

Because I had experienced the wild fluctuations of the recycling marketplace for years at the CEC, I wasn't convinced when I joined the board that markets for most of the recyclables were secure. What if we built a vast new infrastructure and there was insufficient demand for the materials? What would happen in a deep recession when demand fell? Would recyclables like old newspapers end up in the landfill?

The recycling world I knew from my days at the CEC involved selling paper to paper mills in California, such as Weyerhauser's mill in Port Hueneme about forty-five miles south of Santa Barbara, which made liner board paper for cardboard packaging. Or the Garden State newsprint mill that produced new newsprint from used paper in Pomona, near Los Angeles, and the new Ontario linerboard mill located about fifty miles south of Los Angeles. In those days, we still had basic manufacturing industries in California. The distance between the collection points for recyclables and where they were sent for manufacture was typically no more than fifty to one hundred miles.

By the early 1990s, the manufacture of basic products like paper, steel, and plastics was beginning to shift to Asia to exploit the cheap labor, subsidized energy, and lax environmental controls. As I saw this starting to happen, I wanted to buck the trend if possible by identifying and cultivating new manufacturers to come to California. But as I was to learn, this was like spitting into the wind. The body politic in California had embraced so-called clean-tech, represented by the clean rooms and white gowns used in the manufacture of computers and other "clean goods." Never mind that on close inspection any computer manufacturing supply chain, these so-called clean industries, are not that at all. Yes, the engineers housed in beautiful corporate campuses look very clean indeed. A finished computer, an iPhone, and other electronic devices that define our communication age are small, elegant products whose physical presence do not reveal the significant environmental damage that goes into their making: the mining of the minerals to manufacture the guts of the machines, the precious metals, the plastics, the rare earths, and the assembly of the machines abroad— sometimes under terrible working conditions. In fact, for every pound of high-tech product, there are at least seventy pounds of waste that go into the manufacture of that product.[48] This underscores the fact that the pollution effect of producing the electronic devices that we love and cherish has occurred mostly offshore, a fact that is at last beginning to gain the attention that the issue deserves.

But as I learned in trying to give voice to the importance of manufacturing in our future, the message fell on deaf ears. Such is the seduction of "high tech" and "information technology" that the real environmental impacts of this form of manufacturing have been ignored or downplayed. In the minds of the powers that be, in the mind's eye of so many of our citizens, the future of our economy depends on "high tech," and to hell with basic industries and manufacturing! Manufacturing was old-school, old-tech, and the jobs that they produced would be replaced by higher-value, better-paying jobs.

Yet surely the environmental community that stood behind recycling would rally behind the idea of nurturing recycling manufacturing industries in our state.

This assumption was tested in the depths of the 1992–93 recession, when unemployment in California rose to nearly 10 percent; we had a real estate collapse not too different from the one during 2008–2012, though not as long and not quite so deep. MacMillan Bloedel, now MacMillan Bloedel Simpson, a paper manufacturing giant from Canada, and Fort Howard Paper Company, a tissue paper manufacturer based in the Midwest, were both considering locating recycling mills in California, the former near Sacramento, the latter about thirty miles east of Palm Springs. The newsprint mill would be able to utilize a very large percentage of the recyclable paper we were collecting in our growing curbside recycling programs, and a new tissue plant could consume much of the mixed paper that we had limited markets for at that time.

The MacMillan Bloedel plant was to be built in South Sacramento, portside. Located as it was to be on the banks of the Sacramento River, it would release process water into the river after treatment, which would be somewhat warmer than the river water. This posed a threat to the increasingly fragile downstream delta ecosystems. In my view, making a plant like the one proposed, compatible with the demanding environmental standards in California, would be a worthy undertaking. If process requirements needed to be changed to meet the river release standards, or technological innovations were required to do so, this seemed so much the better. Wouldn't it be inspiring if California embraced this type of challenge and was able to encourage the design of basic recycling industries to produce goods and services in a way that was compatible with our regulatory standards? Wouldn't such an achievement be environmentalism at its best? Wouldn't it be an accomplishment if we could learn to manufacture a most basic good—such as paper—here, domestically, and thus capture more of the industrial jobs we were beginning to export to Asia, with workers earning the kind of wages and benefits that the American economy had generated during the 1950s and 1960s when our middle class was thriving?

As I found out, the key environmental organizations dealing with the waste issues and lobbying for recycling—with the exception of Californians Against Waste—gave the project the most tepid support for the plant. The inevitable opposition to the plant emerged, expressing viewpoints that the plant would send warm water into the delta and adversely impact an already anemically reduced salmon run, and that we didn't want heavy industry in Sacramento, just "clean jobs." I felt very isolated in holding to my position and disappointed that we couldn't use the paper mill prospect as an opportunity to deepen our environmentalism. Coming from an organization that had operated programs and built facilities and projects, I was no stranger to the notion that even environmentally beneficial projects have their detractors. What I was surprised by is that the environmental groups in this case didn't seem to want, or care, to connect the dots in the environmental chain of responsibility. If recyclable materials are going to be collected, especially in massive quantities, then it goes without saying that manufacturing must follow. And where and how they were manufactured mattered in my book!

At that time, there were few instances in which environmental groups embraced the responsibility for the full implications of policies that they promoted. The Natural Resources Defense Council did this in the 1980s when it promoted the development of a recycling paper mill in a New York City borough, a mill that it hoped would complement its recycling policies and bring jobs to the Bronx. But such examples have been few and far between.

There were many other instances where I realized that the environmental community lacked interest, insight, or commitment to following through on its goals by taking responsibility for the implications of its policies. I never experienced the environmental community engaging the compost industry to help it navigate the difficult and sometimes insurmountable permitting process in California. And environmentalists were late to recognize (except for the more international-minded organizations such as Friends of the Earth) the consequences of sending electronic wastes to Asia or Africa for disassembly and recovery until international outrage over the pollution from this practice led to eliminating export of so-called e-waste and forced the recycling of these materials within the country of their origin.

Never could I have imagined when I had visited China just six years earlier that, within a decade or less, our paper-making capacity in California and indeed throughout much of the United States would be hollowed out and replaced by massive mills in China and Indonesia. Never could I have imagined that the environmental community from which I came would not seem to care that the recovery of recyclable materials, which so many communities in California and elsewhere lauded, depended on China for a market located halfway around the world. Few, if any, questions were being raised about the sustainability of these markets over decades or the environmental impacts of consuming industries so far away from their point of generation.

Atmospheric scientists have noted that the pollution generated in factories and from coal burning in China rides air currents from east to west, polluting the skies of California in about a week, not to mention the pollution that falls from the skies over the Pacific Ocean. I considered the environmental consequences of our exporting our pollution to China in the form of recyclable materials to be just as real as if we had built paper mills and steel plants in California without requiring proper regulation. What's the difference if the pollution is locally, nationally, or internationally generated? Its consequences are just the same.

Sometimes you realize that the timing isn't right for an issue to take hold in the body politic. This was true of making the case for a manufacturing industry to support recycling in California and the United States. Waste companies were happy to have a buoyant market in China for their commodities, which bolstered their bottom lines and took some of the crazy up-and-down commodity gyrations away. Environmental leaders responsible for waste and recycling issues simply ignored the issue; they seemed more interested in promoting additional recycling programs than in dealing with the environmental consequences of the programs. I figured that I could carry on as a lone voice, but I had a limited time in my position and I wanted to accomplish more than using the bully pulpit to raise an issue. When you're faced with an unmovable object, such as apathy or institutional inertia, you either become like Sisyphus or you adapt. I had learned this lesson twenty years before on the CEC's hilltop site when the easement that we had counted on to connect our site to the city proved unavailable. I didn't resort to consulting the I Ching this time. The lesson was learned.

I refocused on finding ways to move the approximately eleven million tons of organic materials we were landfilling in California every year into compost, soil amendments, or other products. Unlike commodities such as paper or steel, which could move great distances in the world marketplace, organic materials were too low in value and too expensive to transport to make this possible. In the 1990s, the issue of greenhouse gases and climate change were not yet on the national or international agenda, and we hadn't yet made the strong connection between organic materials decomposing in landfills and their contribution to producing methane, a potent greenhouse gas.

ORGANICS: THE MAGIC OF BIOLOGY

There is general agreement that compost is beneficial—it nurtures earthworms and favorable soil microbes, supplies soil nutrients and improves soil fertility, texture, and water-holding capacity. Moreover, compost application can reduce the demand for soluble fertilizers, which can pollute ground water. Many environmental groups and local governments, however, are concerned that compost produced from non-source-separated materials will be unmarketable and will eventually have to be landfilled.

DR. ANTHONY DOMINSKI

Now I was in a position to contribute to the possibilities raised in "Composting Ten Million Tons in California." Working closely with my able advisors, Dr. Howard Levenson and Fitz Fitzgerald, and staff within the organization, we began to map out a strategy increasing the use of compost in California. It involved developing effective compost regulations that would govern the development of compost-making facilities that were to serve as the nexus between the collection of organic materials from our cities and their conversion to compost. Educating farmers to use compost was another part of our strategy, as was the development of some type of compost quality standards.

The regulation-making process is an arduous one; it often takes a year or longer to translate legislative intent into bricks-and-mortar language that has the force of law. Compost-making involves many real and imagined issues that we had to contend with. First and foremost was dealing with the negative impact of the noise, dust, and odor of composting operations. Then there were questions about compost quality. What controls should be placed on the processing of green waste from cities coming into facilities, and how should contaminants such as plastics be cleaned up? And what about public health concerns, such as animal feces, which can be found with lawn clippings making their way into composts, and how can we ensure that the composting process would remove pathogens such as E. coli in a finished compost product? What about the impacts of composting facilities on water quality through runoff into streams or rivers or underground into our groundwater supplies? What about the costs of regulatory compliance and its impact on the composting industry's ability to operate viable facilities in the relatively low-cost waste disposal environment in California? We could regulate facilities to death—meaning that the costs of operation would be simply too great compared with the value of the compost product.

It took several iterations to learn how to strike a reasonable balance between protecting the public and the environment from being damaged by facilities and our desire to promote composting as an important conservation and resource-protection measure. From this experience and other regulation-making endeavors, I gained a healthy appreciation for the complex nature of the regulatory process and how difficult it is to factor in all the relevant considerations and come up with reasonable and enforceable regulations.

With respect to regulations, I came to the 70 percent/30 percent rule: if you can get regulations about 70 percent right, leaving about 30 percent a bit wobbly and to be worked out over time through modifications, you've done a pretty good job. Within the educational system, 70 percent is a poor mark, a C minus. But in governance, where you are balancing a very great number of complex factors, safety, economics, public acceptance, the limits of knowledge, and the certainty of unintended consequences, getting it 70 percent right is a solid outcome. Ninety percent right is a near impossibility, and even 80 percent is a rarity. If you can get to a 70 percent mark, then in most cases and by all means, get the regulations passed. Later you can come back and clean up what has been overlooked or misunderstood.

With the compost regulations now in place, my focus shifted to developing markets for compost. Ten million tons of organics would theoretically produce about five million tons of finished compost a year, because the composting process shrinks by half the volume of the original material. The market for compost was already saturated, and throwing massive new quantities into this market, especially composts derived from municipal waste sources, was a daunting prospect. The only way millions of tons of new compost product could be absorbed in California and throughout the country would be if farmers could be convinced that urban-derived composts had some benefit and were inexpensive enough to use. With this in mind, my preoccupation for my remaining time in office was to find ways of educating and incentivizing farmers to use the stuff.

Anyone who has worked with farmers knows they are a conservative lot, understandably. They "bet the farm" every time they plant in the hopes of bringing to harvest a bountiful crop that commands a profitable price upon sale. They have so many variables to contend with, and the introduction of a new variable—compost—even though it was a time-tested practice a few generations back, would pose serious challenges.

Throughout all of history, the use of composts or equivalent means of building or maintaining soil fertility has been common practice, and it extended up and through the first quarter of the twentieth century. Then came chemical agriculture and with it vast monocultures and industrial-scale farming. Compost was shelved and no longer viewed as a necessity, since fossil fuel energy inputs could generate high yields without any need for organic materials. I was reminded, in facing this challenge, of those first compost piles we made at El Mirasol. A whole generation of post–World War II Americans had skipped lessons previously learned in a more agrarian society: you didn't waste things, you recycled bottles and cans, and you returned what you didn't extract from the land. Waste products from agriculture were plowed back in, or made into composts and applied to the land to help sustain fertility.

Faced with this situation, I thought that we needed to develop demonstration projects throughout California that showed, by example, the value of compost in sustaining California agriculture, a thirty-billion-dollar industry that is powerfully embedded in California politics. With budgetary support from my five colleagues on the board, I obtained enough funding to conduct five demonstration projects that would be developed over a three-year period and led by the University of California's Agricultural Extension Service headquartered at UC Davis, one of the nation's leading agricultural research institutions.

Beyond tapping the UC system for credibility, I needed support within state government to begin to warm farmers up to the prospect of using compost. It so happened that the newly appointed undersecretary of the California Environmental Protection Agency, Jack Pandol, came from a prominent table grape–growing family business based in Tulare County, now the dairy capital of the United States. In his early forties, Jack represented a new generation of growers, many of whom had obtained degrees from the likes of the University of California at Davis. Some of this younger generation of growers were more receptive to the need to find ways of making agriculture more ecologically sustainable. Jack himself was a compost convert, having studied composting methods and applied them to portions of his family's grape orchards.

As is the case when you're guiding an agency and not managing it on a day-to-day basis, you have to be hands-off once a mission is assigned to staff. You hope that the staff understands and is supportive of what you are trying to accomplish, but you are never sure until the "project" is defined and assigned. In this case, the staff got it just right; they identified five projects in the agricultural heartland of California—five of the counties with the largest agricultural output. They constructed the demonstrations to be collaborative, involving UC scientists, compost producers, waste collection companies, and growers covering all the bases from collection, through the composting process, to the applications of compost and the results of the applications on the crops.

Four of the five demonstration projects were located in what some call in California the "Great Valley," one of the greatest agricultural resources on earth, extending some 450 miles from north to south and between forty and sixty miles in width. This region produces much of the summer fruits in our nation as well as rice, most of the nut crops, and just about everything else, amounting to 8 percent of the food produced in the United

States. The growers in the Valley range from some of the largest in the world to small operations of fewer than ten acres who have specialized crops and ship products to the farmers' markets that began springing up throughout the state.

Agricultural scientists, like most scientists, are measured when it comes to drawing conclusions from their research. They take great labors to, if anything, understate the significance of their findings. When it came to drawing conclusions from our compost demonstrations, I remember how obtuse they seemed to me with statements like, "the application of compost would not reduce yields," or "the flavors of the fruit grown with composts were comparable to the fruit grown with chemical inputs." A conclusion from one of the UC plant scientists was that the use of compost had "possible beneficial impact on reducing black rot in peaches," but he qualified his statement by saying that there were problems associated with the application of composts in subsequent years, so no conclusions should be drawn. All these statements seemed neutered to me. And if they struck me that way, what would the public think?

Yes, the scientific conclusions were largely positive, but you almost needed a translator to understand that they were so. For example, what was the significance of the statement, "compost would do no harm"? Doing "no harm" didn't seem like a ringing endorsement for the use of compost. But this statement establishes an important benchmark for farmers unfamiliar with its use. At the least "no harm" meant that compost, properly used, would not be detrimental to plant production.

How to unpack the statement that compost use produces crops comparable in quality to those grown with pesticides and chemical fertilizer? Well, it's actually quite important to a grower to know that the crops grown with compost compared with those grown with pesticides and fertilizers were at parity, since commercial fertilizers and pesticide use were widely considered to produce superior results.

Consider the finding that the flavors of crops grown with compost with those grown with commercial fertilizers and pesticides were comparable. I was sure the compost-grown crops would be more flavorful, since that had been my experience going back to the CEC's early gardens. But, once again, compost-grown crops were equal in flavor, or in the case of the tomato quality, equally flavorless.

Lastly, with the peaches, the use of compost appeared to suppress disease, in this case peach rot. While the conclusion was very qualified, it was consistent with something I learned from John Menge, a mycologist emeritus at UC Riverside. He had experimented with growing avocados using a one-foot-deep green waste mulch and found that this regime suppressed a disease that plagues avocados, phytothra. Phytothra attacks the roots of the avocado, eventually killing the tree. In the organic-rich green mulch environment, mushrooms grew, exuding an enzyme that attacked the cellular structure of the organisms that spread phytothra. Viewing electron microscopic slides of this phenomenon was a revelation: I was watching a biological fungicide at work!

The most persuasive arguments in favor of compost use in agriculture came from Jack Pandol. In an interview in a video we produced to promote the agricultural demonstration projects, he stated that if the compost product was mature, meaning that it had completed the breakdown cycle and was applied at the appropriate rates, it was the "single most effective agricultural practice he had implemented." He encouraged his fellow farmers to adopt its use. Wow! This, coming from one of California's larger industrial-scale growers, who was respected by his fellow growers, was a powerful endorsement.

With the compost regulations in place and the agricultural demonstration projects doing their job, there was still the issue of compost quality standards. All products need standards to gain broader acceptance in the marketplace and compost was no exception. Both buyers and consumers of the products grown with compost need some assurance that they are pathogen-free and free of harmful heavy metals, salts, and other potential problems. Our board did not have the regulatory authority to develop quality standards for products, so I encouraged compost producers and compost sellers to come together and work out a quality-control system. This led to the creation of an organization that was to formalize standards and certify that compost makers were conforming to these standards through lab analysis of products and site inspections.

The development and sustenance of the organization was difficult—there were squabbles between the producers of composts using biosolids from wastewater plants and from material sourced from green and food waste from urban collection programs. The compost makers who did not use biosolids did not want any association with the biosolids industry and the onus of producing a soil product from human waste.

These facets of finding ways to capture organic wastes generated in our cities by the millions of tons per year and returning them to the land was one of the most satisfying experiences of my time in government. I carved this out as my arena, and I was left pretty much alone by my colleagues on the board, members of the legislature, and the administration. During my term, compost production in the state went from about one million tons a year to nearly five million, meaning that nearly half of the organic materials were finding their way into soil products of some sort. I don't claim to be responsible for this increase—it took the efforts of composters and farmers to do that—but I had a hand in encouraging this growth by creating a regulatory system that was supportive of a growing compost industry, and educating farmers to the benefits of compost use.

On the other hand, there were plenty of disappointments. We never developed the kind of compacts with local governments, the compost industry, and the public regarding the design and operation of compost facilities that might have led to broader public acceptance of them. I felt that these facilities were as important to society as wastewater plants, electrical generating facilities, public works yards, bus terminals, and a host of other essential public services. But most officials and much of the public obviously did not see things this way.

Siting and building facilities in general was becoming only more difficult and expensive as California's already complex regulatory process became more convoluted. With the inexorable march of new laws and regulations, the siting and building of compost facilities was especially challenging. And this underscores one of the essential lessons of my story. It's one thing to want a society based on an economy that recycles materials, where the waste from one process becomes the food of another, where renewable energy becomes the basis of our next economy, but a substantive shift to these practices requires a new industrial infrastructure of facilities, paper mills, compost plants, solar and wind farms, and a galaxy of supporting businesses that must be accommodated. California and the nation have yet to grapple with this reality beyond political clichés like "streamlining permits," providing permit assistance and subsidies, where they may be justified, such as tax credits and the like. We are nowhere close to having structures in place to facilitate the changes we profess to want.

One of the ideas I had hoped to develop during my government years was the ability to barge or send trainloads of compost into California's agricultural heartlands. Shipping massive quantities of low-value material like compost by truck to agriculture was, in my view, too energy intensive and expensive. Might it be possible to establish composting facilities in the Bay Area adjacent to the Bay, where barges could be loaded and large quantities of compost shipped at low cost up the Sacramento and San Joaquin Rivers, where they could be unloaded and shipped by truck to farms? Perhaps the state of California could help subsidize the loading and shipping infrastructure for a period of time until the growth of sustainable agriculture would create an interim demand as the value of compost became more recognized? In time, as organic agriculture continued to grow, the role of compost would become embedded to the point where subsidies would no longer be required.

Shipping compost by train from Southern California, located more than one hundred miles from large agricultural markets, may have seemed a stretch at the time, but there was no hesitation in the body politic in Southern California about shipping garbage from the LA metropolitan area to an old mining site in the Southern Coachella Valley, some two hundred miles away. Indeed, the rail hauling of garbage was becoming a common practice on the East Coast, with trainloads of waste from the urban centers going to landfills in Pennsylvania and Virginia with no demonstrable environmental benefit and at a high cost. Why not then send trainloads of compost from privately run facilities strategically located near rail lines and using state-of-the-art composting methods to produce high-quality products with minimal impact such as odor and dust? Why should a hole in the ground to deposit garbage be preferable to regenerating California's soils?

As time went on, I was learning to navigate the strange and convoluted political world of Sacramento, gaining the insights from inside the system that I had hoped to obtain when I began my Sacramento journey. One of the most surprising discoveries I made early on was how just a few well-positioned people controlled environmental lawmaking and regulations, not for a few years but, in some cases, for decades. They were looked to by legislators and the not-for-profit environmental organizations as the "experts" who could navigate the system and deliver outcomes.

Expertise is to be valued in all arenas, including government. But there is a difference between the expertise needed for lawmaking and writing regulations and real knowledge of the subject matter. I found that some individuals who wielded great power had, in fact, a very limited understanding of the field they had so much political influence over, in part because elected officials delegated most of their environmental decision making to these insiders. These individuals rarely, if ever, ventured outside of Sacramento to visit facilities or talk to the people and the industries doing the work to gain a practical understanding of the subject at hand. Well- intentioned and intelligent as they most often were, I found this situation to be extremely frustrating. So insular were they that they would pontificate about how advanced California's waste management and other environmental programs and policies are, even as countries like Sweden, Germany, and Holland put many of our programs to shame.

Having traveled a fair part of the world and especially to Europe, I suffered no grand illusions about how "cutting edge" California was when it came to the environment. Sure, California created among the most stringent air-quality standards in the world. But that was because we had some of the worst air quality in the world that drove these regulations. We also had a progressive recycling law, but we couldn't hold a candle to northern Europe or Japan—in fact, much of the developing world—with respect to recycling. As I noted earlier, recycling in the developing world is a survival occupation, and when survival is in peril, nothing useful is wasted. And yes, we had developed strong laws to preserve the coast of California, some of our most fragile habitats, but only after we had filled in most of our wetlands for urban development and sprawled houses and commercial establishments across irreplaceable farmlands. And when it comes to protecting some of our most precious lands from sprawl, we actually haven't accomplished that much.

I'm not stating this to belittle worthy environmental accomplishments in the Golden State and elsewhere in the United States, but I do tire of the crowing that goes on over how "environmental" California is said to be. I think it's high time we took real stock of ourselves and looked outside of our America-centric world and realized that in many respects California and the United States have a lot to learn from the rest of the world. Like it or not, other nations have stepped up their environmental game—northern Europe without a doubt, and now nations like South Korea, Taiwan, and yes, China, even with its appalling pollution problems.

REGULATION AS ART

The crafting of regulations in almost any governmental domain is an arcane endeavor, often relegated to a very few individuals who understand the intricacies and subtle but important nuances that are invested with the full force of law. My initiation into the role that regulations play in our lives began almost during my first days with the Community Environmental Council. In building our gardens in downtown Santa Barbara, I became aware of the meaning of "setbacks" from a lot line that established where you could place a building and of "hours of operation" that govern how early or late you could run equipment. Later I was to learn the arcana of zoning regulations that determined how many units to an acre you could build, or the square-footage requirements that govern the build-out limitations of a specific lot. I learned about "lot line adjustments," that could determine the size of a parcel and its ultimate use, or an "easement" requirement that established how or if you could access a landlocked parcel of land. The regulatory world is a world of details, where competing interests duel it out and where success is measured by planting a single word or phrase in a statute.

The regulatory arena that I was now engaged in was a much larger one, where the number of players grew and their skills were arguably more fine-tuned than those I had encountered to date. I welcomed the challenge of learning to craft regulations, considering it a necessary skill to master in order to achieve results.

By 1991, when I began my work in Sacramento, the environmental apparatus of the state was well developed following nearly twenty years of environmental lawmaking and regulatory measures following events like the Santa Barbara Oil Spill and the Stringfellow Acid Pits debacle. Twenty years is a long time in the life of governance, even considering that environmental awareness and regulations were a relative newcomer in the governmental realm. Already plaques were building up in the arteries of our regulatory system; a kind of regulatory sclerosis had set in. Regulatory sclerosis is a governmental disease that perniciously invades any organization when it begins to put more emphasis on process than substance, on the maintenance of literal interpretations of statute than on fulfillment of intent, and preservation of the regulatory body as an end in itself. The failings of regulatory bodies are particularly abundant today when every day we read of a failing of every kind of organization to police itself, whether it be a bank, a police force, a planning commission, or a newspaper vested with public responsibilities.

When I went to Sacramento, apart from wanting to advance my environmental goals and objectives, I hoped to participate in the transformation of the regulatory process itself. I thought that the newly created (1971) California Environmental Protection Agency (CalEPA) would stimulate a far-reaching examination of the entire regulatory process. That mission was at the very core of why the CalEPA was created.

But the gulf between idea and reality soon became apparent. Tension quickly developed between the legislative and the executive branches over the role of CalEPA. Because it was now under the control of a Republican governor, albeit a moderate one, the Democrats who controlled both the Assembly and the Senate resisted any encroachments by CalEPA. When a CalEPA measure was proposed that was out of step with the legislature's view, the legislature used the existing boards and commissions, the very organizations that were in need of change, to resist and defeat the measure. These same boards and commissions also served as plum landing grounds for legislators who had been termed out of office or defeated—giving them lucrative salaries that would enrich their retirements, or a platform from which to rebuild their political careers.

Thus it was that the promise of CalEPA was largely unrealized. Instead of being a new and dynamic force for advancing a more integrated regulatory and permitting system, CalEPA became just another layer of government that, if anything, exacerbated the relationship between the executive and legislative branches of government. Environmental boards and commissions would be brought together under one roof (they were spread out all over Sacramento) in an attempt to develop a more collaborative and cross-medium environmental regulatory organization that would replace the entrenched silo system. Within five years, the easiest part of this proposition was realized. The state built what became the largest office building in Sacramento, which houses all of the major environmental regulatory boards. But beyond this impressive edifice, with its attractive courtyard replete with California redwoods and a childcare facility, the policy and regulatory silos that CalEPA was supposed to break down and reform remain; the state's environmental permit and regulatory processes remain obtuse, frustrating, and far more costly than they should be.

During my tenure, I made my views known to other colleagues who had a real interest in improving California's regulatory system and suggested to those who were in a position to try to change the system that we needed to fulfill the promise of the California Environmental Protection Agency. Little, if anything, was done. Proposals to "streamline the permitting process" were introduced every year, citing the cumbersome and costly nature of doing business in California. More often than not, these were in fact foils for weakening regulation. But weakening regulation isn't what I was trying to prompt. In many respects, California's regulatory system needed to be strengthened, not weakened. Strengthening the system would have to come from a rigorous rethinking of a forty-year-old system designed to prevent the worst environmental transgressions. We needed a management and regulatory system that synthesized the best of what we know how to do while eliminating flabby regulatory overlap and blind spots in the regulatory framework that could produce costly regulatory mistakes.

By 1998, I had accomplished what I thought was possible (not nearly as much as I would have liked) and was tired of being a "talking head," with much of the work that I represented actually done by staff and my advisors. I came from a world of linking theory and practice, where I had the creative outlet of building projects that correlated with my ideas. You can't do that as a government official. I was not innately suited to a life in government; my environmental entrepreneurial instincts ran too deep. I wanted to build things again, as I had done with the Community Environmental Council. There were other reasons to move on as well.

Instead of being the dynamic, pioneering, and driving force I thought recycling could be in our economy, it became simply seamless to send recyclable materials to China. By the late 1990s, because of its focus on basic manufacturing and its voracious need for paper, China was well on its way to building a paper recycling infrastructure second to none. Over the decade the paper industry had offshored paper-making. In states like California, with high labor and energy costs, paper-makers, along with other basic product manufacturers, were going out of business one by one. Instead of recycling being a driving force in our economy, we had largely become collectors and intermediate processors of these materials. Indeed, within another ten years, by 2009, 58 percent of all the fiber collected by California's recycling programs was China-bound. Most of the paper mills converting used fiber into paper and liner board for packaging now resided in China. And so it was that China—not the Golden State, with its much-touted recycling programs—was the real recycler. It was our billions of dollars that built massive collections, only to send the product abroad for manufacturing from the Ports of Long Beach, Los Angeles, Seattle, New York, and Boston.

Today, if you buy paper with recycled content, it's more likely to come from China than the United States. Regrettably, at least as I saw it, we in California were in reality a raw-materials colony for China, useful, at least in the present, to feed their appetite for raw materials until we become expendable. Then what? This reality started to weigh on me. I had done what I could to increase the use of organic materials through composting, but what contribution could I make to creating a recycling industrial base in California or elsewhere in the United States?

There were forces at work in the world economy that far transcended anything that I could influence. But that didn't mean that there wasn't important work to be done. There were technologies that I was becoming more and more aware of that could convert into energy materials that were being discarded. I wanted to learn more about them and play a role in bringing technologies that could both further recycling and capture the energy content of waste into being. If I could be part of identifying and developing these technologies, I would very much like to try. Although I wasn't an engineer, I had developed skills that were unique and qualified me, so I thought, to be part of a technological development effort.

I had entered government service as a means to an end. I had wanted to understand policy, regulation, and how the system worked. As a theory/practice person, I wanted to take what I knew and apply it to extracting more recyclable materials from the waste stream and to convert the balance to renewable energy, not the waste to energy systems that had developed a few decades earlier, but a new generation of systems, designed in tandem with waste prevention and recycling programs.

THE WASTE/RENEWABLE ENERGY NEXUS

In the little more than a decade since the incinerator wars in California (they were also fought in New York City, Massachusetts, Washington, and Oregon), we had built a massive collection infrastructure for recycling materials. We had greatly reduced our dependency on landfills and reduced the environmental impacts of managing solid wastes.

Now it seemed fitting that I apply what I learned to taking us closer to a zero-waste society by capturing the untapped energy content in waste in the form of renewable energy. This meant a shift of focus to the private sector, where projects are conceived of and built.

But moving to the private sector, like the other big career transitions in my life, was not an easy one. The company I was to join was located in Orange County, only a few miles from where I grew up, but a world apart from my world in Santa Barbara and my government years in Sacramento. Orange County, California, is one of the last bastions of conservatism in coastal California, a political, social, and economic environment that embraces bedrock conservative principles, limited government, limited regulation, and certainly not much interest in environmental innovation. But if I wanted to participate in the creation of new technology, the nonprofit world wouldn't give me that opportunity, and neither would government. So I made a very practical calculation that I had to be part of a company to do what I thought was needed. I made a pact with Cliff Ronnenberg, CEO of CR&R Incorporated, who had been instrumental in the work of the Community Environmental Council and with whom I had remained friends during my government years. I was given the lofty title of Executive Vice President when in fact I served more as a direct advisor to the owner on regulatory, policy, and technology matters.

My introduction to the private sector went much as it did when I went to Sacramento—it was, in a word, challenging. For the first time in my life, I had a boss, someone I needed to report to. And I was part of an executive team. This was strange, but manageable. A more difficult aspect for me was moving from a close-knit team, consisting of my advisors and executive assistant, to a group of individuals who were operations-oriented in keeping with their operations-based business. They were entirely focused on the here and now, the bottom line. I was a foreign element, accustomed to long-range strategic thinking, and certainly not in a position to establish a profit center like the ones that they managed, at least for some time.

The situation was uncomfortable, but by this time, I was used to sustaining my vision without much of a support base. I could look beyond the constraints of my immediate situation by keeping my eye on the goal, to identify and implement a post-landfill waste management system. For a few years, I commuted between Santa Barbara and Orange County, where I kept an apartment, an experience I loathed. It brought back memories of my years in Sacramento, when I left Santa Barbara for much of each week, a legislator-type life that I never took to.

After a few years, Cliff was comfortable enough with my essentially working from my home in Santa Barbara, reporting in and attending executive meetings and, of course, doing my work. Since I was not involved in the day-to-day operations of what was a very hands-on business, this was a feasible arrangement. Cliff and I had a time-tested relationship that assured him that I was a known commodity who had motivation and discipline.

Cliff left me free to map out my direction, where I could keep in close contact with my CEC colleagues as a board member and my colleagues in Santa Barbara, relationships that I continue to this day. Though I joined the company to pursue post-landfill technology, I had responsibilities, including keeping the company in high standing with the regulatory community. In this role, I was confronted almost immediately with a vexing challenge. Our Material Recovery and Transfer Facility in Stanton, which received and processed eighteen hundred tons of solid waste per day, was located very close to a condominium complex, a situation exacerbated many years earlier by the city fathers who allowed multifamily units to be built within hundreds of feet of an open transfer facility.

BIOFILTRATION

While I knew that one of my responsibilities at CR&R would be to deal with regulatory and compliance issues, I had no idea upon my arrival that there was a preexisting serious problem, with odor complaints from a condominium complex of hundreds of units, some of which were located less than one hundred feet from the sixteen-foot-tall boundary wall of our facility that received, processed, and recycled about seven hundred tons per day of recyclable materials. This facility, formerly an open county dump, predated the condos by several decades. Foolishly, the City of Stanton approved the project with full knowledge of the solid waste facility, thus creating chronic land use conflict that I was about to step into.

Some eleven odor-nuisance violations were made against the facility in the summer of 1998 by the South Coast Air Quality Management District (SCAQMD), one of the most powerful regulatory agencies in the United States. The SCAQMD is known for requiring the most severe air pollution control measures anywhere in the world, but there is good reason for some of its draconian standards. The Los Angeles metropolitan area has the worst air quality in the United States. It's not that Angelinos and their bretheren in Orange, Riverside, and San Bernardino Counties are more polluting than their counterparts around the country. It's regional geography that is to blame. The San Gabriel Mountains, rising to over eleven thousand feet, create a wall preventing air movement, forcing pollution to concentrate in the air basin below, where nearly twenty million people and two of the nation's largest ports reside. The air-quality situation is so extreme that the SCAQMD was given the legal authority to mandate stricter emission standards than those of the US EPA and the California Air Resources Board.

It was with some embarrassment and trepidation that I had to meet with officials of the SCAQMD and deal with the violations that had been issued against the company. But what caused me the most heartburn about this meeting was a real doubt that we could control the odor effectively, given the proximity of the facility to our neighbors.

At the meeting, I learned that odor violations are issued when five people in a neighborhood complain and an AQMD official confirms the problem based on a site visit. Eleven violations were issued in the span of two hot summer months, and there was little doubt that more would be forthcoming. "So," I asked, "the remedy is to control odors to the point where the complaints fall off to below that threshold, simple as that?" The district compliance engineer answered, "Simple as that."

Following the meeting, I met with Cliff and explained to him the difficulty of our challenge and that I needed to try to find a solution to the problem that would protect both the neighborhood and the facility on a long-term basis. Cliff gave me free reign to explore possibilities. As a first step, I decided to attend an industry conference on the East Coast where I knew people who might have insight into systems that could effectively control odors. I was familiar from my work in Sacramento related to composting that there was a technology called biofiltration that was used to remediate odor using a completely biological process. I had met a mechanical engineer there by the name of Jan Allen, who was working for the large international consulting engineering firm CH2M HILL, and ran into him at the conference. Jan had previously managed Cedar Grove composting facility near Seattle. This facility had been under fire for generating odor, and Jan had been on the front lines of that battle. He had experience with biofiltration. As we talked, I began to sense that biofiltration might be a way out of our dilemma, considering that the other alternatives, a wet scrubber that strips odorous compounds out of the air, and carbon filtration, using activated charcoal to filter the air, would be high maintenance and potentially cost-prohibitive given the voluminous quantities of air that would have to be treated.

I came back from the conference and introduced the idea of biofiltration. It was met with much understandable skepticism. Our company executive team didn't know a thing about it. Why would they? They were not exposed to the compost and wastewater industries at the time. I think my first explanation to them about biofiltration fell on deaf ears. But Cliff was a very open-minded, intellectually curious individual who never dismissed out of hand something brought to him by a respected colleague. As I saw it, our regulatory situation and our responsibility as a corporate citizen required nothing short of a fundamental air-treatment approach that would have a long-standing, beneficial impact on a problem that we owned. Short of such an approach, the company might find itself in a maelstrom of controversy or a lawsuit. At the least, I argued, we needed to begin experimenting with the biofiltration option. Cliff agreed. Working with Jan Allen, we decided on a year-long biofiltration testing regime.

To test the feasibility of biofiltration, we set up an experiment consisting of five containers filled with different media product—gravel, wood chips, and blends of the two—and piped odorous air from the buildings to the containers. Then five of us, including one city councilman, smelled the air once it had passed through the test biofilters. This might seem simplistic, even primitive, but in fact this approach was the most realistic way of determining the effectiveness of the process. The effectiveness standard we were to meet is one of the oldest of standards in the law: "Don't create a nuisance."

In the realm of science, high-sensitivity devices have been developed to detect odors of various sorts and, naturally, the most refined of these have been applied to matters of national security, such as detecting explosives or chemical or biological weapons. The district had been looking into the application of such devices to odor, but it had yet to find one that was practical and affordable. As it turns out, it's challenging to come up with a device as sensitive as the human nose, so in our case, the "smell test" was the right one.

Now the question was how to scale up, to go essentially from a bench-scale application of biofiltration to full scale. We needed a filter large enough to treat the air generated in two one-acre sized buildings ranging in height from thirty-five to sixty-five feet—or, in scientific terms, more than

120,000 cubic feet per minute. Design drawings were prepared for a filter of nearly one acre in size, at a height of some twelve feet. In composition the filter could be made of high-performance synthetic materials, light in weight, and capable of holding a sponge-like wetness, but the cost would be very high, perhaps close to two million dollars (far too expensive for our company to incur). Instead of costly synthetic materials, we decided to construct the biofilter out of concrete rubble and wood chips, mixed with some so-called zoo-doo generated by animals at the Los Angeles Zoo that had been composted.

Biofilter, Orange County, California. Environmental odor control technology built with recycled materials.

To Cliff's and his son David's credit, they brought to the task of designing the biofilter their innate engineering sensibilities, their understanding of materials handling, the properties of the different materials like ground wood and broken concrete, and their ingenuity in identifying and executing ways of reducing costs. In essence, they made an unaffordable project feasible.

When it came time to construct this biological colossus, we had stockpiled broken concrete that we would normally receive at our waste facility, and we ground orange trees that were felled in preparation for another residential development in Orange County (sadly, one of the last remaining groves in a county where the word Orange has more to do with hype or nostaligia than with reality).

The project was contracted out, but the work was basically performed by the rarest of the rare of heavy-equipment operators who, armed only with skip loader with a bucket, almost single-handedly constructed the massive biofilter. He skillfully placed several thousand tons of broken concrete rubble between and over a network of plastic pipes, factory drilled with twenty thousand holes, laid out on three-foot centers for the entire six-hundred-foot length of the biofilter. The purpose of the holes in the pipe was to distribute air that was sucked out of the building by three 75 horsepower fans. Once the plastic pipe network was laid, he placed the concrete rubble around the pipes, careful to not to do anything that might damage them, to a height of about four feet. This created a porous environment to allow the air from the building to circulate freely, rising upward. Above the concrete rubble was placed some five feet of wood chips from the ground orange grove, to which we added the "zoo-doo" from the Los Angeles Zoo. It was a marvel to watch the tractor man work. He moved his skip loader around like an artist day after day, working alone, self-contained and determined. He was an inspiration!

By design, the air that is drawn into the biofilter rises through a four-foot-deep rock bed and a deep layer of wood chips within roughly thirty to sixty seconds, depending on internal conditions. In the moist and warm environment within the biofilter, billions of microscopic organisms grow on the surface of both the rock and wood, though mostly on the wood. As the odorous air drawn from the building works its way from the bottom to the top of the filter, these organisms feed on the odor compounds passing through and remove them, thus cleansing the air. By the time the air exits the filter, it is essentially odor-free, provided the biofilter is maintained properly. If it becomes too wet, the microorganism activity is reduced and foul air can be emitted. If it becomes too dry, the microorganisms die and the filter becomes simply a medium through which odorous air passes into the atmosphere. So attentiveness to the inner environment of the biofilter is a continuous issue because it is, after all, a living system.

It was a cool October morning in 2000 when the biofilter was first started up. The electric fans began to hum, and we could see the air being drawn in from inside the building. The warmer air that exited the biofilter hit the cool ambient air, both moist, creating a vapor cloud that must have risen to nearly one hundred feet above the biofilter and just hung there. If you didn't know otherwise, it looked like smoke, and I was waiting for the fire engines to roll up just as they did twenty years before when we made our first large compost pile at El Mirasol.

For more than fourteen years now, that biofilter has done a yeoman's work in controlling odor—the first large-scale application of biofilter technology at a solid waste transfer and processing facility that we know of in the United States. And while the filter in and of itself cannot eliminate odor entirely, coupled with good on-site management it made a critical difference, transforming a facility that was a chronic nuisance to one that greatly reduced its impact on the surrounding community (while performing its vital function of receiving waste from nearly a dozen Southern California communities, recovering recyclables, and sending the unrecoverable materials to landfill).

The design, building, and operation of the biofilter is one of the most satisfying experiences of my career. Here was a technology that had not been applied to a situation like ours; we took it from the realm of ideas, tested it, built it in its entirety from recycled materials at a fraction of the cost it would have been if it had been built by customary means, and we put it into operation. We had built another piece of a much-needed environmental infrastructure, another piece of the pattern language.

You might say that the creation of the biofilter was a detour from my primary mission, to find and develop technology that could greatly reduce our dependence on landfill that would not be dependent on markets in distant China, one that would be entirely homegrown. Detours often offer important opportunities for learning and evolving in the difficult task of creating complex new environmental infrastructures. In our case, the building and operation of the biofilter gave us confidence that we could tackle one of the most difficult challenges facing new waste technology and the expansion of composting: odor control. Without effective odor control, new systems would have to be relegated to remote sites, meaning long trips being made with lumbering low-mileage trucks spewing emissions.

Among the benefits of biofiltration was that the very substance of the biofilter, the wood chips themselves, become a habitat for red worms. They, along with other life in the filter environment, eventually break down the wood mass. After about four years of life, the breakdown was affecting the performance of the biofilter, so it was dismantled. We found ourselves with a rich soil product full of millions of thriving red worms.

It was heartening to see this because it demonstrated, to me at least, that biofiltration is more than an odor-control system; it literally processes and cleans diesel emission–saturated air, detoxifying it. I don't have proof of this, but I would expect that it would be proven true if subjected to study.

Odor remains a great regulatory challenge in our increasingly dense urban society. Bakeries, fast-food establishments, restaurants, coffee houses, salsa-production plants, and any number of other establishments produce odors that may seem on first blush pleasant, but they become annoying and sometimes unbearable. I believe that biofiltration systems, where there is room for them, offer, in many cases, the best means of controlling odor and, in the process, allow otherwise incompatible activities to coexist.

THE END OF LANDFILLS?

As I was skirmishing with the biofilter development and learning the ropes of being in the private sector with its laser-like focus on operations, winning city contracts and, of course, the bottom-line, I began my search for a credible postlandfill technology.

The search started with a seminar at the Community Environmental Council. As with the many seminars that the CEC convened, it was preceded by a white paper that a colleague and I had prepared to frame the issues. The issues were these: There would still be an immense amount of solid waste materials going to landfills, even with strong recycling efforts and growth in the compost industry in California. By now it was abundantly clear that the California-grown recycling industry, which recycling pioneers like myself had thought would happen, had failed to materialize, as California, and indeed the nation, let many manufacturing industries go offshore. What could be done with the remaining waste to prevent it from going to landfill? Couldn't we find technologies that could convert this waste to forms of energy, including electricity and biofuels—or, better yet, bio-based chemicals?

The seminar brought to Santa Barbara inventors, engineering companies, technology vendors, government officials, and non-governmental organization leaders to discuss the technologies, their state of development, the economic and technological challenges people faced, and other considerations such as their compatibility with recycling and their emissions' profiles. These technologies included systems with the most grotesque names like "pyrolysis" and "gasification," which were thermal technologies that the companies claimed could reduce waste by 90 percent or more while producing green energy and low air emissions as well as biological systems like anaerobic digestion. Collectively, we called these systems "conversion technologies" because, in addition to creating energy from waste, they could create fuels and chemicals through thermal or chemical conversion.

At the time, I had only the most general understanding of how conversion technologies worked. I knew that some of these technologies were considered promising. During the Carter presidency, when the nation was embroiled in energy crises, they were in a very early stage of development, more like research and development projects. The question now was whether there might be a role for them in handling residual waste from material recovery and other types of recycling facilities such as contaminated paper, cardboard, and low-grade mixed plastics. It seemed to me that, if they were viable, there could be several plants that could convert these residual wastes to energy from perhaps a twenty-five-mile radius, rather than have these wastes trucked to remote landfills. Such plants could reduce the energy footprint from shipping waste and generate energy that could go right into the grid or be suitable for cogeneration applications. At least we wouldn't be sending the waste to be landfilled, hauling it as much as two hundred miles to desert locations by train and truck.

Following the seminar, my first serious study of a conversion technology began in Fayetteville, Arkansas, where a former professor of chemistry at the University of Arkansas, Dr. James Gaddy, was developing a conversion technology to convert municipal waste and green waste to ethanol through fermentation. Gaddy had developed genetically engineered microbes that he claimed could accelerate the conversion process and thus drive down the costs of making ethanol.

Cliff had earlier provided some seed funding for his process, but the majority of it came from the US Department of Energy and later from investors. After studying this system, I concluded that while the technology appeared promising, the commercialization of the technology was still years off, and that substantial research and development funding would be needed to sustain the development effort until it could be

Schwartze Pumpe: Last energy stand of Nazi Germany.
Coal gasification tries to morph into modern waste management technology.

commercialized. We didn't have several millions of dollars to commit to open-ended prototype development, so we discontinued support.

I turned my focus to waste technologies in Europe. Germany has been and remains one the world's leading centers for innovative recycling, waste prevention, and waste-to-renewable energy programs. I was fortunate to connect with a very helpful staff member of the American Chamber of Commerce in Berlin, Stephen Dahle, from Colorado, who arranged for me to visit several gasification and compost technology companies, along with the Brandenburg State Environmental Protection Agency, to gain a better understanding of Germany's current and future approaches to recycling waste.

I had been to Berlin ten years earlier when I was in government, as a US Information Service speaker to Germany. In the early 1990s, Germany had introduced a bold measure to reduce waste packaging. Known as the Green Dot program, it placed responsibility on the producers of products to ensure that their packaging material would be recycled, and it offered incentives to eliminate excessive packaging (such as placing a tube of tooth-paste in a box and then wrapping it in plastic). This was the leading edge of what has come to be known as "product stewardship," a policy framework that places responsibility on the manufacturers of products (from cosmetics to cars) to ensure that their products are recyclable and that the use of toxic products is minimized.

During my four days around Berlin, I spent most of my time on the German autobahns with Stephen, traveling great distances to facility sites. One site visit I shall never forget took me near the Saxony/Polish border to a town with the ghastly name Schwarze Pumpe, which means "Black Pump." Schwarze Pumpe, in addition to its grim name, had an even darker history as the center for Nazi deployment of coal gasification. Coal gasification technology was developed by the Nazi war machine to extract the energy content from coal and transform it into a liquid. The process was cumbersome and costly, but the Nazis were forced to develop it when vital oil supplies from the Black Sea region were cut off by the advancement of the Red Army.

Following World War II, coal from the region was a source of energy for Eastern Europe, but with the fall of the East German government, subsidies for energy development were being curtailed. I was taken to the sole surviving gasification plant. Plant engineers were desperately trying to adapt their technology to handling municipal solid waste or any other source of waste for that matter. For them, it was a terrifying time, as the economic safety net provided by the East German government was unraveling, and the Federal Democratic Republic was absorbing East Germany.

I didn't find the technology at all appealing; it seemed as grim as the region, all broken-down and crumbling as the Soviet Empire cratered and collapsed. The only sign of newness in this vast, forested flatland region was an enormous new natural gas energy plant, built, I was told, by a Swedish firm—architecturally bold and gleaming, an almost ethereal-looking building in this otherwise forbidding, drained, and depleted landscape.

On our way back, Stephen and I stopped in the nearby small city of Forst, famished from not eating all day, and stepped into a pub, the only establishment that was open in town. Suited up as we were and very foreign-looking in this remote place, we found ourselves glared at by four big men huddled at the pub's rear. Their faces were out of a Bruegel painting.

There was no telling what could happen to a couple of errant travelers in this most unwelcoming of environments.

We hightailed our way out of the pub and out of Forst. As we drove away, I saw a young Chinese woman walking alone along a road. I stared at her, wondering what on earth she could be doing here in this seemingly racially homogeneous and no doubt xenophobic backwater of a still barely unified Germany. I wanted to snatch her up, rescue her from what seemed to be an appalling fate. Then she was gone, vanished from the rear-view mirror.

The next day, I visited a very sophisticated gasification plant near Dresden that was using waste to produce Fischer-Tropsch diesel fuel. Fischer-Tropsch diesel is also a synthetic diesel fuel that companies like Volkswagen and Volvo have banked on as a future source of lower-emission fuels compatible with the continued use of the diesel engine. Unlike the United States, Germany and indeed much of Europe have committed research and development and their engine technology to a diesel-engine platform. While this plant had much going for it, including impeccable German engineering, when I asked for a quote on plant costs the sticker price was so far beyond what would be feasible in the United States that we didn't pursue it any further.

I concluded my trip with a visit to Brandenburg, the headquarters of the state's Environmental Protection Agency. I took the short train ride from central Berlin to Brandenburg and briskly walked in the cold to Brandenburg EPA. The famed Albert Einstein Institute was located next door.

The director of the EPA's solid waste division explained his group's approach to managing waste. In advance of what became the European Directive, which essentially banned organic waste from landfill because organic waste produces the potent greenhouse gas, methane, Brandenburg was going to take all organic materials from cities like Berlin, compost them and then landfill the spent organic waste so it couldn't produce methane. I was shown an impressive three-dimensional video about the plant they were planning to build to accomplish this. This plant would first compost green waste collected within Brandenburg and then deposit the composted green waste, now inert, with its greenhouse gas content removed, into a landfill. I was taken aback that the Germans would go to such lengths and expend such sums to remove greenhouse gases from the environment. This project certainly underscored how serious Germany was taking the threat of global warming.

In the course of our discussion, I explained to the director that in California, perhaps America's greenest state, it would be impossible to propose such an intervention. In 1999, the subject of global warming and climate change was still largely off the radar, and even were it not so, there was little likelihood of getting state and local governments to spend the kind of money that Brandenburg was committed to.

I shared with him the state of waste technology and the interest that our company had in finding technologies that could manage the wastes we couldn't recycle. I told him that the mere mention of thermal systems, such as waste incineration, gasification, and the production of forms of energy like Fischer-Tropsch diesel from waste products, provoked almost hysterical fears in some of California's environmental organizations and environmental justice groups. Bearing out the depth of these fears in our state was a recently enacted piece of legislation that required any proposed gasification facility to pass a test of producing zero emissions. The German official was astounded that there could be such a law, since from a scientific perspective no technology could have "zero emissions." How, he asked me, could a sophisticated state like California, known for its environmental leadership, put such a standard into law? All I could say was that it was an embarrassing admission of a mind-set that prevailed among influential environmental leaders and officials.

The explanation for this state of affairs in California casts light on how convoluted and unscientific the legislative process can become when it's driven by what I consider to be an ideologically based environmentalism. The genesis of this story goes back to the incinerator battles that were waged in California in the mid- to late 1980s.

In those days, waste-to-energy companies were eager to sell their technologies to local governments, a move driven in part by renewable energy subsidies created during the 1982 oil crisis and by the US EPA, which was promoting the technology as part of a government effort to develop domestic energy supplies. In 1978, Congress enacted the Public Utilities Regulatory

Policies Act (PURPA) as part of the National Energy Act. This law was in response to the US oil crisis of 1973, when oil-producing nations in the Middle East imposed an oil boycott in response to Washington's support of Israel in the Yom Kippur War. The Act provided substantial subsidies for producers of electric power from municipal waste, solar, and biomass sources. The subsidies were guaranteed by the government for a minimum of ten years, providing electricity rate enhancements of as much as six cents per kilowatt hour, about double what the price of electricity was selling for in the marketplace. With this level of subsidy, massive incinerator plants, which would otherwise not be economically viable, became feasible.

Costing upward of $150 million or more, waste incinerators were big business, and the industry had eyes on development in California because of the massive quantities of waste going to landfills. Cities such as San Francisco and Los Angeles, and counties including Los Angeles and San Diego, were courted by the companies, and several projects were in an advanced stage of development. In addition to the power purchase agreements from the utilities that subsidized the price of power and the length of the purchase contracts, project developers needed one more thing—agreements from local governments participating in the projects guaranteeing that their wastes would "flow" to the facilities through what are called "put or pay" agreements. This guaranteed waste flow to an incinerator assured project developers that they would have adequate supplies of waste to generate the electrical revenues needed to pay off their debt and produce a rate of return on the investment that would support the project financing. If for some reason the amount of waste required for the facility wasn't forthcoming, local governments and their rate payers would be on the hook to make up for the lost waste and revenue.

Such agreements were correctly viewed by pro-recycling and environmental interests as an anathema to future recycling in America. Although it was now more than a decade since the incinerator battles had been waged and the technology defeated in California, and the state of the incinerator industry was now moribund throughout the country, due to the sun-setting of PURPA, the psychological scars from the epic political battles were still fresh. Proponents of technologies like gasification were desperate to overcome the stigma associated with incineration. Gasification was one technology, they claimed, that would result in minimal emissions, significantly below historical waste incinerators and even some forms of recycling. One company from Australia, Brightstar, now deceased, went so far as to make the claim that its technology did not produce any emissions. Its bosses shared this claim with one of the legislature's leading consultants and he, being a shrewd fellow, worked with a legislator to incorporate a "zero emission" in a new statute governing conversion technologies. This was how California adopted its scientifically indefensible definition in statute that has withstood more than a decade's effort to change it.

What is particularly galling about this is that Germany, Sweden, and other European countries, which have more comprehensive recycling laws and product stewardship practices than we do, have long since resolved the battle between environmentalists and technology developers over, for instance, the use of waste incineration. They don't understand why we continue to pit recycling and product stewardship against alternative technology and continue to rely as heavily as we do on the most primitive of waste management systems—landfill.

Twenty years ago in California, we were able to engage in complex policy issues, such as conversion, by establishing blue-ribbon groups representing science and academia, public interest groups, local governments, and the public at large and allowing them to consider and work through the points of contention. Political leaders placed their trust in the findings of such groups and often subordinated their own previously held positions to them. But in today's hyper-ideologically driven environment, with its lockstep conformity, I have observed, in other words, that knowledge and insight have taken a backseat to prejudice. This represents a sweeping change in our body politic and is a severe departure from the past, when diverse opinions were debated honestly and knowledge was respected. In this environment, it's no wonder that we can't forge critical policies to deal with energy and climate change, along with many other critical issues.

Like most of the American public who are disgusted with the state of politics, many nonprofit and business leaders no longer regard Congress as a functional institution capable of delivering reasonableness, predictability, and the long-term view, all qualities that citizens and business alike should expect from their government. Businesses, which we need to fashion our infrastructures and implement technological innovation, must navigate development without reliable government partners. They are increasingly forced to rely on internal means, along with industry associations that offer some sense of unity and kinship. Maybe in the longer run, the combined frustration between the public and progressive businesses will forge powerful new relationships that can galvanize into a strong enough political base to achieve desired ends using unconventional means. Perhaps they will be able to create a popular base of public interest that begins to wean out the extremes and reintroduce a body politic in which common sense and decency are more the norm than an anomaly. In the meantime, in the absence of national guidance, leadership is forced to move more and more to the state and local levels where many strange, sometimes awful, and sometimes exciting and ennobling experiments in governance play out. But even at state levels, as I have tried to argue with the case study of conversion technology, attitudes and ideologies that promote narrow thinking and thus narrowly conceived laws and policies are difficult to unseat.

BIOGAS

After studying many conversion systems, though by no means all of those available, and taking stock of the political and policy context in California, anaerobic digestion (AD) technology for reducing the amount of waste going to landfills emerged as the most feasible option. Anaerobic digestion is a simple biological process that operates at "body temperature." Organic waste such as food waste and grass clippings are ground and fed into a big tank (digester) that acts just like our stomach by breaking down the compounds and producing a waste product known as digestate and biogas. The digestate, provided it's clean enough, is used as a soil amendment in landscaping, and the gas is cleaned and used to produce electricity, or a biofuel called biomethane, which can be used to power natural gas vehicles.

By the 1990s, anaerobic digestion was starting to develop in Europe. By 2000, AD development took off in northern Europe, driven by the European Union's ban on the disposal of organic wastes in landfills, and Europe's move to develop renewable energy sources, among them low-carbon transportation fuels. The most powerful catalyst for development was Germany's Feed-In Tariff (2004), a policy that gave German farmers a very large subsidy to produce electricity from anaerobically produced biogas. The subsidy meant that prices of up to eighteen cents per kilowatt hour were available to AD facility developers. It prompted German farmers to become renewable energy producers, sending a new around-the-clock source of renewable electricity into the electrical grid. By 2010 there were more than eight thousand AD facilities in Germany, mostly small, mostly on farms. Germany has now made AD development one of the cornerstones of its effort to become the world's first fossil-free country. German scientists and policy makers believe that with AD applications that produce renewable natural gas instead of electricity, up to 10 percent of all of Germany's transportation fuels can come from farm and urban organic wastes.

We have no comparable incentives, which is why there has been little development of these technologies in the United States. Landfill costs in Southern California range from about thirty dollars per ton disposed to upward of sixty dollars per ton. By contrast, landfill costs in Germany, Sweden, and other northern European nations are well over one hundred dollars per ton.

Great Britain is the latest European nation to embrace the possibilities of anaerobic digestion. As recently as a decade ago, Great Britain was Europe's laggard when it came to recycling and developing alternatives to the landfilling of waste. But beginning in 2000, the country decided to impose landfill taxes that were quite punishing, making landfilling of waste less and less economically attractive, to the point where an AD industry is taking off as in northern Europe. Political leaders in Great Britain had the courage to enact high landfill taxes, seeing them as the most effective means of changing both waste management and renewable energy practices in the country. This is something US policy makers have been loath to do. In less than a decade, England went from being an outlier in forward-thinking waste management practices to becoming a leader on the world stage.

Our path to AD development has had many turns and twists—not untypical in the story of developing new environmental technology. As I learned over the past decade, sometimes painfully, identifying, choosing, and developing new environmental technology is complex, full of risk, and can only be accomplished if critical development conditions are in alignment. The technology must prove itself to be capable of operating for decades on a commercial scale, at a size where companies like ours can invest in, with the expectation that they can become a core part of our business platform, not a research and development project. And it must be able to be permitted in a timely way, without incurring costly lawsuits and other forms of delay.

My journey into the world of AD, and by extension the world of bio-energy, began in 2005 when we were approached by an Israeli firm that had developed a pilot AD facility producing electricity on the outskirts of Tel Aviv, next to the city's giant landfill, which was in the process of being closed. The firm had been in the water treatment business, based in the port city of Haifa, where much of Israel's energy sector resides. Water clean-up is a technology associated with the oil industry.

The late Dr. Mel Finstein, a professor emeritus from Rutgers University and consultant to Arrowbio, and Yair Zadik, the company CEO, took me to lunch in Santa Barbara to explain why they thought our company and theirs should join forces and submit a proposal to the city of Los Angeles, which had recently issued a Request for Proposals to build a noncommercial scale "emerging technology" for the city. Under the leadership of Los Angeles City Councilman Greig Smith, the city had recently passed a plan to wean itself from landfill, and in the process create renewable energy technologies that would improve the environment, eliminate deep-seated frustrations from the public impacted by landfills receiving city waste, and create green jobs. Antonio Villaragosa, the city's first Latino mayor with national political ambitions, signed on to Smith's plan. The city directed its powerful Board of Public Works, working through its Bureau of Sanitation, to undertake the RFP.

ArrowBio invited me to come to Tel Aviv, see their facility, meet their engineers, and discuss how we might collaborate. I made the long trip to Israel, my first, where I was put up in a Sheraton Hotel on the lively Tel Aviv waterfront. The following morning, having worked through some jet lag, I was met by Yair at the hotel and taken to the ArrowBio plant.

The Arrow system involved separating organic materials from nonorganic waste in a water environment—essentially an artificial stream. Waste was dropped into a large water tank by incoming trucks with little by way of materials sorting or separation. Yair described the process as that of a river, with quiet pools and rapids. The light materials, such as plastics, floated and were skimmed off while heavier materials, like metals and glass, sank. Organic materials such as pieces of food would either break up into small particles in the water, or in the case of, say, an apple, would be pulverized by high-velocity water into finer, nonorganic particles that would pass through and be removed via a series of ever finer screens. At the end of the process, organic materials suspended in water would go to a "wet" series of anaerobic digesters, where they would be converted to biogas. Then the biogas would be cleaned up and used to run electric turbines for the production of electricity. The "digestate," the byproduct of digestion, was to be used as a soil product.

This process was completely counterintuitive to waste separation practices that we were familiar with. To put waste in a water environment seemed to present all kinds of problems: contamination of recyclable materials, weighting them down with water, possible contamination of the organic materials separated in the process, and other concerns. As skeptical as I was when I arrived, I left believing that, lacking an AD technology alternative, we should continue to explore the Arrow option. We had so much more to learn about AD options and not much else to consider at that time.

Arrow had won a contract with a quasi-governmental agency, Waste of New South Wales (WSN), providing solid waste recycling and composting services for greater Sydney. In the fall of 2008, I visited the grand opening of the plant that was still under construction, a massive facility that was designed to process up to 480 tons per day. I met with the consulting engineers hired by the agencies and local governments who were participating in the project, and with the principals of WSN. From these meetings Arrow's abilities seemed to be confirmed. The officials at WSN had high praise for ArrowBio's performance during the construction phase, up to the point of the grand opening.

The Australian consulting engineers who had been hired by WSN to evaluate the viability of the technology presented a favorable picture, along with an assessment that the digestate's use as a soil product would meet Australian regulatory requirements. And the public officials who had committed to sending waste to the facility from local communities nearby spoke with conviction that they had made the right technology selection. The facility would be a world-leading effort to minimize the landfilling of waste and would, by virtue of converting the methane in waste to energy, greatly reduce the release of greenhouse gases into the environment. All in all, the picture was a favorable one. But the technology was still to be proven.

Since the construction of this plant would reveal the strengths and weaknesses of the technology soon enough, I felt it was essential that I establish a strong communications link with the WSN officials so that after my return we could find out, from time to time, how the project was proceeding. In the meantime, we continued with our own due diligence and hired a major engineering firm with expertise in AD technology to further evaluate the system. They had projects in Israel and visited the facility. The feedback was again generally positive.

But as time went on, I learned that there were problems with components of the system. The conveyor belts that carried materials from site to site within the plant proved to be flimsy and had to be replaced at considerable cost. Later, there were concerns that some of the recyclable materials recovered by the ArrowBio system were unmarketable and that the gas output was not what was expected.

Unraveling just who was responsible for the difficulties was too complicated for us to determine. This was because under its arrangement with Arrow, WSN had assumed responsibility for the construction of the facility. Without a forensic analysis by a third-party engineering firm, it would be virtually impossible to sort out who was responsible for the problems that were emerging—WSN or Arrow, or a combination of the two? But it was clear that serious problems existed, so we began to retreat from the technology. We opened up other channels into the AD world to find a more suitable technology. Fortunately, by 2010, AD development had progressed greatly in northern Europe—specifically in Germany, Sweden, and Belgium—where hundreds of facilities were now in use. European vendors were now beginning to market their wares in the United States.

Our experience vetting the ArrowBio process and many others over the course of years underscored just how hazardous it can be to try to apply a new or foreign technology in our industry. There are so many aspects that must be mastered in order to have a viable technology. In the case of AD development, feed materials must be clean and relatively homogeneous to allow the digester to work properly. Then the gas cleanup systems, which were still relatively new, needed to produce the right quality of biomethane so that it could be used for either fuel to run trucks or be injected into the natural pipeline system. One also had to make sure that the digestate was of a suitable quality for use by agriculture, nurseries, or landscapers and that the product could be sold year-round. This latter point is of enormous concern, because a successful project cannot leave hanging the question of whether the digestate can be marketed as a soil amendment on a 365-day-a-year basis, year after year after year.

Assuming these factors could be satisfied, there were issues securing financing. Could our banks be convinced that the systems, though relatively mature in Europe, would work here? Would there be available equipment components in the case of breakdowns that were readily available to maintain the system in operation? Was there a sufficient market for the biogas, and at what price? Could the final capital cost of the facility be pinned down enough to be accurate, and would the cost of the system, including its operation, warrant a bank loan, given projected revenues? And what about the regulatory impediments, obtaining permits from the local government, from the state, from the air-quality district and a myriad other agencies? Even if all these hurdles could be surmounted, would the local governments that we provided long-term services for agree to utilize the technology, and at what price?

As I saw it, if companies like ours and local governments could get the technology right, AD could become a dominant platform for managing the organic fraction of solid waste in the United States, producing the cleanest transportation fuel possible, eliminating greenhouse gases, and reducing reliance on primitive landfill as our primary waste system, just as northern Europe had done. Instead of trucks being powered by diesel fuel, or even so called "clean" natural gas, they would run on biomethane, the treated biogas produced from anaerobic digesters. Which brings us to the subject of transportation, the lynchpin in waste management operations and the core of so much commercial goods transportation in the United States.

A company like ours operates hundreds of heavy-duty trucks. In the United States there are an estimated eleven million to thirteen million heavy-duty diesel trucks that are licensed and operating, which consume about fifty billion gallons of diesel fuel per year. The health risk from the burning of diesel fuel is 7.5 times greater than the combined health risk of all toxic air pollutants combined. About eleven thousand cancer deaths per year are attributed to diesel combustion, and it's one of the largest contributing factors to asthma in children. Until the early 2000s, most trucks operating in the waste industry were diesel powered, getting fewer than five miles to the gallon while producing large amounts of particulate emissions, nitrous oxides (a smog precursor), and greenhouse gases.

In the early 1970s, it was the AQMD that introduced the catalytic convertor to capture emissions on cars sold within the LA Basin. The catalytic convertor and a host of other technical innovations stemming from the needs to reduce emissions have been developed and imposed on businesses operating in the South Coast, but even so, the district has been unable to reach federally mandated clean air standards for emissions such as nitrous oxide (NOx).

Although I had served as a state regulator and was familiar with California's powerful Air Resources Board, I didn't appreciate the power and reach of the AQMD until I came to the company and witnessed a public hearing process that led to the passage of Rule 1193. This rule requires bus, waste truck, and fleet operators to progressively replace diesel with natural gas engines. It was passed by the AQMD Board of Governors over the strenuous objections of the giants in the oil industry, including American Petroleum Institute, ARCO, Chevron, and Exxon.

The "fleet rule," as it's called, launched a significant experiment in changing heavy-duty engine platforms away from diesel to natural gas and in providing a new infrastructure to fuel these vehicles, a transformation that is still very much a work in progress. With grant-making authority, the AQMD has dispensed several hundred millions of dollars over the past fifteen years to companies and local government fleet operators to enable them to pay for the extra cost of natural gas engines and fueling stations. This experiment was initially fraught with problems. The on-board natural gas fueling tanks for Liquefied Natural Gas (LNG) vehicles were problematic, suffering from leaks and other issues that produced on-the-road breakdowns. There were other technical difficulties that plagued natural gas truck fleets for the first few years, but with time these problems have mostly been resolved, and fleet operators today are generally satisfied with the engine and fueling storage technology.

But even with the large fleet transformation underway, the AQMD realizes that this is only a transition, that to truly clean up the air it will be necessary to develop zero-emission transportation technology. A zero-emission transportation platform needs zero carbon fuels to power vehicles, electrification of cars to an increasing extent, the utilization of hydrogen fuel-cell vehicles and any number of other possibilities. The transformation of the transportation sector coincides with the transformation of the waste sector, and it underscores the growing interrelatedness between environmental regulation and environmental technology.

Biomethane is refined biogas produced through the anaerobic digestion of organic waste. To meet natural gas standards for domestic use, raw biogas must be cleaned up to be between 98 and 99 percent pure methane. At 97 percent or better, the biomethane meets the fuel specifications for natural gas engines and as such it's a new renewable fuel source. Biomethane produced from food and green waste, as well as other forms of biomass constituents, such as farm and organic residues from food processing, are available to produce biomethane. According to the California Air Resources Board, biomethane is the cleanest transportation fuel available, six times cleaner than natural gas, producing no net increase in carbon. In fact, it's a carbon negative fuel.

According to the California Energy Commission, natural gas provides more than half of the state's heating and cooling and a growing share of transportation fuels. California could produce enough renewable natural gas to replace one quarter of all the diesel fuel used by motor vehicles in California.[49] In the United States, food and green waste represents about 40 percent of the solid waste produced in our towns and cities. By my reckoning, the biomethane potential of these abundant and renewable materials is more than three hundred million gallons (diesel equivalent annually). In California alone biomethane could be powering some nine thousand heavy-duty trucks and buses. The organic materials needed to produce the fuel has an existing collection and processing infrastructure already in place in terms of collection containers, vehicles, and recycling facilities. Southern California has enough organic materials to produce enough fuel to run the LA City and County bus systems, plus all of the trash trucks that pass through it. There's more than enough fuel to run the trucks that serve the Los Angeles and Long Beach harbors, which presently befoul the air breathed by thousands of adults and children who live along the freeways that carry the harbor freight to market.

In 2009, I went to Sweden on a trip organized by the Swedish Consulate in Los Angeles. This trip involved site visits to biomethane facilities in Gothenburg and several small cities nearby and meetings with the mayor of Gothenburg, the Swedish Environmental Protection Agency, Volvo, and the city of Stockholm. The site visits and meetings were nothing short of a revelation. Unlike the United States, which has a history steeped in gas development and a well-established natural gas grid, Sweden lacks natural

Goran Johansson: Powerful Mayor of Gotenburg, Sweden and proponent of using biogas for buses, trucks, cars, ships and jets.

gas resources and a distribution system. Moreover, Sweden has a troubled political history with Russia, which has been its principal supplier of natural gas as with many of the European countries. About twenty years ago, Sweden decided that it would do everything within its means to develop domestic renewable energy resources to bolster national security. One of the measures taken was to set incentive pricing for non–fossil fuel electrical and transportation energy resource development, not for a paltry few years, as we tend to do in the United States, but for decades.

During my visit, I began to see the outlines of transportation systems propelled by biogas produced from the anaerobic digestion of municipal organic wastes, wastewater plants treating domestic sewage, and the wastes from dairies and food waste processors. Göran Johansson, the mayor of Gothenburg at that time, was perhaps Sweden's most famous politician, an irascible mover and shaker of the old style of hard knocks, the kind who uses friendly persuasion and, failing that, isn't beyond becoming an outright bully in pursuit of his purpose. He explained to me that Gothenburg, Sweden's second largest city (and its industrial heart where Volvo trucks and automobiles are made and where Sweden's main port is located), was going to be running all of its buses and waste collection trucks within a few years on biomethane from its food waste and waste water plants. He'd told Volvo's top management that he wanted them to produce, in short order, engines that could run successfully on biomethane. When Volvo's top bosses balked, he told them, by God the city's trucks and buses would be built by Mercedes, not Volvo, causing a national disgrace. Volvo got with the program.

A few days later in Stockholm, visiting the Stockholm City Hall and the Swedish Environmental Ministry, I heard a similar message. Within a few years, all of Stockholm's buses and trucks would be running on biomethane. By 2011, this became a fact. By 2020, Sweden plans to meet all of its transportation fuel needs from biogas plants by tapping all of its biogas-generation potential.

Compared with the United States, Sweden is a small, even tiny country of some nine million. It has a large welfare system and its citizens are, in general, more committed to environmental protection. This is all true. But as I traveled about Sweden, taking a very fast train from Gothenburg to Stockholm, eating at wonderful restaurants, walking the glorious Stockholm waterfront, visiting the visionary city within the city Hammarby Sjöstad, and sampling the countryside and seaside villages on the rugged West Coast and the Stockholm region's archipelago, I was mightily impressed by the beauty and quality of life that modern Sweden has achieved. Economically, it's one of northern Europe's powerhouses, with a per household income of $46,380, compared to the US household income of $57,160.[50] It weathered the banking crisis better than almost any country in the world. It is home to some of Europe's most advanced high-tech and consumer products companies. In many respects, it seemed to me that Sweden's decision to exploit its biological and truly sustainable resources was an intelligent and necessary response for a country that values its natural environment, takes climate change seriously (in both conservative and liberal circles alike), and has accepted the fact that clean energy costs more and is worth the price.

I visited Sweden's two largest cities, met with business leaders, politicians, and government officials, and spent time meeting with friends and new acquaintances, experiencing what I could of their priorities in governing the country, including their commitment to the development of renewable energy. There was much to learn from this small but sophisticated country about how to make renewable energy work. Why not exploit the gas released from wastewater plants and inject this gas into the natural gas grid, as they were doing in Gothenburg? Why not capture the gas from lowly food wastes and farm residues and convert it to valuable liquid fuels to run cars, trucks, buses, and planes? It seemed like sanctified common sense to me.

Sweden's big neighbor to the south, the mighty manufacturing machine of Germany with its leading companies, its powerful economy, and its high standard of living (at income of $43,740 per household with eighty-two million people, nearly nine times the population of Sweden) is taking a similar path. Germany too has very limited fossil fuel resources, the result of more than a hundred years of coal consumption and a lack of oil and natural gas.

Denmark, Belgium, and the Netherlands share environmental values with Sweden and Germany, and they too lack fossil fuel resources. It's understandable that these countries would seek a shift to a more renewable energy base, making them less dependent on Russia and the Middle East for their energy resources. One could argue that, if they had a fossil fuel resource base like the United States, they too would be less sanguine about spending the additional sums to develop renewable energy. But this logic holds only if you accept the premise that relatively low-cost fossil fuels, with their irrefutable environmental impacts on public health, the climate, and on nature itself, are indispensable to our future. If you don't accept the premise, then what these countries are doing to develop renewable energy resources seems eminently sensible.

As I see it, they are making necessary and important investments in securing as stable an energy future as they can, one that leads to self-generated industries such as wind, solar, and biogas, tapping the resources that they have without plundering their lands, polluting their air, and contaminating their soils while maintaining their standard of living. If, in another twenty years, they are able to reach high levels of renewable energy development while maintaining their advanced standard of living, they will have shown us the way toward a post–fossil fuel world. And if they are unable to attain this, it won't be for lack of effort, as in the case with the United States.

Hammarby Sjöstad, Stockholm: An ecological city within the city.

While in Stockholm, I was given a tour of Hammarby Sjöstad, an ecological city within the city, by a staff member from the mayor's office. With its triple-glazed windows, its vacuum-tubed waste collection systems that deliver recyclables and garbage to depositories within the complex and eliminates the need for clunky trucks with their noisy hydraulic equipment to have to pick up and transport waste, Hammarby Sjöstad was clearly a leading-edge urban sustainability experiment. The visit added to my appreciation of how much northern Europe has to teach us about practical environmentalism and how, in so many ways, they have advanced well beyond us.

I met with industry, government, environmental, and academic experts alike. I found a refreshingly different approach to thermal systems among technical and opinion leaders. In contrast with the policy and legislative makers in California, where ideology can trump science, Swedish policy seems steeped in science. Waste policy, for example, is based on extensive public health risk studies and the pragmatic recognition that some waste materials such as plastics are not easily recycled and are preferably burned to heat water and provide space heating.

How refreshing it was to learn that Swedish experts from the academy, government, and NGOs had long ago worked through the politics of incineration while we in California debate its efficacy endlessly and with often baseless reasoning.

When I toured Hammarby Sjöstad with a well-informed tour guide furnished by the City of Stockholm, I marveled at the vacuum-tube waste collection systems that deliver recyclables and garbage to depositories within the complex, thus eliminating the need for clunky trucks with their noisy hydraulic equipment. I learned that heat from the nearby waste-to-energy incinerator was providing hot water natural gas for the homes and commercial establishments with their triple-glazed windows that provided optimal energy conservation.

America has had the luxury to develop insular ways. It is so big, relatively unpopulated, and so rich in natural resources that it hasn't needed to place limits upon itself, how people moved about the land, where to dump its trash, or how to sustain its natural resources. However, throughout the Northeast and now in the South Atlantic states, in pockets of the Midwest, and along the Pacific Coast, we've become as crowded as Europe has been for more than a century. Transportation, housing, and food are no longer cheap compared with the rest of the world. And so it seems like it's time to look not only to experiments around our country, but to those around the world for insights and practical measures that can help us cope with change and make us a better country.

We have much to learn from Sweden and Germany when it comes to biogas development. We have much to learn from Mexico City and cities in South America about traffic management. We have much to learn from France and China about bullet trains. When it comes to charting an environmental course for the United States, I don't believe in American exceptionalism. I don't think we are at all exceptional in preserving and protecting the environment and preparing for global warming impacts that are now upon us.

We were exceptional at the birth of the modern environmental movement when we put in place national and state policies to address pollution of the land, the air, and the water. No country did more in this regard. We were exceptional when we decided to make the catalytic converter mandatory in automobiles to curb NOx emissions. But most of this innovation is decades-old now, and in the meantime many parts of the world have caught up and surpassed us. Let's not begrudge this fact. Let's accept it and realize that we have much to learn from the world and get on with learning and applying those achievements by others that make sense for us.

ON THE MATTER OF SCALE

If there is anything I have learned on the environmental frontier, it is the importance and power of small enterprises, the work of a few individuals, the innovations that happen at the local level, and their ability to influence over time the larger society. I think this is true now more than ever. We live in a time when we are overpowered by bigness, the bigness of corporations with their immense reach into so many aspects of our lives, decisions made by remote people to whom we have little, if any, access. We have become, like much of the world, an urban-based civilization where the people who govern are often remote. If you live in Los Angeles County for example, the seat of power is in downtown Los Angeles, which can be as far as fifty miles from where you live. Each of the five county supervisors presides over millions of citizens—many more than live in states like Montana, Wyoming, and the Dakotas. While they have "field offices," these too can be difficult to access, and, besides, the voting still takes place at the seat of power, where it may take you a full day to participate. What do these facts tell you about governance in the urban regions of our country? Big beyond measure, physically and psychologically remote from the governed, they are a living testament to how deeply and dramatically the political geography of America has changed.

It was James Madison who was entrusted by the framers of this nation to make a study of governmental and political systems that could provide important lessons for how we should govern our new nation. When he reported on his findings, high among the societies in the history of the world that had important lessons to offer the Congress were the Athenian Greeks in the time of Solon. Madison found inspiration in the emphasis the Greeks placed on citizen participation in the governance of the Athenian city-state, and on the idea of the polis. At the core of the Athenian experiment in democracy was its small and intimate scale. At the time of the Founders, America was a country of small towns where many of the citizens knew one another and could participate meaningfully in their government. As a nation of thirteen colonies, with a population of fewer than about three million people, living mostly in small rural communities, America could relate to the ideal of the Greek polis.

Could the framers have envisioned that the thirteen colonies would become, within 225 years, a nation of more than 300 million persons living in urban regions with populations as large as 20 million, with states like California approaching a population of 40 million? Could they have imagined that one county (LA County) would have nearly 20 million people, some six times the size of the United States in 1776? Could they have imagined, when they allocated two senators to represent each state, that there would come a time when one state with nearly 40 million people would have the same number of senators as one with 600,000 people?

Senators from sparsely populated states like North and South Dakota, Wyoming, Alaska, and Montana wield as much power over energy policy as senators from the largest states combined, and sometimes more. Moreover, there are sharply different views of how energy should be developed between the states, even between cities in the same states.

California, Oregon, and Washington are favorable to renewable energy development, in contrast to states like Oklahoma, Louisiana, Kentucky, West Virginia, and Pennsylvania that resist renewable energy incentives and development. These latter regard any attempt to reduce fossil fuel use as a threat to their economy, and the influence in those states by the powerful fossil fuel industry has successfully thwarted renewable energy development.

After more than forty years of trying, the country is hardly closer to having an energy policy that secures clean energy resources and improves the prospects for our national security than it was in the mid-1970s. And now with fracking, which has inadvertently established the United States as an emerging fossil fuel giant once again, the prospects for forging a renewable energy future become even more challenging.

In the mid-2000s, the prospect of climate change emerged. Climate change raised the specter of environmental alterations that a decade earlier seemed unimaginable: the retreat of the ice caps, the warming of our oceans, growing acidity in the sea, the loss of our coral reefs, loss of snow pack in the Sierra, and rising sea levels. These projections of conditions to come were mind-bending, almost beyond comprehension, like the Cold War prospect of nuclear winter.

Climate-change issues seeped into the deliberations of the Board of Directors of the CEC that I was serving on. We had led our community and region toward a more sustainable path—sometimes we led the State of California—but now, as we looked around and measured ourselves and our resources, we realized that our works were inadequate, that we needed to rethink the why and what of our vision. At the time, we were managing three recycling centers, our small green campus headquarters, and three community gardens, plus a house that had been donated to us for our executive director.

Several of us, especially our former executive director, Jon Clark, presented the case for recasting the organization to focus solely on the energy question, to apply all of our resources, human and capital, to the reasoning that if society would not embrace renewable energy, within a few more decades everything else we were doing would count for naught. Besides, most of our programs and projects were no longer cutting-edge. Recycling was well established by this point. The private sector could do what we were doing and do a better job of it because of its singular focus on making a profit. Green building had come of age. As much as we loved our wonderful Gildea Center and its spectacular setting on the hilltop overlooking the city, in the end it was just a building and a place, and besides, we were falling behind in the maintenance of the physical plant.

Community gardens had also come of age. The truth was that we were perpetuating activities that could be done, in some cases better, by others while the burning and critical question of how to wean ourselves from fossil fuels was largely ignored—too controversial for the body politic, too complex for most local organizations to delve into, and as a public issue, too big and too obtuse.

Several members of our board came up with the radical idea of selling all our assets and using the money to launch a campaign to push energy conservation and renewable energy in our region, and get back to the model that had served us so well, merging our environmental theory with practice. This generated intense and sometime vitriolic debate within our board. Some argued that it would be selling our legacy, letting down the donors who had contributed to building the infrastructure that was ours. I admit that I was troubled deeply by the prospect of selling it all off. I could feel the proverbial blood, sweat, and tears that had built the council. The idea of jettisoning all of this to launch a difficult and uncertain campaign to end dependency on fossil fuels was unnerving.

As a board, we struggled with abandoning the environmental artifacts that defined us. Perspectives differed sharply; however, there was an underlying consensus that it was time to change course.

After months of sometimes heated exchange, we made a decision that was monumental for us. We would do nothing less than recycle our very own organization, turn it inside out, sell everything and apply all our resources to combat climate change. Once we had accomplished the selling of the assets, we would embark upon the preparation of a detailed plan to show the way toward the fossil-free future that we would now single-mindedly pursue.

The selling of the assets took about a year. The sale of the recycling operations was the least painful move because everyone on the board realized that this was now a mature business and that its sale to MarBorg Industries, a local waste company with which we were on good terms, would benefit our bank account and result in our employees gaining better wages and benefits. MarBorg seamlessly took over the operations and employed most of our employees, giving them an economic bump upward and generous health and retirement benefits that were beyond our means.

We sold the beautiful Estes home with some sadness. It had been donated to us by Genevieve Estes, a local artist who designed and built the home herself and who typified the kind of person attracted to the CEC, especially in our formative years—creative, individualistic, and eccentric. Would Genevieve have been happy with the sale of her home? Probably not, but perhaps she would have appreciated the courage of our convictions, the imperative we felt to break with our past so that we could once again be the beacon into the future that we once were.

The most wrenching sale was of the Gildea Center, such a beautiful facility, so powerful a force in stimulating environmental innovation near and far in its early days. Its loss was, in some respects, heartbreaking. Literally every inch of the plateau of this property had been worked over so lovingly, time and time again, by staff and volunteers who built the road, the first garden building, the gardens themselves, and the Gildea Resource Center.

I had often referred to the Gildea Center as an institution of hope that transformed you and put you into another frame of mind. It had that special quality you sense when you're in the rarefied air of a fine university, an art gallery, or a lovely park, a place where the human imagination and nature converge and conspire.

If anyone experienced the sense of loss over the Gildea Center, it was me; I had lived and breathed the place for nearly a decade, first as an act of the imagination, and then clothing the idea of it. But as important as the center had been for me, I was fully prepared to let it go, if it would help all of us focus and commit to the urgent task of our time, making the transition away from fossil fuel.

Leaving the Gildea Center was an emotional and seminal event for many of us. I've always thought that endings are as important as beginnings, and that the vitality one experiences at the outset of a personal relationship or a new job or initiative should be sustained to some degree to the end. Given what a large role Gildea had played in the lives of the staff, the members of the organization, those who had designed it, and the interns who had lived there during the first few years, we needed to conclude our relationship in a fitting way. To this end, we invited all who had played an instrumental role in its creation to gather and bid farewell, as if we were leaving a dear friend, a cherished family member, for the last time.

The Gildea tribe gathered from far and wide, and for three days and nights we celebrated with dinners, parties, song, and dance as well as with reflective conversations over what we had accomplished together.

We closed with a solemn ceremony that began near sunset and continued until darkness enveloped the site. An accomplished singer sang the great Gayatri mantra, a Hindu hymn to the sun that I had learned many years before. As the sitar droned and the tabla beat to a kind of cosmic rhythm, we sat in the open, in chilling silence, shuddering, even weeping. As the music went quiet, the last light faded, and we just walked away.

The community gardens were placed in the hands of the City Parks and Recreation Department; the Art from Scrap program that provided reject products from manufacturing and businesses from town for sale for artistic creations, mostly those of children, was given back to Kay Sanchez, who created it before we took it under the CEC's wing; the Watershed Resource Center that we had built as Santa Barbara's first platinum green building to house programs to restore and protect Santa Barbara's creeks also went to Art from Scrap. We let go all of the programs that we had begun and nurtured over thirty-five years.

The Gildea Center was purchased by Hospice of Santa Barbara, an organization that has helped thousands of community members and their families at life's end. Today, where the Gildea Center stood there is a sixteen-bed hospice facility, one of the finest in the nation, where the spirit of the Gildea Center lives on and where many of us may well spend our final days.

FOSSIL-FREE?

The fossil fuel age has been with us now for a little more than one hundred years, or about four generations. There's hardly a soul alive who has not been touched in almost every aspect of his or her life by the power of oil. As Buckminster Fuller noted, oil enabled an ordinary family to have at its disposal the kind of horsepower that only kings and royalty could command in the past.

But as we know, there is a shadow side to all things that blaze with light and power. We have been slow to recognize in full measure this shadowy aspect to oil, but it was there all along. As a small boy more than fifty years ago, I experienced its shadow. For others, the menacing aspects of oil were far worse. Today, ask the families residing along the freeway corridor to the Ports of Long Beach and Los Angeles about how they've been harmed by oil, and they'll reveal a sad litany of statistics concerning the high incidence of air pollution–caused cancers, statistics compiled by the University of Southern California's School of Public Policy.

Ask former Secretary of State George Schultz about the shadow side of our dependence on oil, and he'll speak to the threat it means to our national security each and every day. Ask a US general what it means to the military, and he or she will reveal the strain our dependence on oil places on the entire military enterprise, about how it puts troops needlessly in harm's way around the world. Ask a prominent economist, and he or she will talk about the immense export of dollars abroad, dollars that are badly needed for investment in job-producing industries in the United States. Ask the scientists, the 97 percent who have validated human-induced climate change, not the flabby-headed noisemakers on television who spew their cretin bile that denies the human impact on the natural world and climate. Let these scientists explain what understanding they have gained when they measure the snow packs in the Sierra for water content, the ice sheets in the Arctic, the temperatures of the world's marine currents, the rising acidity in the oceans, and what this portends for the coming decades as climate change seizes the world stage and the migrations to cope with its effects begin.

WHEN CERTAINTY IS THE ENEMY

When faced with problems, there are two basic courses of action. For those so inclined, there is the action of inaction, denial, resistance to change, admonitions of fate, and statements that there are forces at work that are beyond our insight and beyond our control. Under the guise of caution, of "not knowing enough," not being "certain," the case is made to wait and see—to act only if necessary under extreme duress. Such equivocation in the face of overwhelming scientific evidence is analogous to a family, its finances going under water, wishing against all evidence to the contrary, that its members will be rescued, that a check will arrive in the mail, or an aunt will die just in time with a bequest to relieve them of the heavy burden of having to change their lives.

We only have a couple of options before us. One is to retreat and cower before the task, to conclude that it's just too big and too difficult to address. Isn't this the prevailing view at the national level? Doesn't it reflect an attitude that is characteristic of people faced with an overwhelmingly abstract yet existentially threatening situation? It's like being in a city when an enemy is still somewhat distant, but inexorably on the march toward you. You retreat inwardly and hang on to the world as you know it by pretending that other world that's about to take over isn't real. It's simply too psychologically difficult to bear what is about to happen.

The second choice, and the one that I'm most comfortable proposing—one that is a product of my experience—is to consider this immense and still-abstract problem and break it down into understandable and manageable pieces. One must understand the scale of the problem, the scale and nature of the decisions that can impact it, and the conditions and time frames required to attack it.

In terms of scale, the age of oil gave rise to the need for coal mines, electrical generating plants, refineries, rail and pipelines, and other distribution systems—most highly centralized, extremely capital-intensive, and, by most measures, very large constructs. Enterprises of this sort required government subsidies in a myriad ways: oil-depletion allowances and the construction of roads and railway lines to help build the oil infrastructure, along with supportive taxation policies and laws.

Where and how this oil-based infrastructure can be altered in a timely way is the central question of our time. Fortunately, the architecture of the oil infrastructure is no mystery, and the elements of a postoil future have long been mapped out by academics, policy makers, and technologists. Intellectually at least, we have command of the field. And we have much more than that—we have the elements of the future in various stages of development in both blue and red states and an increasingly aroused public that is coming to the recognition of what is at stake.

So the task of realignment, the task of building bridges to a renewable energy future, is actually underway, and in some cases further along than we have been led to believe. Throughout the world, in all climes and contexts, urban, rural, from the biggest nations to the smallest, the work to build an energy system no longer dependent on fossil fuel has begun, and there are many indications that the work is gaining momentum.

Unlike forty years ago when I began to experiment in finding ways out of our fossil fuel dependency, there were few technical and policy tools available for making a transition. How different the present is, equipped as we are with an array of powerful tools to build this new world.

We have an impressive toolbox of proven renewable energy technologies available at a commercial scale. We have laboratories at major universities and within numerous companies that are working to make these systems better and more economical. We have decades of home-appliance development delivering water heaters, refrigerators, dish washers, and heating and cooling systems that use much less energy than their predecessors; we have transport vehicles today that can run reliably on alternative fuels like renewable natural gas or electricity produced from the sunlight; we are designing buildings that are mimicking natural systems, buildings that are pointing the way to the creation of living environments that can photosynthesize and purify air and water in ways that we could barely dream of forty years ago. More importantly, we have countries like Sweden and Germany and states like California that are well along in building a renewable energy infrastructure that are undeniably changing the substance and face of how we meet our energy needs.

Despite the absence of federal leadership, states like California are pointing the way, doing what our paralyzed federal government will not do. California's climate-change law, passed in 2006, has withstood many challenges, the most recent of which was a campaign to overturn the laws resulting from an initiative supported by the oil industry. That campaign was decisively defeated in 2011, thus embedding the law more deeply in the state and making it absolutely clear that doing business in California requires compliance with AB 32's renewable energy and greenhouse gas emissions standards.

COMMUNITY ENERGY BLUEPRINTS

Let us look now at a more localized consideration of how a post–fossil fuel economy can be created. In 2006, in the aftermath of selling off all the assets of the Community Environmental Council in order to focus our resources on energy, we prepared a blueprint for how our region could move away from its dependence on fossil fuel over about three decades. At the outset, we knew the proposition would be exceedingly challenging on every front: financial, political, technical, and social. Our view was that it was more important to articulate a bold, overarching roadmap pointing toward a fossil fuel–free future than to present some short-term, incremental activities in the absence of a larger objective. This boldness was consistent with so many of our earlier efforts. In our view, Santa Barbara, one of the birthplaces of the environmental movement and a victim of oil pollution, was precisely the right community to foster such a plan. Once again Santa Barbara could serve as a laboratory for the development of policies and programs that could in time prove useful to a broader societal effort to achieve renewable energy self-sufficiency.

We committed about $500,000 of our hard-earned capital to undertake what at the time was perhaps the most comprehensive and ambitious study of its kind in the country. We hired a young lawyer, Tam Hunt, who had the commitment and the drive to carry out the assignment. Tam hired UC Berkeley's Dan Kammen and his graduate students along with several private consulting firms with specialized knowledge of the components of renewable energy, solar, wind, biomass and biofuels, and electrification of the transport sector, to prepare the plan.

The Blueprint,[51] as it came to be known, written by Tam and the CEC's assistant director, Sigrid Wright, took about one year to develop, organize, and publish, and in 2007 became one of the first regional energy plans of its kind. It began with an assessment of the perceived issues and problems that would justify a local government to embark on such an undertaking: "We have witnessed the effects of increased greenhouse gases for many decades. In the last century, global temperatures have risen an average of about 1.3 percent F, and twice that in the polar zones. This may not seem like a large increase, but on a global basis, this increase in incredibly fast. While scientists don't always agree on the details, they overwhelmingly agree that we are already witnessing rapid climate change due to human-related greenhouse gas emissions." We could see by the end of the twenty-first century, if not sooner, the depletion of our Sierra snowpack by between 30 percent and 70 percent, and the loss of precious water that our forty-billion-dollar agricultural industry depends upon to farm the San Joaquin Valley that in turn provides water to our cities and so many of the recreational amenities that Californians enjoy, such as lakes and rivers and the natural species that depend upon the heretofore reliable snowpacks. Health-related concerns include an increase in the number and intensity of heat waves and the scourge of much of California's drought-induced fires that threaten our landscape and our cities alike.

The Blueprint was cast in the vein of so many of our other projects—with a pragmatic and economic focus. It included a strong fiscal analysis of the fossil-free prospect. By 2020, the county could be saving about $430 million per year, equivalent to $830 per person per year, and by 2033 that number would increase to more than $1,200 per capita, or $1.5 billion per year.

Any good planning effort begins with a hard look at the facts on the ground—in this case our sources of energy, the quantities consumed, the costs of the energy, and the available alternatives. This is the all-important foundation work. But unlike working on a small and focused project like building a home or a shopping complex, a park, or even a community's general plan, where it's possible to "true" the foundation, truing our assumptions presents a more elusive challenge given the comprehensive nature and the complexity of our task: designing a thirty-year energy transition plan. There are simply too many variables, changing energy costs, and economic conditions within the country and the region that impact the availability of capital, public opinion, and technological and other forms of innovations.

But this is no reason for paralysis, nor should it lead to what has become a prevalent disease in our country, overwrought analysis that supplants clear-thinking decision making. We delude ourselves into believing that by gathering and analyzing information endlessly, we will make better decisions, or we will avoid mistakes and possible failure. Decision makers at all levels seem to be cowering behind "the need for ever more information." But in the end, our ability to comprehend, digest, and make sense of it is questionable.

I often find myself asking, when confronted with complexity, what the Founding Fathers would have done in the face of our predicament. How might Jefferson, Madison, Washington, or Adams have taken on the challenge of weaning this country from fossil fuels? Surely, they would find the motivation to do so from a national security point of view. They had taken the colonies to war against England as a matter of sovereignty and freedom. A 70 percent dependency on oil to them would have been like relying on the rest of the world to provide wood to build our ships or the paper to write our correspondence and books. They simply wouldn't have stood for it.

Then there would be the more prickly issue of how they might have approached the use of domestic resources in lieu of a dependency on imports. No one can answer this question conclusively, but here I would like to offer an opinion. Fully 40 percent of the framers of the Declaration of Independence were college graduates, an astounding figure given the small number of colleges in the colonies and how few citizens of the new republic possessed a college education. More importantly, perhaps their education was far more rigorous and rounded than today, steeped as it was in world history, mastery of the English language, Latin, and Greek, combined with strong skills in mathematics and the science of the times.

When the framers were faced with crafting a form of governance, what did they do? Did they look to religion to define the way the republic would be governed, since most of the framers were Christians? No! Did they resort to ideology as a basis for designing government? No; they did what came naturally to them. They called on their powers of reason and their practical bent and asked perhaps the smartest man among them, James Madison, to canvass the world's history for examples of governmental structures that comported with the ideals of our emerging nation and report back on his findings. Madison mined the wisdom of ancient Greece, statesmen like Solon and Pericles, for insights. He looked to the polis, which the great classical scholar H. D. F. Kitto described in his landmark book The Greeks as more a "state of mind" than a place, a state of mind where participation in the governance of a city-state, in every sense of the word, was a duty, a right, and an honor.

While much attention has been paid to the development of renewable energy systems and the accompanying need for an updated energy grid to exploit renewable energy resources for compelling reasons such as efficiency, there is a tendency to think large and to assume that solutions to our energy problem must replicate the development pattern that delivered our fossil fuel infrastructure. Why couldn't it develop differently, tapping rather than overriding regional differences? Why not resort to the development of an approach to energy generation that taps the renewable powers found in the natural world—the sun, the sea, the wind, and the land?

When I traveled about California in my role with the California Environmental Protection Agency trying to understand how best to craft regulations that could apply to recycling, composting, and renewable energy facilities, I came to appreciate the enormous regional differences that exist within California, let alone the nation. Within the state are the underpopulated and forested northern regions, rich with biomass and water. There's the Great Valley, the most fertile and productive agricultural area on earth. There are desert environments, vast and also unpopulated like the northern part of the state, replete with sunshine and ripe for solar development. There's the coastal region running north–south for nearly one thousand miles, densely populated in the southern third and dotted with small towns to the north. And within these broadly defined regions are a host of subclimates and even microclimates. The design of recycling and composting programs—and in the future, renewable energy projects tapping waste as a resource—will, by necessity, need to reflect these regional characteristics.

As far back as the 1970s, the work of Amory Lovins at the Rocky Mountain Institute and state organizations like the California Energy Commission identified the importance of making more efficient use of our energy resources as a first-priority focus. The California Energy Commission's work demonstrated how powerful a tool energy efficiency can be. In the mid-1970s, industry energy forecasters argued for rapid deployment of dozens of new nuclear reactors to meet growing energy demand in California. The California Energy Commission (CEC), created in 1976 by Governor Jerry Brown, developed an independent forecast that posited a markedly different conclusion. This forecast projected that if California adopted energy efficiency standards for new buildings and appliances, energy demand would fall on a per capita basis.

California was the first state in the nation to adopt new building and appliance standards. The cumulative impact of these standards on energy demand supported the commission's findings. California's population grew from some twenty million in 1970 to about thirty-seven million by 2009 without needing one new nuclear reactor. In the process, the state became the most efficient consumer of energy on a per capita basis in the country.

Drawing on the state's success in wringing efficiency from the built environment and recognizing that building standards can be improved upon by local fiat, the plan examined the prospects of achieving higher building performance energy efficiency. The critics of such measures argue that they raise the cost of buildings, and yes, they do. But as the statistics show, the initial investment in efficiency reaps substantial energy savings dividends over time. Like disciplining the family to save rather than spend, a virtue nearly lost in America until the recession forced savings rates to rise, savings multiply over time and result in greater long-term prosperity and that elusive but important quality called peace of mind. And, as anyone who has lived or worked in a more energy-efficient building equipped with double-glazed windows knows, they are more comfortable spaces by far than their less-efficient counterparts.

The Blueprint proceeds to detail the investments needed to achieve the desired results sector by sector, taking into account that much of Santa Barbara is already built out, and that the savings will be realized by retrofits, remodels, and some tear-downs, the natural course of the built environment in more mature communities.

TRANSPORTATION FUELS

Natural gas fueling stations like this one will soon switch to renewable natural gas.

When it comes to meeting the needs for transportation, the plan calls for a predictable array of personal choices and decisions that impact how we move about our community. We could walk more, take a bus, or ride a bike rather than always resorting to using a car. These "lifestyle choices" are the butt of jokes of critics who decry any sort of life change as a direct affront to our personal freedoms, to the very idea of America as a place of unlimited access to anything we need as long as we have the means to do so. These lifestyle choices are, like waste prevention and energy efficiency, the low-hanging fruit when it comes to change, but that doesn't mean that people adopt energy-efficient habits and measures. In the hierarchy of waste management, reducing waste through the use of less packaging, or even the substitution of nontoxic materials, has been at the top of the priority list, but the United States, unlike Europe, has been very slow to practice waste prevention.

Other strategies to significantly reduce the use of fossil fuels in Santa Barbara County will take personal investment. In a community that personal wealth has blessed, Santa Barbara County had the fourth-highest use of hybrids per household in the country. Critics will point to the relative affluence of the area, but another way of looking at communities in the coastal zone of California where hybrid ownership is high is that we are early adapters, using technologies that will spread throughout the country.

In 2001, I was among the early purchasers of the newly marketed Toyota Prius, which had been in the development stage in Japan for years prior to entering the American market. I remember that it was only a decade ago that, when I would drive about town, other drivers and passersby would look at this strange-looking new vehicle and give an occasional thumbs-up. When I parked my car in a large parking lot, I would have no trouble finding it, for it stood out like a sore thumb. Today, I'm in my third-generation Prius; the car is so commonplace that there are dozens of them in the parking lot.

Electric car lineup, Earth Day 2014.

I must admit that apart from the novelty of driving a Prius then, it felt good—as did collecting my recyclables, making my compost, and getting fruit from my home orchard—that I was contributing in some small way to a long-overdue adjustment in the way we live for the sake of nature and for our future. That little engine under the hood took me wherever I wanted to go while using about half the fuel of a standard car, generating near-zero emissions. Using a Prius then was the equivalent of taking eight conventional cars off the road.

In 2001, there were only two hybrid automobile platforms on the road: the Toyota Prius and the Honda Insight. Today, there isn't a major car manufacturer that doesn't have one or more hybrid models. In fact, hybrids are almost passé as the electric car begins to emerge, perhaps to be followed by the long-anticipated hydrogen platform.

I am by no means an expert about the engine platforms of the future, but there is clearly growing interest and investment in the electric vehicle. Some experts I know think that the hydrogen platform holds the most promise because it doesn't pose the battery-storage challenge that longer-range electrical vehicles do. We shall see.

The Blueprint stressed the importance of making a "rapid shift to vehicles that run partially or entirely on electricity, and then generating the electricity through renewable resources such as wind or solar." If Santa Barbara were to tackle the transportation sector head-on, it could cut transportation petroleum demand by 50 percent or more.

As I stated, I'm not sure what the optimal transportation engine will be: hybrid, plug-in hybrid, hydrogen, or all electric. I have close friends who are experts who claim that we are still a long way from having the batteries that will reliably support electrification of the transportation sector and that hydrogen may be the more viable option. I leave that to the experts and to the marketplace, but the focus on moving expeditiously away from fossil fuels is what we need to adhere to.

At the heart of the future of transportation is the question of the fuel. For more than one hundred years fossil fuel has been cheap and abundant. Cheap and abundant because the costs of obtaining and burning it have been grossly undervalued, and remain so. It's familiar, and like all things familiar, it gives us comfort. Like comfort food, it may not be the best for you, but it sure tastes good and you somehow feel better knowing it's there.

The plan for fuel pointed to biofuels typically derived from plants to provide the most immediate opportunities for significantly reducing petroleum demand because both the cars and the fuels already exist. Locally grown biofuels can be made from switch grass and poplar trees, both fast growing, requiring less water and fertilizer in a landscape that isn't blessed with abundant rainfall. Also cellulosic ethanol can be made from waste products like straw husks, wood chips, and municipal solid waste. As I reread the plan prepared some four years ago, it treats too lightly the potential of converting food, agricultural, and biosolids to renewable natural gas, a path to transportation energy. Municipal organic wastes, including food, leaves, and grass clippings, are now recognized as the proverbial

low-hanging fruit for making renewable fuel. The collection system is in place, the trucks are there; the only missing piece is the anaerobic digester component to tap the biogas potential found in waste. The Santa Barbara region, the community, could run all of its buses, garbage collection trucks, and street sweepers by exploiting a perennial resource: green and food waste.

Bikeway, Long Island, New York.

The plan suggests a pathway to a fossil-free future that encompasses many factors, including those that cannot be affected by local actions, but there are many that can be. The local actions that can be taken are in so many ways so prosaic, so pedestrian in a world that is motivated by "breaking news" and gadgetry that they produce flatline emotions. The acts of walking, biking, carpooling, and riding buses and trains have been pushed by environmental proponents for a good forty years, without much impact. But I'm reminded that this was the case with environmentalists pushing to "reduce, reuse, and recycle." Like modern-day Sisypheans reciting this mantra in the face of an avalanche of consumer-generated products rapidly converted to waste, over time the innate wisdom contained in this simple phrase connected with more and more people to the point where it became an irreversible force that has moved individuals, cities, and countries throughout the world to begin to move away from the throw-away mind-set.

Start with small, mundane moves—occasionally take your family downtown on a bus, or forego a trip by car around the block to the grocery store and walk there. As many of us know, these simple actions are discouraged by the antipedestrian, antibicycle, car-based monoculture. I for one rarely ride a bicycle in my part of town in Santa Barbara, and I will not encourage my child to ride because we don't have safe bike paths here. And we don't do a good job of policing the rights of pedestrians. As an avid walker, I'm startled by the lack of responsiveness by many motorists to a pedestrian in a crosswalk. I've literally been in a position to touch a car as it roars by me as I'm half way out in a marked pedestrian crossing. Not exactly confidence-builders for persons seeking other paths of mobility. But with persistence on the part of pedestrians and cyclists, there is growing evidence that transportation diversity is gaining ground across the country.

If we recognize the importance of what individuals can contribute to lowering demand on fossil fuels by life habits, but don't support the infrastructure to encourage these life habits, we are left, like the recyclers of earlier times, having to make extraordinary efforts to live our values. Only a small percentage of the residents of a community will do so. But making change convenient, like placing a bin for collecting your recyclables or an envelope to mail your old cell phone back to the manufacturer, that's a different story indeed. So, the importance of walking, of riding bicycles, of accessing other modes of transit has to reach that critical point, as it has apparently in the cities of Portland and Eugene, Oregon, and now Austin, Chicago, and New York City, where thousands of people embrace this way of living and don't consider it in the least a step backward in the quality of their lives. They are achieving quality-of-life multiples by gaining fitness and health in the process. Once embraced, they wouldn't do it any other way.

And so it is with the choice of vehicles to circulate in. If you need a car, consider a smaller one, a more fuel-efficient one. And maybe, even in the absence of a federal government that lacks the nerve to, dare I say, "incentivize" the public toward such an investment, local and state governments can find ways to provide their own incentives, rationalizing such moves in the name of local economic development, keeping precious dollars recycled within the community and improving public health.

To wean our region off fossil fuels, as the plan states, "we will need additional options beyond driving small cars, hybrid vehicles, or using the increasingly discredited biofuels such as ethanol made from food crops, while the verdict is still out on the development of biodiesel. There is the prospect of "electrifying" the transportation sector by actively transitioning to vehicles that run on electricity. This is advantageous, even if we remain with today's sources of electricity, because vehicles that use electricity are two to three times more efficient than those that run on petroleum. These include the plug-in hybrids, electric-only vehicles, and hydrogen vehicles. As we read from the sparkling advertisements from the world's car makers, the transportation sector is in the midst of a dynamic transformation, its biggest since the automobile went public.

Bold new products based on at least a partial electrification platform are being introduced and promoted. Ford, for example, has introduced a plug-in electric hybrid, a stunning machine that may be the equal of the Mercedes and BMW platforms.[52] The number and variety of vehicles demonstrates that electrification of the auto industry has now moved well beyond the introduction of Honda's zero-emission vehicle—the now legendary EVI of movie fame. Tesla Motors, though still very small and "boutique," has designs on a more mass-market SUV Tesla. Elon Musk of Tesla is engaged in multiple business ventures, including electrical battery production, that have the potential to turn the automobile market on its head if technical progress and revenues can sustain the momentum.

There are also fueling infrastructure challenges that will be difficult to overcome in towns like Santa Barbara and elsewhere. Charging stations will need to be built and made convenient; home charging systems will pose an additional expense to consumers, along with the network of pipelines and pressurized on-board equipment that will be required for the hydrogen fuel option.

Although the challenges are many and in some cases daunting, I'm heartened by the year-to-year progress that I measure when I attend each Earth Day Festival in Santa Barbara. What began a decade ago with a smattering of alternative-fueled or -powered vehicles has mushroomed into a full block long on two sides, and I expect that year after year it will grow. There's the gleaming and glorious Tesla, the marquee electrical vehicle statement, next to the understated Nissan Leaf, the car that portends a more Everyman electrical vehicle, and now the GM Spark. We are witnessing the unleashing of the technical and entrepreneurial talent of the world auto industry increasingly disassociating itself from the petroleum economy with vehicles that either are stingy on petroleum fuel use or don't need petroleum at all.

What about the government sector? What is its role in promoting a postpetroleum transportation sector? At the federal level, the industry-supported increase in the mileage standard will reap large dividends in reducing fuel consumption. Equally important are policies, such as the Renewable Fuel Standard (RFS), that provide a subsidy for renewable fuels over fossil fuels. One would think that the RFS would enjoy broad bipartisan support given that much renewable fuel will be developed in red as well as blue states, but no such luck in the polarized and paralyzed world of Washington, DC.

Businesses hate uncertainty in policies because uncertainty adds greatly to the risks associated with innovation. The Renewable Fuel Standard (RFS) will likely survive and remain an important component in driving the progress of renewable fuels. But another key policy driver, the Federal Investment Tax Credit (FITC), has been terminated. This tax credit allowed companies that made investments in renewable energy technologies (electricity) to claim a 30 percent tax credit once the project became operational. That's a 30 percent tax credit directly against the project cost. For profitable companies this was a powerful incentive, making marginally profitable corporate investments profitable enough to warrant a go-ahead. Reauthorization of this tax credit is a priority of the renewable energy industry and should be a priority for the nation.

Using California as a bellwether state, we are beginning to see just how important government can be as an instrument of change. In 2006, Governor Arnold Schwarzenegger and the California legislature came to a meeting of the minds and enacted the California Global Warming

Solutions Act (AB 32). AB 32 required the state, the world's twelfth largest emitter of carbon worldwide, to set out on a path of reducing its greenhouse emissions to 1990 levels by 2020 by essentially committing California to unwind twenty years of carbon emissions build-up.[53] AB 32 introduced several measures that are beginning to be implemented. One is a carbon trading system, the largest in the world next to the European system. California's carbon trading went into effect in 2013, with the first trade generating more than 533 million dollars[54] from major carbon emitters, such as refineries and power plants. The idea behind the trading system is that heavy carbon emitters have to purchase credits from essentially a carbon bank. It's estimated that if the system proves workable, billions of dollars will become available for investments in low or zero carbon emission technologies.

Another measure of AB 32 is what is called the Low Carbon Fuel Standard (LCFS). The LCFS requires that oil refiners in the state use renewable liquid fuels to make up 10 percent of the refined fuel sold in California by the year 2020. Challenged both politically and in the courts, the LCFS 10 percent requirement is a potentially very large boon to renewable fuel producers. It's significant to note that at least politically the LCFS withstood, only a year ago, a concerted effort by the oil industry and political operatives like the Koch Brothers, with their Texas oil commodity vested interests, to unravel AB 32 through the initiative process. They ran a full-fledged campaign to win the hearts and minds of the California electorate in 2010, only to find that in spite of all the money they spent on ads decrying the LCFS, the California electorate wouldn't buy it and trounced the initiative by a margin of 61 percent to 38 percent. At the end of June 2014, under another challenge by the oil industry, the US Supreme Court upheld the LCFS, making its prospect for a long life very strong.[55]

Other measures initiated by the California legislature to promote renewable energy include a requirement to purchase biomethane, which is biogas that has been cleaned up to natural gas standards, and to inject it in the natural gas grid for the purpose of generating renewable electricity. Additionally, the legislature has committed more than $120 million a year for projects within the state that further renewable fuels and

Architect's rendering of CR&R Anaerobic Digester under construction in Perris, Riverside County, California (2015). This facility will convert municipal organic waste to renewable natural gas and soil products.

transportation. It's possible that this legislation, in tandem with pending legislation, will be enough to jump-start one new renewable energy option for California that has significant national and international ramifications. This option involves the development of a biogas industry whereby the energy content found in municipal green and food waste (some seven million tons in California and sixty-seven million tons nationally, according to the US EPA in 2012) can be exploited and converted through anaerobic digestion (AD) into biogas. According to the Biomass Collaborative at UC Davis, there are enough organic waste materials in California to meet the estimated two billion gallons needed to satisfy the LCFS. The municipal waste sector alone could meet some 30 percent of the required annual low-carbon fuel demand. It's not difficult to imagine that within ten to fifteen years some 10 percent of California's liquid fuel needs could be met from biogas plants producing fuel. Creating this biogas industry is feasible by several means.

The most straightforward path to the development of a biogas industry is to ban organic wastes going to landfills by 2020. And in 2014, that's what the California legislature did with the passing of bills to restrict green and food waste going to landfills.[56] There is growing consensus within the state that this makes sense because commercial-scale anaerobic digestion tech-

CR&R Anaerobic Digester facility under construction, March, 2015.

nology is now available to process this material into biogas. There are several pathways to generating this material such as stand-alone biogas plants built and operated by the solid waste management sector and waste water facilities that can receive food waste as part of their wastewater operations to produce electricity from biogas.

For the past seven years I have been developing, as a private-sector executive, the option of building anaerobic digestion technology at one of our company's solid waste processing facilities. This project will receive approximately 80,000 tons per year of source-separated municipal green and food waste. Using proven, commercial-scale German technology, it will convert this waste to biogas. The biogas will then be cleaned up to fuel-grade biomethane or what we are calling renewable natural gas (RNG). Some one million diesel fuel equivalent gallons of RNG will be produced at this first plant scheduled for completion in the fall of 2015 in Riverside County, California. This is enough fuel to power, on a daily basis, an estimated seventy to eighty heavy-duty trash and recycling trucks. What this means is that RNG produced from nonfood plant-sourced feedstock reduces carbon emissions, according to the California Air Resources Board, by at least 35 percent over petroleum-derived fuels. According to the California Air Resources Board, which governs air quality in the state, RNG is six times cleaner than fossil fuel–derived natural gas, making it the cleanest transportation fuel available, bar none. The beauty of RNG is that there is a ready market for the fuel; natural gas vehicles, of which there are now thousands in California, can utilize it, and the fueling stations have already been built to deliver it.

In April of 2014, the Costa Mesa Sanitary District that contracts with CR&R to provide residential waste and recycling services for the City of Costa Mesa with a population of about 110,000, modified its long-term contract with CR&R to allow its organic waste to be converted to biogas using the CR&R AD facility. This outcome resulted from several factors. CR&R was a trusted service provider for the district, with more than a twenty-year contract history. The district also wanted to be on the front lines of providing advanced waste management technology. After many presentations to the district's board of directors and some four public hearings, the district voted to increase its service rates by $1.87 per residential customer per month to enable the district to use CR&R's AD facility. Now $1.87 per month might seem like a small sum to the average reader, but in Southern California where waste service rates are ultralow, gaining a $1.87 rate increase is no easy matter. Based on this experience and exploratory meetings with other cities that we service, the combination of regulatory and legislative pressures directed to remove organic waste from landfills coupled with a desire for the lowest-emissions heavy-duty vehicles running on city streets is likely to produce a snowball effect where one city after another will sign up for an AD component of their waste system. In this way AD development will unfold, much as it did with recycling.

Recently I estimated, based on our companies' experience with biogas development, what it might cost to develop a biogas industry that would utilize 75 percent of the organic materials found in California's waste stream. About sixty-seven biogas plants would be needed to process the approximately five million tons of organic waste available. At an average cost of $20 million per facility, the capital cost for this, by far the largest component of a biogas infrastructure, would be about $1.3 billion. Fueling stations to compress the fuel and deliver it to trucks would add about $66 million to the infrastructure cost. The approximately seven hundred million gallons of diesel equivalent RNG (probably a conservative number) that would be annually produced as a result of this investment would achieve an estimated annual greenhouse gas reduction of 1,280,500 tons of GHG along with measurable reductions in smog-making NOx and lung-damaging particulates known as PM10. Imagine a green industry of this scope made possible by an investment of about $2 per household per month.[57]

The role of local government in stimulating an RNG industry cannot be overestimated. When recycling was the domain of small nonprofits some twenty-five years ago, local governments in California took the lead in making it a standard practice in the state. Once local governments began to adopt aggressive recycling programs in cities like San Jose, San Francisco, and Los Angeles, recycling snowballed to the point that within a decade it became common currency. Based on my past experience in participating and facilitating changes in the waste management system, I am convinced that an RNG-based municipal waste management system will be led by early adapters at the local government level. Once the first projects are built and operating, proving the efficacy of this recycling approach, others will follow. The rate of adoption, of course, will be greatly accelerated now that California has implemented a phasing-out of organics going to landfills.

In terms of the impact that local governments can have on other forms of renewable energy development, particularly solar, there are many contributions to be made. These include making solar photovoltaic development design and building approvals simpler and quicker, permitting fueling stations, and providing incentives for companies willing to build them; providing parking incentives for ultralow- and zero-emission vehicles and informing the public about them; and as always, leading by example by employing these vehicles in the public fleets to the extent that it is financially feasible.

WIND

Wind is ubiquitous worldwide, but it isn't economical to develop wind systems everywhere. Financially, viable wind farms require an abundance of wind consistency more than velocity. In Santa Barbara County's case, offshore wind is pegged for development to produce about 20 percent of the energy required for a fossil-free future. The lion's share of the wind energy that would be tapped is far offshore, beyond the Channel Islands some twenty-six miles distant from the mainland where the wind energy potential is abundant.

The Blueprint identifies wind energy as the most economical source of the renewable energy options stating that it is competitive with and sometimes less costly than fossil fuel–based electricity. With the discoveries of natural gas reservoirs now being tapped through fracking, the cost competitiveness of wind energy is less attractive, but fracking is in its early stages of development and has been allowed to proceed with scant regulation made possible by the so-called Halliburton Amendment to the Federal Energy Policy Act of 2005. This policy exempts fracking from compliance with provisions of the Safe Drinking Water Act, Clean Water Act, and CERCLA, the Comprehensive Environmental Response, Compensation, and Liability Act of 1980, the so-called Superfund law that was passed by the Congress following several toxic waste disasters.

We will find out in the coming few years if it will actually be the low-cost option that it is now, or if contamination from wells results in greater opposition to it, including bans, or much tighter regulation that will translate into higher costs for developing fracking resources. Ironically, recent discoveries of natural gas and oil potentially recoverable through fracking have made the County of Santa Barbara one of the potential epicenters for fracking exploitation in the country.

Santa Barbara County is blessed with enormous wind energy potential on land of some 3,800 GWh, according to Professor Daniel Kaman of UC Berkley, who was a lead consultant for the Blueprint's wind power section. But this pales in comparison to the offshore wind potential that he estimates at 290,000 GWh, theoretically enough to meet our current demand for electricity by a factor of 100.

To access this energy onshore, large wind farms would need to be built. The first of these was identified in the Blueprint—a farm proposed by Acciona, a Spanish wind energy company that would have produced 120 megawatts, enough power to meet 10 percent of Santa Barbara's demand for electricity.

In order to exploit the offshore wind potential that resides far out in the Santa Barbara Channel, floating wind machines would have to be built and then connected to the energy grid by an underwater cable—no small technological and economic challenge! Building three-hundred-foot-plus tall wind turbines can certainly be done. We've built massive structures offshore to exploit oil resources for nearly fifty years now, and the technology to exploit oil in ever more difficult environments is evolving still.

As for the proposed land-based wind farm, it wa located in a remote, mountainous area near the coastline, the development called for the construction of sixty-five wind turbines, each a height of some 370 feet, or about thirty-seven stories. The highest reaches of the towers would be seen slightly from an ocean-front state park and from several home sites in a sparsely populated area. The huge sweep of the turbines (the diameter of a football field) would generate some noise and cause a relatively low number of bird kills per year, according to the environmental assessment for the facility.

It took more than three years for the project to be approved, followed by a lawsuit by one of the neighbors of the project citing adverse environmental impacts. The suit was dismissed in 2009, and the project was expected to be built and operating by 2012. But it never happened. The conditions of approval that called for closing down the turbines if there were excessive bird kills proved problematic to securing project financing along with concerns over the future of the Investment Tax Credit. The drawn-out permitting process ran the clock out on the project developer. The window of opportunity the project had in terms of favorable utility rates, a competitive construction environment, and secured project financing was lost. Time, a factor ever so important for any project, let alone a more economically fragile renewable one, took its toll to the point where the wind farm was abandoned by the developer.

Although in the end the project didn't materialize, the CEC took the environmentally responsible position of supporting it through the planning process, once it had been vetted by the staff and the CEC board of directors. Working with other environmental organizations, the project gained the support of the Santa Barbara Audubon Society, the Santa Barbara Environmental Defense Center, and other organizations known more for project opposition than support. The CEC's position of support was consistent with its historical commitment to stand behind a project in keeping with its values and necessary to accomplish a desired end. This position reflected a core philosophy that sustainability isn't brought about by blueprints, polemics, and advocacy. All three are necessary, but ultimately sustainability necessitates on-the-ground tangible projects. The wind farm was to be part of a bricks-and-mortar renewable infrastructure, one of a number of projects that collectively would comprise a post–petroleum energy generating system.

SUN

·Lancaster, California: Solar City USA?

The Blueprint suggests that solar power could meet nearly 16 percent of Santa Barbara's future energy demand. Solar photovoltaics, passive solar design, and solar hot water heating are mature technologies with decades of experience behind them. In addition to the possibility of ubiquitous solar-cell applications in the residential and commercial sectors, the Blueprint identified "concentrated solar power," a younger technology with only a few applications in California and around the world and none, as yet, in our region. These technologies use mirrors or lenses to focus sunlight on either a central point or a tube filled with oil that turns water into steam, which drives a generator to produce electricity. Of all the solar power options that the CEC analyzed with the help of its consulting teams, concentrated solar power seemed to be the one that could probably provide the most power reliably and at the lowest cost over the long term, with a cautionary note that I will discuss shortly.

The most significant barrier for some solar technologies, as it has been for decades now, is cost, although cost can vary widely between technologies and even between different installations of the same technology. On the whole, passive solar design (suitable for new construction, mostly) and solar water heating are, relatively speaking, inexpensive options within the economic reach of many. By contrast, photovoltaic and concentrating solar power systems remain relatively expensive, though costs for these systems continue to come down, and as they do they will become more prevalent. Indeed, today, instead of being a visual rarity, one sees photovoltaic systems on rooftops across America—in new subdivisions, on many government buildings, and increasingly on commercial buildings as well.

Several large dish systems are now built and others planned for very large concentrated solar projects in California, sized at 850 and 900 megawatts—enough to provide electricity to more than one million homes when they come on line. These projects concentrate the power of the sun through calibrated mirrors that track the sun's course through the day and focus the energy to run turbines that generate electricity. Recently I've become aware of alleged large numbers of birds that are incinerated as they pass through the concentrating field of these systems. Unintended consequences are a reality in renewable energy projects, and they must be carefully considered and avoided, if possible.

Topaz Solar Farm, at 550 megawatts (enough power for 160,000 homes), is one of the world's largest proposed facilities for a site of some 9.5 square miles in San Luis Obispo County that abuts Santa Barbara County. In 2012, the project received approval and as of this writing is under construction. Santa Barbara does not have the availability of sites like the one on the Carrizo Plain, illustrating the regional idiosyncrasies that characterize renewable energy development. A smaller industrial-scale array (40 MW) was approved by the courts in October 2014.

For solar to become more mainstream, once again like recycling, access to the technologies must be made easier and more affordable. Various tax credits have been in place for years, but these haven't proven sufficient to spawn a large market. Santa Barbara and other communities are looking into various investments that include financing solar through a locally generated revolving loan program tied to one's property taxes. Instead of trying to finance a system through a combination of steep cash outlays, which are very difficult to justify and afford, given the challenges facing most people in meeting the necessities of life, one could receive a loan that is repaid through the property tax bill. The loan amount and interest are added to one's property tax and paid semiannually. This would mean that for no entry cost, home improvements—whether solar, energy efficiency, or other approaches—can be financed, which would enable more people to participate. Importantly, this type of program is predicated upon a property owner first making the important smaller investments in upgrading energy efficiency such as lighting, eliminating cracks and fissures that let warm and cool air seasonally impact energy use, and other relatively low-cost measures. Only when these investments have been made could one qualify for such loans. I have learned recently that this option has run into approval problems with the Federal Mortgage Agency, so its future is in doubt.

The private sector for the past several years has offered homeowners and landlords alike the option of financing solar with no capital required. They assume ownership of the solar system and are made whole by claiming the homeowner's monthly utility. Only those home or property owners who have large enough monthly bills are eligible for this program.

Another option for accelerating the pace of renewable energy development is called Community Based Aggregation (CBA). This option harnesses and enables municipalities to contract for renewable energy with private renewable energy providers, thus creating investment-grade renewable energy projects secured by the purchasing power of local governments. Publically financed utilities, based on a centralized energy production and delivery model, have understandably resisted the CBA option because it fractures their business model. But the centralized model is more than one hundred years old now and reflects a time when the production and delivery of energy required large-scale power plants and single-source energy grids. The desirability of maintaining this centralized model in our time that is atomizing so many of life's essentials, like information, telecommunications, and retailing, is open to question.

With solar cells and greatly improved energy management systems, not to mention the vulnerability of centralized systems to security issues and climate change, it seems fitting that local governments might find sourcing their energy more locally an option whose time has come.

Marin County near San Francisco has adopted CBA, and other local governments, including Santa Barbara, are being pressed to do so. Time will tell if this option takes hold. If it does, we're in for a bold new renewable energy future.

In the meantime, progress in solarizing Santa Barbara and most other communities, though steady, remains slow. It will take political will and leadership to accelerate progress. Temporarily, at least, Santa Barbara will have to look to exemplar communities like Lancaster, California, for political and economic inspiration. Lancaster, a sprawling desert city of some 157,000 located about fifty miles north of Los Angeles, bedrock conservative and anti–big government, is emerging as perhaps the nation's leader in solar development. Its mayor, R. Rex Parris, has publically stated that Lancaster could become one of the first cities, if not the first city, to be powered exclusively by the sun. Hard-hit by the 2008 deep recession, the community has struggled to right itself and find a way forward as it shed once-prosperous jobs related to the defense industry and NASA. The mayor's website includes the following statements, which could have been made by the most radical of environmentalists—chiding as they do cities like Berkeley and San Francisco for not having the political courage to do what he and his city are doing to develop solar energy.

"Mayor Parris has led the City with forward thinking unique partnerships with leaders all over the world…The City of Lancaster worked very closely with eSolar to bring its 5 MW Sierra Sun Tower solar project to completion in just fourteen months. In August of 2009, eSolar proudly held the grand opening of the nation's only operating solar thermal power tower plant in the United States. The solar journey continued when all of the city's municipal buildings were converted to solar power. This jump-started the Solar Lancaster Program…to provide an affordable solar financing program for home and business owners and nonprofit organizations."[58]

Its business leaders have recognized that with their abundant high-desert-sunshine days they have the ability to solarize more economically than many other local governments. Its political leaders have embraced solar by mandating that every new building must generate solar electricity. This is a policy commitment one would never have expected from conservative elected officials, based as it is on pragmatic self-interest. Lancaster could tap its most abundant resource, the sun, and by so doing help itself to dig out of an economic quagmire with the prospect of creating new jobs and recycling more money in its cash-strapped economy. Who could have thought that the most far-reaching renewable energy decision would be made by the conservative city of Lancaster?

SEA

Much of Santa Barbara County abuts the Pacific Ocean, and for decades scientists and entrepreneurs have looked to the various forms of energy within it to exploit for power.

The Blueprint suggests that ocean power could contribute about 8 percent of the region's power needs. But tapping ocean power by exploiting wave or tidal energy is very experimental at this stage. The most likely source of ocean energy in our area is wave power, as we don't have the strong tides, ocean currents, and thermal gradients found in other parts of the country or the world. A study referenced in the Blueprint found that there is theoretically enough wave power potential for about six hundred thousand homes in Santa Barbara and neighboring San Luis Obispo Counties. The first such facilities to use wave and tidal energy were installed in 2000 and 2006 in Scotland and Portugal, respectively. These are of a commercial scale. Most other proposed projects are of a pilot scale to determine if commercialization is viable.

As one might imagine, the development of projects of this ilk on the California coastline would face severe constraints related to visual impacts; interactions with marine life; conflicts with other uses of sea space, such as boating, fishing, and diving; and permitting from a phalanx of more than ten regulatory agencies with a say in ocean or shoreline developments. Nevertheless, the CEC has begun to work with local agencies and prospective project developers should this option take on more significance in the coming years.

POST-PETROLEUM ECONOMICS

What will it cost, and is it affordable? These are the questions that are central to individuals, businesses, institutions, and government at all levels when considering our energy future. Cost and affordability are not one-dimensional calculations. They must be understood in their broader context: Cost compared to what? Affordability compared to what? This is the heart of the matter. The price we are currently paying for our fuel at the pump and for the goods and services we receive doesn't comport with their real costs, or in cradle-to-cradle terms, their effectiveness quotient. Environmentalists have argued this point unsuccessfully for the most part for forty years. They have made the case for consideration of what it costs to park the 7th Fleet in the Persian Gulf to protect the flow of oil. They have made the case that fighting the wars in Iraq and Afghanistan have been excluded from the cost of oil, as those costs have been borne by the US taxpayer. They have contended that the direct and indirect environmental costs of oil production and consumption are not fully reflected in the price at the pump.

Even when you exclude these other costs and boil them down to strict and narrow traditional economics, the Santa Barbara County Blueprint suggested that the county would be in better financial shape by adopting renewable energy technologies than continuing to burn fossil fuel. How can this be so?

Working with Professor Dan Kammen and his team at UC Berkeley and Professor Peter Schwartz of the California Polytechnical University at San Luis Obispo, a scenario was developed whereby Santa Barbara County produced the equivalent of 100 percent of the energy it uses. Their analysis showed that if this was accomplished, county residents on a per capita basis would save about $830 per year by 2020 and $3,015 each year by 2030. This amounts to $418 million in savings by 2020 and $1.52 billion by 2030, factored in 2007 constant dollars. This is due to the fact that energy efficiency in the electricity, natural gas, and petroleum sectors saves consumers money and to the fact that fossil fuel prices are projected to continue to rise, whereas renewable energy sources are projected to continue to fall, or at least rise more slowly than fossil fuel prices due to factors such as economies of scale as their development increases. Since the Blueprint was completed in 2007, the numbers and assumptions must be recalibrated in the context of rapidly developing domestic oil shale and natural gas resources—the result of the fracking phenomenon. We are very much in the early stages of development, where a wide range of regulatory standards are in play from state to state that will impact the costs of these new fossil-based energy resources.

To further evaluate the economic dimensions of the Blueprint, the CEC commissioned a study from the University of California, Santa Barbara's Economic Forecast Project, drawing on the local university's expertise to evaluate the cost of implementing the Blueprint. The university economists confirmed the savings previously mentioned, based upon the "business as usual" scenario in which current price trends are projected to continue. In the low-cost scenario, net annual savings are $389 per year by 2020 and $1,487 per year in 2030. So even if fossil fuel prices don't rise as they have been, say in the case where at present natural gas prices have fallen significantly due to relatively low demand accompanied by abundant supplies, there remain very real benefits. And remember, these benefits are based upon "efficiency" rather than "effectiveness" economics.

Should oil shock pricing come our way as a result of scarcity pressures created by growing demands from the likes of India and China, Brazil and Turkey, or should the environmental or development costs of fracking rise from increased regulatory requirements, it's conceivable that the energy savings could be as great as $6,112 per year by 2020 and over $30,000 per year by 2030. That, of course, would render energy essentially unaffordable for most and would usher in radical changes that are almost too horrific to contemplate. I am loath to make such predictions. Having tried to do this with recyclable commodities, I learned that forecasting is a necessary but treacherous business. Core values and considerations such as national security should trump energy cost prognostications.

The core of the Blueprint analysis was predicated on business as usual, not on externalities like climate change or the prospect of regulatory measures such as carbon trading and carbon taxes, because projecting such costs is such a speculative exercise, given our dysfunctional American politics, that it would greatly lessen the Blueprint's significance as a guidepost for current and future actions. These factors are, nonetheless, gaining credence in certain parts of the country and most definitely in California. Should carbon trading and California's low-carbon fuel standards prove durable and effective, the economic feasibility of the renewable path developed in such local government renewable energy framework will be stimulated.

Let's look further at some of the findings in the Blueprint that bear upon its practicality. To begin with, it's important to look to on-the-ground evidence of implementing different Blueprint measures. One need only consider California's experience in fostering building energy efficiency standards to gain perspective on the building efficiency recommendations. As a result of these standards established in 1976 by young and far-sighted Governor Jerry Brown, in a state that has nearly tripled its population and increased its physical plant enormously over these near forty years, electricity consumption is basically the same as it was in the early 1970s—at only 40 percent of the per capita energy consumption of the rest of the country. Much-debated public policy drove these measures—the efforts of the California Energy Commission and the Public Utilities Commission.

In 2004, the costs of electrical energy efficiency measures implemented in the residential, nonresidential, and new-construction sectors averaged 1.4 cents per kWh, about one-sixth of the wholesale cost of new electrical generation, while California's economy grew robustly.

Similarly, the cost of increased energy efficiency measures in the transportation sector have been very cost-competitive. Fuel economy standards that increased from 13.1 miles per gallon in 1975 to 20.6 miles per gallon in 2000 saved consumers ninety-two billion dollars, according to the Union of Concerned Scientists, when gasoline was selling on average at $1.54 per gallon.

If today's prices were factored, the annual savings would balloon to around $300 billion per year, assuming a price of $3.00 a gallon. I don't know what it cost the auto industry by way of expenditures to achieve the higher fuel standard, but that investment has long since been made and the costs have long since reaped huge savings for consumers—and that's at an average of 20.6 miles per gallon, a pitifully low fuel efficiency given today's hybrid, diesel, and conventional engine and chassis technologies and despite the new fuel standards negotiated with the major automobile manufacturers in 2011.

As we look forward to the price of energy, a report by the California Energy Commission helps frame our options in terms of cost/benefit. Future renewable energy options are varied; each has its own capital investment requirements that reflect current technology pricing, economies of project scale, and other factors.

Real-world experience with wind power finds it to be competitive with fossil fuels throughout the United States, although with the current natural gas glut, a price gap has emerged. Moreover, wholesale costs are not the best measure of factoring future costs. A better measure is to compare the electricity cost of building a new wind farm to that of a new natural gas or coal-fired electrical generating plant. Using new plant cost data in building, a California standard combined cycle natural gas plant is slightly greater in cost than the cost of a wind farm. Essentially, they are on par with each other. And once again, it's important to note that the costs associated with natural gas and other fossil fuels exclude the effectiveness criteria put forth in the emerging cradle-to-cradle economic development framework that include environmental costs to life on the planet.

Trying to forecast what energy pricing will be a few years out, let alone decades, is a wilderness best left for speculators to hang their fate on. Although pricing is relevant to decision making, we are rapidly approaching a fork in the road in our country where we must choose a path to the future. When Sweden chose a future less dependent on fossil fuel, they decided it was more important to stimulate renewable energy than to remain dependent on gas and oil from Russia and other parts of the world. Such choices are not all that foreign to our national experience. When our waters became so foul and polluted, we decided to build wastewater treatment plants, and in so doing we vastly improved our public health. It cost a lot more money to build wastewater treatment plants than pipe sewage directly into our rivers and the oceans, but we came to a fork in the road where we chose not to do that anymore. We chose so at similar forks in the road with respect to emission controls on our vehicles, energy standards for our appliances, and recycling solid waste.

In the provocative book *Cradle to Cradle*, architect William McDonough and chemist Michael Braungart argue for a design framework based on effectiveness rather than the current one of efficiency.[59] This is a revolutionary idea, one that marks a fundamental break with the design paradigm that characterized the twentieth century, which the authors note is one based on brute force using massive quantities of fossil fuels, goods, and services that reflected little if any regard for their impact on public health and the environment. That twentieth-century paradigm, which had its roots in the latter nineteenth century, served to lift much of mankind out of its predominately subsistence- and rural-based life, bringing about a revolution in the means of mobility and creating a standard of living that had never before been realized on earth. But as we now know, all those benefits were not won without a price.

Building a renewable energy infrastructure involves more decisions than just building new plants. There has been much discussion about the need to modernize our energy grid that delivers energy from where it is generated to where it is consumed. Although an important factor, the Blueprint's analysis showed that adjusting our energy infrastructure to accommodate a higher use of intermittent energy generated from wind, solar, and tidal and/or wave sources is relatively small, no more than 0.5 cents per kWh or less than 10 percent of the total cost of electricity to consumers. The fundamental challenge and barrier facing renewable energy is rolling them out at a sufficient scale to warrant changes in the electrical grid system to distribute the energy.

Concerning our transportation future, the clear economic winners will be the producers of more fuel-stingy vehicles. The fact that there is a rapidly growing segment of the car market in the more affordable range bodes well for substantial cuts in fuel use and fuel cost controls in the uncertain future world of petroleum supplies. The University of California, Santa Barbara Economic Forecast Project found that gasoline costs would likely rise from a $3.35 per gallon mid-2007 rate to $6 per gallon by 2020 and double that by 2030, not factoring inflation. If such projections prove remotely true, the marketplace will be transformed on its own with little need for government intervention—affecting every aspect of the transportation infrastructure in communities throughout the country. Market forces will spin out alternative vehicles only a few years from now that will be very different from the vehicles we are driving today. Small two- and three-wheeled vehicles operating on battery power will emerge in our cities. Indeed this is happening even with a $3.00-a-gallon fuel cost. These changes in the nature of vehicles themselves are developing hand-in-hand with remarkable sociodemographic changes. Young professionals who will increasingly make up the work force are demanding new live/work arrangements, and consumer and consumption patterns are taking hold that are far less energy-intensive than those that have prevailed for the past fifty years. Ownership and use of the private automobile could well fall as a result of these demographic changes, moving society more in line with energy effectiveness rather than energy consumption. Thus it's not technological changes alone that are impacting fossil fuel use; it's a demographic change reflecting a profound shift in personal needs and values.

But what about the all-important job-creation dimension? The metrics between status-quo fossil fuel reliance and energy efficiency and renewable energy are stark for us to consider. According to Worldwatch Institute, the natural gas sector requires 0.01 to 1.2 person hours per kilowatt hour produced; biomass requires 0.1 to 0.5 person hours; wind, 0.01 to 1.2 person hours; and solar, 0.8 to 2.1 person hours. The meaning of these statistics is that renewable energy is more labor intensive—an upward triangle modest contributor of job growth.

Translating these general statistics to a local community like Santa Barbara means that on a very conservative basis, about five hundred jobs would be created in our county (really not that many), the equivalent of adding one major new employer capable of paying middle-class wages and benefits. On a nationwide basis, this figure would extrapolate to about 150,000 new jobs—again, not that many. These job numbers are small compared to what renewable energy supporters bandy about. By far the most significant and sustainable economic benefits come from the cycling of dollars that we will no longer pay for energy—or fracking or other fossil fuel development—domestically, and the ripple effect of renewable expenditures on local economies throughout the country.

A POSTOIL PATTERN LANGUAGE

Having set forth the blueprint for a fossil-free future, what is the prospect that such a future could unfold within a generation? Can a community or a region realistically restructure its transportation infrastructure and its residential, commercial, and industrial-built environment to produce renewable energy systems that are both reliable and affordable without massive government intervention and subsidies? Cynics will sneer that such a prospective enterprise is poppycock—too far-reaching, too expensive, too structurally difficult to achieve. But I argue that such a transformation is more probable than not, not likely in twenty-five years but perhaps within fifty years.

Let me preface my following remarks with this observation: Robert Garcia, Mayor of Long Beach, California, reporting at the January 2013 Conference of Mayors in Washington, DC, said that the three hundred mayors in attendance put climate change on the top of their civic agendas. The mayors understand that local government will be the generators of programs to alter how we address greenhouse and other pollutants, and that they are resolved to act in the absence of federal leadership.[60]

There is a rapidly developing nexus of technologies and values that are changing the energy equation. As noted earlier, we have a literal outpouring of technologies and devices that are game-changers when it comes to energy use. Within another decade, the numbers of these vehicles will be dominant as the older, less fuel-efficient cars are cycled down or replaced altogether. A similar transformation can be expected in the heavy-duty vehicle sector, especially in states like California that are focused on reducing diesel emissions. I believe that people will be dazzled by the outpouring of creativity and ingenuity that the personal transportation sector will experience. As long as the vehicles are high quality and appealing to aesthetic tastes, they will be embraced by a public that doesn't want to be vulnerable to fuel shock and wants a more conservative approach to projecting their household budgets. An investment in these technologies will give people greater fiscal predictability in a time of resource pricing uncertainty. If electrification takes off for the in-town or shorter-range vehicles, then our utility companies, working with the auto producers and the building trades, can quickly respond to a very powerful business opportunity. And the political leaders in our communities can facilitate the required physical facilities through the permit-approval process, hopefully easing the current burdens that property owners and businesses face when it comes to adopting innovations.

The ability to transform the built environment—the single family and multifamily homes, businesses, and industry—is a more diffuse challenge but one that can be facilitated by the adoption of the aforementioned loan programs tied to the property tax bill. Improvements ranging from a few hundred to tens of thousands of dollars can be financed this way, with paybacks to the users in a few years, well within the typical loan-repayment framework, or by innovative private-sector offerings such as those in place for selling solar photovoltaic systems.

In the case of the normal turnovers of properties, the loans would carry forth with the buyers without requiring a new and potentially expensive home equity loan. Other financing mechanisms will likely arise as more and more consumers realize the cost-effectiveness of making efficiency investments. They will increasingly understand that such investments are the best means of stabilizing the fixed costs in one's life related to providing modern life's essentials—lighting, heating, cooling, and connectivity with communication systems. As with the transportation sector, a few more decades will see massive turnover in the built environment, and with each turnover, new products and features will be incorporated in the modernization of buildings (even very old ones) that, once made, are essentially permanent.

As for the development of large renewable energy projects, the picture is clouded by the lack of a predictable policy framework, and uncertainty over incentives, as well as vexing permitting problems. The story of the proposed 90 megawatt wind farm in Santa Barbara County exemplifies the hazards of project development. As one rancher who would have been the beneficiary of a lifetime of revenues from the facility put it, "You can't make it as a cattle rancher and leave anything for your family, but with a few windmills on my property, I have the annuity that I need." How is this any different from the way we developed our fossil fuel resources? Derricks, iron horses, and refineries were taken for granted in the run up to the fossil fuel century; instead of these we will have better-placed facilities with far fewer environmental impacts.

As the previous generation drew considerable wealth from holes in the ground tied to vast pipe networks; as whole industries were born to provide the pipes, the motors, the pipefitters, and the electricians, so will be the case with the building of larger renewable energy projects, stretching, using the Santa Barbara example, from the outer Santa Barbara Channel, where the most efficient capture of wind energy can occur, to the higher remote plains north of Santa Barbara, where solar energy is most abundant.

Where will the financing for all of this come from? It will be propelled, at least in California, by the policies set in Sacramento requiring a robust development of in-state renewable energy development, an emissions-reduction policy, and a low-carbon fuel standard. These policies create the investment framework for developing large facilities such as the wind farms, the centralized solar energy projects, and biogas development. Capital is and will continue to flow to such projects from within California's powerful capital markets and from abroad, from Europe, and from Asia.

Also, in California at least, we have massive investments underway by the publically regulated utility giants, especially Southern California Edison. Edison alone has budgeted nineteen billion dollars over the next five years to develop new energy grids. According to Hal Conklin, a former executive with Southern California Edison, this is a larger investment in energy conservation and renewable energy than that of the entire federal budget. More importantly, it's already paid for because these investment numbers are built into the current energy rate structure. Within a few years, 450 megawatts of wind-generated energy may be generated from the Tehachapi Mountains north of Los Angeles and the 377 MW Ivanpah Solar Electric Generating System about fifty miles northeast of Needles, California, in the Mojave Desert and distributed using newly constructed transmission lines.[61] The entire Southern California grid system is being rejuvenated and updated so that it is able to transmit energy from the new renewable energy generating plants that are more diverse and decentralized than the fossil fuel–powered generating plants.

Additionally, several billion dollars have been invested by Edison in smart meters, most of which are now deployed in most homes in Southern California, providing real-time energy metering that residents can program to predict what their energy costs will be for the month and year. In theory, these smart meters are appealing, but to some, giving the kind of information that they can generate to a utility smacks of Big Brotherism and possible privacy concerns. Be that as it may, to an increasing degree, "smart metering" will allow for the ongoing regulation of appliances such as dishwashers, washing machines, and furnaces to be run to coincide with off-peak energy pricing—highest during the work day and lowest in the early morning and evening hours. Smart metering may prevent the need for the construction of many more "peaker energy plants" like the ones that were built quickly following California's Enron-induced brown-outs and exorbitant energy prices in the late 1990s. The reasoning goes that with the new smart-metering, energy consumption will be tempered during these times, thus eliminating costly capital investments in these plants. Along with the smart metering and the upgrades of the energy infrastructure, the California public will soon be able to plug in the new electric vehicles at home—making possible what many of us only dreamed of a few years back.

RENEWABLE TECHNOLOGY DIFFUSION

We have a tendency to focus on the big infrastructural changes that will mark a transition from our fossil fuel dependency to a fossil-free age. But a singular focus on big infrastructural change misses a myriad of actions, large and small, that in total will contribute significantly to the transition. These are diffusion factors, and they include recycling, gardening, localized farming, the development of walkways and bikeways, and product stewardship, all very popular and important markers of a shift in the values and lifestyles of modern living. The builder of my home, one of the larger custom builders in Santa Barbara, notes a trend in that market toward smaller, green structures. Custom home sizes that had steadily grown in square footage since the mid-1960s are smaller today, no doubt driven in part by the economic hardships following the financial meltdown. The twenty-five-hundred-square-foot custom home of prerecession America is decreasing in size by hundreds of square feet, an indicator of a larger restructuring underway. But it's too early to tell if this is a long-term trend or, should the economy gain full steam again, if housing sizes will creep up once more.

In California, recycling rates have now climbed into the 70 percent range in several cities like San Francisco, San Jose, and Los Angeles. These rates exceed those prescribed by state law and underscore the role local governments can play, should they choose to do so. The rising recycling rates are having a ripple effect—creating peer pressure, if you will, for other cities to stretch themselves. By the time the state gets around to officially raising the recycling rates, many local governments will have done so already. Why? Because changing values become political and policy drivers at the local level. People don't want to have their waste delivered to a land-fill. They want to see the resources that they discard tapped to become useful products once again. This move to increase recycling has driven, and continues to drive, changes to the waste infrastructure in profound ways. The city of Edmonton in Canada is pursuing a zero-waste agenda where landfill costs are relatively cheap. Why? Because that is what the community wants to do with its resources.[62]

Landfills are trying to exploit the energy within their giant mounds to produce fuel for transportation. They will inject the fuel into the natural gas pipeline if our public investor utilities make that feasible. (They haven't so far.) Attempts to bypass the landfill gas to pipeline option have thus far proven economically infeasible, at least in California, where project development costs tend to be greater than in many parts of the country.

By 2020, we will see organic wastes essentially banned from landfills, as is the case in Europe. For the run up to 2020, there will be a proliferation of projects throughout California that will tap the unrecoverable portion of the municipal waste stream and convert the waste to electricity or fuel. In California, perhaps first, and in communities throughout the country later, we will see anaerobic digesters proliferate to produce renewable natural gas and electricity from food waste from residences, restaurants, and institutions. Such facilities will be built for food waste processing.

One sterling example of this is found in Oxnard, California. Gills Onion is the largest onion processor in the United States. They produce fresh-cut and canned onions for the domestic market. Their facility was facing increased regulatory pressure to not apply waste products from their process--onion discards and water--on the land. Today the facility uses an anaerobic digester to convert the onion wastes to electricity through fuel cells.

The energy provides about 30 percent of the energy to run the onion-processing plant. This elegant project was made possible by alternative technology subsidies found in California. The technology is largely homegrown, built by a local building contractor using components, including the fuel cells, built in California. A revolutionary battery-storage system has been installed at this plant that enables the facility to store electricity during off-hours so that it can be tapped during peak hours, and as a result reduce the cost of the electricity that the plant has to buy from the utility.

On a national level, product manufacturing, packaging, and the associated transportation account for 40 percent of all greenhouse gas emissions, a startlingly high number and one that is underappreciated in public policy directed toward reducing greenhouse gas emissions. The high number becomes understandable when you consider the life cycle of a Coca-Cola can. The story begins with the mining of bauxite in Australia. The bauxite is refined in Norway, where energy prices are low because of abundant hydropower. Rolls of aluminum leave the factory and are shipped many thousands of miles to an aluminum-can fabrication factory, where cheap hydropower makes aluminum-making viable. The raw aluminum cans are then shipped many more thousands of miles, where they are painted and become the aluminum can we all recognize. The finished cans then travel to the bottling plants, and from the bottling plants the product is shipped once again to supermarkets and convenience stores, where it is purchased by the consumer. This story is replicated in product development, whether we are talking about computers, cell phones, apparel, or foods of all sorts. The carbon footprint of the product chain is massive. We are in the early stages of appreciating the impact of this product chain and determining if there are ways to affect its large contribution to the warming of the planet.

Extended Producer Responsibility (EPR) is a mechanism that may lead to significant reductions in the GHG emissions from this product chain. EPR is a well-developed system in Europe that places the responsibility on the manufacturers of products, from packaging to cell phones to batteries, to establish collection and recycling programs to "take back" these products and keep them out of the municipal waste stream. The system started in Germany with the then revolutionary Green Dot program aimed to encourage the reduction of packaging while mandating strong recycling quotas by material. Given the prodigious economic influence of Germany, the Green Dot system was essentially adopted by the EU through the Organization of Economic Directives (OECD) and has become a European-wide effort.

In the United States, local governments are responsible for collecting, recycling, and/or disposing of these products. There is virtually no leadership at the national level to implement such a program here. In the absence of federal leadership, states—and even more importantly, local governments—have been developing their own forms of EPR. More than one hundred cities in California have passed bans on single-use plastic bags since 2007. [63] The removal of these one-use plastic bags made of petroleum that litter the landscape will reduce fossil fuel use, albeit almost insignificantly, given the amount of petroleum produced. Even so, with this locally induced ban, people across the country have demonstrated a willingness to adapt and use either the paper bags or reusable bags instead. Adoption of EPR measures like this will increase our ability to recycle materials and reduce the amount of waste going to often-remote landfill sites requiring energy-intensive transportation.

BIO-BASED PACKAGING

Bio-based packaging and the beginnings of so-called green chemistry to provide goods that have historically been manufactured from petroleum are starting to show up more and more in the marketplace. We're still very early on in the development of such products; there have been many false starts and failures, but in time, as the products improve and the demand for fully recyclable packaging increases, the use of petroleum as the building block for so many packaging materials will decrease. As noted, much of the impetus for these measures is coming not from the federal or state government, but from local governments, and in many cases from the private sector, from the gigantic chains Walmart and Target to medium and small businesses.

In *Cradle to Cradle*, the authors suggest a time when green chemistry might deliver the prospect of making products that, like leaves and other organic matter, can simply be cycled into the earth without harm to the environment. Imagine the prospect of product chains, transportation fuels, and transportation systems that don't produce GHG emissions and where disposal is no longer associated with pollution of land, air, or water. It's not the least bit unreasonable to think that the fertile young minds coursing through our university system—the business leaders of tomorrow—will doggedly pursue these types of product possibilities, seeking competitive business advantage in a world of more than seven billion people, where the survival of people and ecosystems will depend on such inventions.

LOCAL FOOD

Gardens and local agriculture: yes, it may seem questionable to project meaningful reductions in fossil fuel use from small-scale gardening and farming. But there is a powerful local-food movement underway throughout the United States—one that's not limited at all to the "ecotopia" States of Washington, Oregon, and California. The public's food palette is changing, as evidenced in a growing interest in consuming locally grown fruits and vegetables, meats, poultry, and fish. As with recycling and Extended Producer Responsibility, these activities translate into less fossil fuel use on a per capita basis and more local expenditures that have a positive impact on local economies. The interest in the presence of local farming done organically or sustainably is underscored by recent marketing efforts by one or more developers to place new home projects adjacent to organic farms. The farms become integral to the development, just as co-locating developments adjacent to parks and wild areas such as estuaries now command a premium in development value. Such developments are, more often than not, energy intensive in nature because they are essentially suburbs, and, as we have learned from such developments over the past fifty years, they are rarely accompanied by employment opportunities nearby and lack essential services that reduce the need to drive. Even so, the fact that people are recognizing that being located near a farm can be a positive rather than a negative experience suggests the kinds of consumer shifts that appear to be emerging.

BICYCLE AND FOOT POWER

Pedestrian, bicycle, and public transportation infrastructure investments are thought by their critics to be ineffectual and inconsequential for significantly reducing fuel consumption. Harsher critics think that policies to promote pedestrian, bicycle, and public transportation are examples of social engineering, reflecting a growing and unwelcome intrusion of government in people's lives. There are interest groups that strenuously resist such measures as being "anticar" with organizational titles like Cars Are Basic. They argue that every dollar spent on the development of bicycles and pedestrian ways is a dollar that won't be spent on filling potholes or resurfacing broken-down streets and highways. But times are changing and so are the values that drive public policy and investment, along with consumer preferences. Isn't it the role of government to reflect such changes? After all, the highways and street systems we enjoy were the product of a consumer and industrial world that demanded expansive highway and street systems that delivered great mobility, which society has prized for much of the past seventy-five years. Public investment made possible the far-flung development that we now call sprawl, making possible commutes of up to one hundred miles per day or more to reach the suburbs. Based on changing demographics and the values expressed by younger people, and the economic challenges facing many retiring baby boomers, a less car-based living model is becoming feasible and attractive to many. This trend isn't being propelled by public policies or by social scientists, planners, and environmentalists—code words of "social engineers." It's emerging because of decisions made by individuals, by groups and associations, and by businesses and local governments responding to changing economics, values, and quality-of-life concerns.

Fewer young professionals are buying into the suburban paradigm of owning a suburban home and driving half an hour or more to the workplace. More of them want safe bicycle lanes to ride or walk to work, or take a bus or shuttle. With the tools of information at their fingertips they can accomplish tasks like reserving a car for a trip in a moment's time, determining restaurants within walking or biking distance, or any number of other functions, provided that safe and convenient means of transportation are available. Shifts in values and accompanying technologies become the engine of transformation. No longer amorphous, they result in consumer signals, followed by investments that conform to them. The bicycle rider wants a bike rack where he or she goes out to eat or shop. Riders want separated bicycle lanes that protect them from traffic. They want housing that offers amenities like places to store bicycles and the latest communications tools built into their living spaces. In time, these new amenities become strong, perhaps even dominant, economic factors that define the future urban infrastructures. They have very real implications for fossil fuel use, driving down personal energy consumption by reducing the number of vehicle trips made and even the numbers of vehicles needed. They drive us away from fossil fuels. When they become wedded to wanting to live in buildings that produce their own renewable energy or utilities that provide an expanding choice of renewable energy to power their information and entertainment tools, the impact they will have on lowering our need for fossil fuels becomes synergistic and powerful.

Today, designing buildings on the basis of their life-cycle impact on the environment as embodied in the US Green Building Council's LEED program (Leadership in Energy and Environmental Design) and other current green building standards is almost the norm in learning institutions. For example, all new buildings within the University of California system must meet at least the LEEDs Silver Status. On campuses throughout the country, LEEDs standard buildings have become commonplace. Government and corporate buildings are becoming greener as well.

The LEED program and corporate green building innovation have recently been bested by the State of California. The California Energy Commission has adopted a Zero Net Energy standard for new buildings, the most far-reaching building energy standard in the world. By 2020, all new residences in California must add as much energy as they consume, resulting in a Zero Net Energy equation. By 2030, this same standard will be required for all new commercial buildings. Compliance with this standard is achieved by utilizing solar photovoltaic systems for electricity production and a wide range of conservation technologies, from the mundane to the sophisticated. Taken together, they make it possible to construct buildings that produce as much energy as they use. By 2020, California's Zero Net Energy requirement for the building sector will be the law and Zero Net Energy buildings will become the norm for new construction.

A host of green energy building features can be found throughout Silicon Valley and within San Francisco and San Jose. Greenness has spread to more staid manufacturing firms like Ford Motor Company; William McDonough's cradle-to-cradle design ideas were adopted in rebuilding Ford's cavernous Rouge manufacturing plant in Detroit and in the new building creations of many other prominent national companies. This quiet, transformational building revolution is happening, and not at the instigation of environmental activists or only because of corporate visionaries like the late Ray Anderson, the CEO and corporate sustainability pioneer at Interface, a large carpet and flooring manufacturer. Changing values, perspectives, and aesthetics that favor a lighter carbon footprint and an eye to the long view are the drivers of this quiet but profound building revolution.

Within the span of a few decades, the adoption of a fossil-free worldview and behaviors that support such a worldview may become the new normal. More likely than not, this won't be solely the result of public policy initiatives and accompanying regulations, though they are helpful. The big shift will be cumulative—the result of a growing drumbeat of news and direct experiences with climate change, and the product of millions of consumer purchases, government procurements including the purchase of renewable fuels by the Department of Defense, and corporate procurement practices for the goods and services they need. The university sector will likely remain the leading edge of change because much of what they do is increasingly being influenced by the values of students. But it's possible that government and the private sectors will become just as innovative and, in some cases, take the lead because, simply put, an entrepreneur can implement a design by fiat.

Corporate public relations campaigns that have produced so much "green washing"—environmental "feel good" sloganing and marketing—will be forced to demonstrate a deeper green commitment as the generational change in values seeps into the corporate boardrooms and spreads throughout corporate management, resulting in greater public scrutiny of green claims versus practices. Greater transparency through information sharing makes corporate greenness claims more subject to accountability.

Taking the bus, bicycling, or walking won't be something you do once a year to feel self-righteous on your way to celebrate Earth Day. Take a page from the City of San Jose, where much of the core of the city has experienced a remarkable transformation in less than twenty years. The hollowed-out, sterile, and car-dominated downtown of yesterday has emerged as a vital and hip central city, where new public transit thrives and where people now don't give it a second thought as long as the trains and buses run on time. They're clean, quiet, and affordable.

When one thinks about it, the car has had a relatively short life—fewer than seventy years—as a primary means of mass transportation, driven by subsidies like the gasoline tax and the nefarious designs of companies like General Motors, who spent heavily to influence decision makers in cities like Los Angeles to abandon their popular trains (the Red Line) in favor of buses and cars. Investments toward transforming cities to compensate for the one-dimensional transportation system called the private automobile are slowly but surely occurring, favoring more transportation diversification through the support of rail lines, new subways, dedicated and safe bicycle lanes, and improving the pedestrian environment.

How ironic it is that developed nations are trending away from car to trains, bikes, and walking, while developing countries like China, Thailand, and Vietnam are becoming more car dependent. When I first visited China some twenty-five years ago, Beijing was a sea of bicycles, with hardly a highway. People moved on foot, by bicycle, and by motorbike. Visit Beijing or any other major Chinese city today and it's a gridlocked city of cars with few bicycles evident and massive rings of freeways, frantically constructed to accommodate China's burgeoning car growth. Some consider this trending toward Western-style consumption a reason for downplaying the prospects for sustainability. They see a tidal wave of fossil fuel growth paralleling growing prosperity. They observe that China has become the world's number-one consumer of oil, gas, and coal, eclipsing US consumption, and note that the country is on a worldwide buying binge to secure fossil fuel energy sources far into the future.

But will the on-the-ground realities of a country as big as China deepening its use of fossil fuel wane under domestic pressures to address quality-of-life concerns? China's thirty-year run on fossil fuels has fed the worst and most sustained pollution in the world with potentially unimaginable health impacts as the population of China ages. Aping the consumerism of the West and the huge, pent-up consumer demands to mimic in some way the lifestyles of the rich and famous may prove short-lived. After a less-than-a-decade-long rush to the private car, many Chinese cities are bogged down in the worst of traffic congestion, characterized by mindlessly sitting in cars that hardly move. Just under the surface of China's wonder of prosperity is a potential rebellion-in-the-making as its people gasp for air in their increasingly air-conditioned, car-choked nightmare cities, where particulate matter can exceed five hundred parts per million and sometimes go much higher than that. No wonder, then, that those who can afford it flee cities like Beijing to places where the air is cleaner. No wonder that the bad air is increasingly the determining factor in the decision of China's best and brightest not to expose themselves and their families to life-shortening air pollution. In a conversation I had recently with a Chinese professor from Dalian, China, I was told that some nine million affluent Chinese have left China in pursuit of a cleaner environment. As she put it, the "rich can buy organic food and bottled water for drinking in China, but they can't buy clean air." Horrible air quality, rapidly shrinking water supplies, polluted land, constant noise and dust, and the unsettling nature of the country's unrelenting rapid growth—the chickens have come home to roost and challenge the Chinese economic miracle.

Trending patterns in the West suggest deeper changes afoot that will transform the way we live, what products we buy or don't buy, what we choose to eat, the amenities we select for our homes and work places, and how we move about our communities. All of these will increasingly be expressions of what we value, based on the menu of options from which we can choose, and these values, in an increasingly interdependent world, will spread.

The top waste industry executive at Browning Ferris Industries (now Republic) who twenty-five years ago made the disparaging comment that recycling was for "Boy and Girl Scout paper drives" is long gone. Today such a boast would be laughed out of the room, as the ubiquitous three-can recycling bins found in urban areas in California, Oregon, Minnesota, Rhode Island, New York, and Massachusetts attest. And this example only touches the surface of the transformative forces that are in play. Cities and states throughout the country are exploring and developing more comprehensive approaches to the problem of waste that will increasingly lead them to using these wastes to produce renewable energy, including fuels to drive our children to school and electricity to run our appliances and communications tools.

I don't believe it's a reach to think that, over the next few decades, bikeways, walkways, and a better environment in general will become embedded in the urban fabric. And it's in the urban fabric, the dominant infrastructure of the twenty-first century, where the most robust shift away from fossil fuels will happen.

RETHINKING OUR REGULATORY SYSTEM

At the Verdexchange conference in Los Angeles on January 26, 2015, the former mayor of Long Beach and CEO of Southern California Edison called for a new regulatory paradigm to foster the transition to renewables. An inhibiting factor that will slow down this transformation is the regulatory apparatus that has built up over decades, coupled with a legacy of incentives that propelled the advance of the fossil fuel age. We have built a massive regulatory machine that now consists of a maze of departments and agencies who oversee a galaxy of laws and regulations intended to prevent environmental abuse and deliver environmental protections. In states like California that have embraced environmental values, the regulatory system is a phalanx that must be engaged, consisting of numerous public hearings and appeals, fees, and stringent standards that must be met to win project approval. It has become a kind of Fifth Estate. Nonprofit environmental-advocacy organizations, government agencies charged with implementing and enforcing regulations, consulting firms that help companies and governments navigate through the complexities of the permit process and regulations, and attorneys who litigate on behalf of environmental causes comprise this Fifth Estate.

The regulatory system has driven many of the necessary environmental protections achieved over the past forty years, and it performs a vital check and balance in the governance of development in our country. But the relevant question today is, is this system up to the task of ushering in a post–fossil fuel age? Is a system born out of the need to protect us from the worst of environmental abuse capable of delivering the depth and breadth of change within a compressed time frame? This system, with its blind spots and internal conflicts of mission, is confounding our ability to make timely progress implementing a renewable energy and sustainable infrastructure.

In December 1997, the California Air Resources Board, charged with protecting the state's air quality, permitted the chemical compound MTBE (methyl tertiary-butyl ether) as a gasoline additive that was found to be effective in reducing air emissions. I was serving in Sacramento at the time that the regulation was enacted, and I recall asking a high-level US EPA official if this regulation had been thoroughly thought through. The answer was affirmative. The agency had done its due diligence. But within less than a year of its implementation, there was a rash of water-well contaminations where MTBE was found, having leaked out of stationary fueling tanks. The most publicized case involved water wells in Santa Monica, where one well after another quickly became contaminated. In Santa Monica alone, lawsuits against Chevron and BP resulted in clean-up settlements that cost some $423 million. Another case in Jacksonville, Florida, was settled for $150 million in claims against Exxon Mobil. Within a few more years, as the evidence of MTBE-based water contamination mounted, it led to an Air Resources Board ban on MTBE use in the state. Ethanol was substituted for MTBE, and its use has been ongoing since the ban.

At a more micro scale, when I was in the private sector, MTBE was detected in the area of an old fueling tank on our premises. The contamination area was fewer than four hundred square feet, the size of a couple of bedrooms. It took nearly fourteen years from the time of its detection to remediate this site at a cost of nearly $500,000. The threat to groundwater was negligible, and that became apparent after several years of water testing. But the local health department was reluctant to let the site self-remediate (just let natural ambient conditions work to eliminate the pollution), and so treatment was continued for another ten years. Had the groundwater and potable water contamination proved to be a demonstrable threat, the remediation costs of prevention would be completely justifiable, but the threat wasn't there and overly cautious staff dithered, forcing the company to tie up substantial working capital to treat a very minor problem. These types of costly, low-performance environmental mitigations are widespread and are indicative of a system that fails to discriminate between substantial and minor environmental concerns. The result is squandered private capital, a waste of regulatory staff time that could be more meaningfully deployed, and private-sector disdain for a government that, at times, seems clueless.

There are, of course, no guarantees that even if a more "integrated" regulatory framework had existed when the MTBE rule was enacted the blind spot in the regulatory equation would have been caught in time. But it might have been if more effective insight and information had been shared across the regulatory silos—in this case, the water/air boundaries, preventing serious water-well contamination and hundreds of millions of dollars spent correcting the problem. As critical as I am of the regulatory system, I want to pause and make it clear that environmental regulations overall have served our country very well. We only need to look at parts of the country where regulation has been slack, such as the Elk River release of crude mctim, a chemical foam used to treat coal impurities, and the Dan River Spill from Duke Energy's coal ash and wastewater holding ponds, to appreciate the importance of strong regulations and equally strong enforcement of regulations. Coastal protections such as those afforded by the California Coastal Commission and similar agencies elsewhere in the country include wetland and sand dune preservation, along with public access to beaches. Had there been such regulatory agencies in place in Louisiana, perhaps the impacts of Hurricane Katrina would not have been so devastating. Regulations have led to farmland protection, landmark energy building standards, recycling and composting, urban limit lines, and innumerable other worthy achievements.

The importance of a strong regulatory system is critical in our increasingly complex world. But, as the expression goes, "one man's ceiling is another man's floor." Today's regulatory system is that floor. We need to rise above the floor and establish a future-oriented regulatory framework that can facilitate the rapid deployment of renewable energy resources. We need to move like we did when we built our railroads and energy grids and brought roads into our national forests to cut trees and mine.

Deterrence, keeping environmental impacts at bay, is yesterday's regulatory news. We're beyond that now. Let's consider the critical need to develop biofuels that generate near-zero CO_2 emissions. The South Coast Air

Quality Management District (SCAQMD) must do everything feasible to comply with the Federal Clean Air Act, and that requires some draconian measures to constrain emissions from stationary sources like limiting outdoor barbecues and volatile emissions from petroleum-based painting and finishing products. The district has even considered banning open fires on beaches to reduce emissions. Given the almost impossible task that the district is charged with, one would think it would do everything within its power to encourage emission reductions. No doubt it would, but for the inherent inflexibility of the Clean Air Act. Let me illustrate the problem.

If one is developing a bioenergy project within the district boundaries and it produces emissions, even if very low, the project will be treated like any stationary source of pollutants, such as a factory or a refinery. There is no ability at present for the district to reward projects that, in their totality, reduce emissions. The Clean Air Act is rigid; it doesn't permit the district to value emission reductions from a technology to offset so-called new source requirements, meaning that any new emission source must be mitigated even if the technology producing those emissions more than offsets the new emissions with emission reductions. In effect, the district must turn a blind eye to the project's emissions benefits, even though all parties know that the project is resulting in net energy benefits. Opening up the Clean Air Act to make it a more effective instrument of change is fraught with danger because of vehement antiregulatory views in Congress. But failing to do that means that it remains a blunt-force instrument that results in too one-dimensional regulation.

Another example concerns composting facilities. A pollutant of great concern to the SCAQMD is nitrous oxide (NOx) because it contributes heavily to smog. Ammonia, released from composting operations, especially food waste, is an NOx precursor. The district has therefore placed severe restrictions on the release of ammonia, essentially requiring releases be captured. This forces composting operations to be fully enclosed, or at minimum, if conducted in the open, that a system of pipes and fans draw the air out of the compost pile for treatment. Given the relatively low value of compost products and the low-margin profits of compost producers, the economics imposed by these regulations are, at best, challenging. And now California is upping its recycling requirements to 75 percent. Without composting facilities, California cannot meet its recycling mandates. And without the application of compost, our depleting soils cannot be enriched. In addition, the water-conserving potential of applying compost to the land cannot be realized. How does one value the various environmental goals that are being pursued and arbitrate between them so as to avoid direct conflicts where one agency stifles or kills the mission of another? So the growing question is how can the regulatory system better sort out and support multiple and synergistic environmental improvement measures?

Another example of challenging regulatory hurdles facing renewable energy development is exemplified by the controversy over the proposed wind farm that would be located between five and fifteen miles off Martha's Vineyard. The project calls for developing 457 megawatts of wind energy produced by 130 wind machines 285 feet in height. It would be the first large offshore wind farm in the United States. Supported by the Department of Interior and the State of Massachusetts Department of the Environment, the project would produce enough energy to meet 75 percent of the electrical power needs of Cape Cod, Martha's Vineyard, and Nantucket Island—clearly an important contribution to making that part of the country a low CO_2 emitter. But this wind farm faces formidable opposition from some of the most influential families and individuals in the country, including the Kennedys, Kerrys, Bill Koch of the Koch Brothers, and Mitt Romney—a tough cast of opponents indeed. They claim that the aesthetic costs of the enormous wind machines are too great; they will create a visual blight in one of the most picturesque settings on the Eastern seaboard if not the country. The project was first proposed in 2006 and has been stalled for years now as the opponents apply the full complement of regulatory process protections against it.

At the opposite end of the country, in California's Mojave Desert, solar farms planned to contribute heavily to meeting the state's renewable energy goals are being challenged by desert-protection advocates. Protectionist interests don't see the desert as the empty, desolate, low-environmental-impact setting that project proponents consider it to be. They don't want the desert tortoise and other species victimized to make way for solar farms.

They see a blaze of solar collectors as an eyesore in the desert. "Can't they go somewhere else?" they argue. These stories, whether they relate to a compost facility, a wind farm, a solar installation, or solar arrays on the rooftops of homes and commercial buildings are repeated over and over again as the goal of sustainability comes up against regulatory reality of gaining permit approvals. Between the idea and the reality stands the power of the Fifth Estate that can, and often does, unwind the best-laid plans.

The historical criticism of the regulatory system typically comes from business and economic interests of every sort, from the usual suspects: the American Chamber of Commerce, the conservative think tanks like the Heritage Foundation, state and local chambers of commerce, and industrial giants like Big Oil. Their mantra for decades now is to cut the red tape in the process, "streamline and fast-track" the permit system. But this so-called permit fast-tracking has been tried many times and largely without success in regulation-steeped states like California. Critics of fast-tracking see it as code language for trashing the protections afforded by the existing system.

To underscore the regulatory challenge, take a look at California's regulatory system as it stands in 2014. There is a State Air Resource Board that enforces the nation's Clean Air Standards and is the lead agency for implementing the California Climate Change Act known as AB 32. Then there is the state's Water Resources Control Board that enforces the nation's Clean Water Act. The California Energy Commission (CEC) is a state agency that has the responsibility for long-range energy planning, permitting energy facilities of fifty or more megawatts, and for implementing appliance and building conservations standards. CalRecycle is the agency that, among its many functions, regulates the state's solid waste facilities, including landfills, recycling plants, compost facilities, and waste incinerators. The California Department of Toxics regulates, as the title suggests, toxic substances produced within the state and their disposal. The State Coastal Commission has planning and permit authority for a coastal band that extends down California's eleven-hundred-mile coastline; there is a California Department of Food and Agriculture, a Department of Forestry, a Department of Conservation, and Department of Fish and Game. Have I missed any? These agencies, departments, and commissions are over brooded by the California Resources and the California Environmental Protection Agencies. These are overarching agencies, conceived to function as coordinators and interpreters of regulatory functions of the agencies and departments they oversee. However, in the California system, they don't fundamentally control them because the departments, boards, and commissions are the creations of the California legislature. As such they have statutory authority, meaning they are independent of the executive branch. Of course "independent" may be something of a misnomer because this labyrinth of entities has a director, a group of commissioners, and/or board members who are appointed jointly by the governor and the legislature. Many of these appointees owe their positions to the appointing authorities.

Under this regulatory morass are yet other layers of regulatory authority. There are air districts throughout the state that have their own regulations and issue their own permits. There are regional water boards throughout the state that also have their own regulations and issue their own permits. And, of course, in California alone, there are more than four hundred local governments who have their own project review authority, which include architectural review boards and panels, planning commissions, and a myriad of local water and sanitation districts, many of which are political powerhouses in and of themselves.

One could throw up one's hands looking at the magnitude of the challenge and say change is impossible. Let it stand. Give it a rest. Live with it. But in a society facing calamitous climate change where, in California's case, its water supply is at stake, its forests and many of its suburbs reaching into the forests and brush lands could burn up, and its agricultural resources without water are rendered useless, can it indulge these shortcomings? Short of resorting to executive orders issued during times of emergency (which I suppose is always an option if conditions get bad enough and they are there already with the water supply), this is the system or rather the gauntlet that forging a renewable energy future faces.

A renewable energy future brings forth new and interrelated demands. Consider the regulatory dimensions facing a biogas development project to make renewable energy. The plant itself is regulated by CalRecycle with its authority over solid waste facilities. But the regional air quality agency (as previously mentioned) has authority over the gas flares and any other air-borne emissions from the facility. And the state and regional water boards have authority over the land application of the digestate or soil product made of composted digestate with other materials such as manures. Then the Department of Agriculture may have authority over the soil products produced if commercially sold in the marketplace. The developer of a biogas project that produces energy, whether electrical or fuels, such as renewable natural gas, must also interact with California's Public Utilities Commission that regulates California's powerful, investor-owned utilities, who wheel renewable energy through their transmission systems. The waste wants to become renewable electricity and fuel and soil products, all of which have considerable and synergistic environmental value. But our regimented, silo-based regulatory system, in which air, water, waste, energy, and soil products are the domain of a single regulatory agency, has great difficulty valuing their cross-media benefits. They blur the regulatory boundaries of single-purpose entities created decades ago to address singular environmental problems.

Clearly we need the expertise that resides within these agencies, commissions, and departmental disciplines along with the checks and balances that come from viewing projects through their multiple lenses, but isn't there a more intelligent regulatory design, capable of capturing and integrating the cumulative knowledge gained and delivering a yes/no decision in a matter of a few months rather than many months or years? We're in a pre-iPhone, pre-Internet regulatory world, and the system is, simply put, obsolete!

Critics will howl at this proposition as naïve—claiming that it's a pre-scription for top-down big-government authority with the powers to crush local interests. I don't deny the dangers that a redesigned regulatory system may pose. It could well translate to scenarios like this. The opponent of the wind farm that's going to damage pristine views and make noise could lose more readily to wind farm development interests. The solar farms in the Mojave would obliterate some of the desert landscape and flora and fauna and still be allowed to proceed. The compost facility a mile away might send whiffs of odor now and then that pose a real nuisance, but it couldn't be threatened or closed down by a few neighbors for whom it was a nuisance.

But when you think about what has been allowed in pursuit of fracking and other forms of oil extraction of late, the kind of reform I'm proposing is modest. It would have at its core reliance on the highest of standards for project development, including environmental sensitivities, based on science as well as project technology, deployment, and operating standards. The insights and knowledge that we've gained from the near countless project analyses would be applied to a reformed regulatory design. Data and core analyses undertaken in project reviews are to be mined and synthesized, distilling our key scientific, policy, and procedural insights.

Where might the seed ideas for a new regulatory design come from? They will not likely come from within government or from the consulting world whose bread and butter is the status quo. Rather they're more likely to emerge from an unexpected source—a graduate student, perhaps, or people from within the technology and business communities who are unconstrained by habit, training, and allegiance to the prevailing regulatory paradigm. My guess is that the keenest innovation ideas will be the work of a university student who finds the regulatory conundrum to be an exciting problem to unravel and offer insight and alternatives. Perhaps a budding mathematician, who instead of inventing a new algorithm to enrich arbitrageurs, can devise a numeric system to apply to project review and decision-making options. Might a clever young law student, instead of drilling down to reveal a lucrative loophole in our arcane tax system, give us insight as to how we might simplify the information overload and redundancy associated with the review process? Maybe a young economist can devise more effective performance-based incentives for solar, wind, and biogas projects and pedestrian and bicycle paths.

In 1993, serving as a US Information Agency Speaker in China on US environmental policy, I was giving a lecture at Chengdu University. I was describing the environmental decision-making framework, a subject sure to put a room filled with students and faculty to sleep. After all, this was China, where "public process" was as remote to the average student or professor as a man on the moon. My wife Kathy, who was then

324 • Out of the Wasteland

chair of the Santa Barbara County Planning Commission, was seated next to a Chengdu University professor of sociology. After the lecture, Kathy explained to her and the students who swarmed around her how the planning commission process works. Both professor and students were dumbfounded and defensive about what she described. Finally, in a state of exasperation, the professor asked Kathy with all seriousness, "Why don't you just use a computer to make decisions?" We often laugh about that conversation, how revelatory it was about the state of public participation in China. But between that extreme of the professor's question and our byzantine and arcane system, there should be some way forward that will improve our understanding of complex information, reduce the volume of written documents, much of which is redundant, and capture the essence of the decision options at hand. So many complex functions today are expressed numerically—why not some application of this to decision making in the public arena?

SCALE

The great social and architectural historian, Lewis Mumford, in his signature work, *The City in History*,[64] argued that getting scale right was critical for the health of cities. He feared the metropolis of yesterday would become the megalopolis of tomorrow, where nodes of urbanization would fuse into one another and become indistinguishable. He observed that people living in such cities would feel increasingly alienated from each other, and politically would feel estranged from their government. The megalopolis that Mumford feared is commonplace today in Shanghai, Mexico City, Sao Paolo, Manila, Jakarta, and Beijing. It's here in the Washington to Boston Corridor and on the San Diego to Los Angeles flood plains.

Scale was at the very heart of the question that Santa Barbara asked itself some forty years ago: how big should we be? So simple a question, so straightforward. And yet so very few cities have raised it, let alone deliberated or tried to answer it. Why? When it comes to so many questions about our future, the cities and communities we live in, the water we use, and the energy we consume, most people and their civic leaders believe that the environments beyond their homes are shaped by forces largely beyond their control. The prevailing view is where growth is a factor it just happens—that efforts to guide, let alone limit, are made by a developer, by shifting demographics, a decision by a company to move in or move out or because fracking development is possible. All these factors of course bear on the question, but at the heart of the matter, as we learned in Santa Barbara, communities can indeed play a large role in how they look, how they feel, how they grow or, for that matter, shrink, as is the case with Detroit. And when a community engages in such matters, the public sphere intensifies; people engage as they realize that they can indeed make a difference.

By most measures, Santa Barbara's insistence on preserving its small scale has contributed to a vibrant community life. There are said to be more nonprofit organizations in Santa Barbara than in any community of its size in the country. By preserving the beauty of its surroundings and its older, cherished neighborhoods, it has remained a magnet for those seeking a refuge from the nearby Los Angeles metropolitan area with its twenty or so million residents and from other parts of the country and the world. It boasts a top-tier public university, UCSB, the esteemed Music Academy of the West for exceptional young musicians from throughout the world; the Santa Barbara International Film Festival, one of the finest film festivals in the country; a top-flight community college and adult education program; and many other cultural and civic attributes. In a recent call for candidates to run for a vacant seat on the Santa Barbara City Council some forty-six candidates surfaced, many highly qualified individuals seeking to contribute to Santa Barbara's tradition of community involvement.

Critics of Santa Barbara's choice about its future can sneer and say it's a decision made possible only because of its wealth, not so much because of the wealth that resides in the city proper, but by the enormous wealth of individuals living in proximity to the city, in the rarefied confines of Montecito and Hope Ranch and atop the Santa Barbara Riviera. Without a doubt wealth has played an enormous role in preserving open space and parks, creating and sustaining cultural institutions, and providing support for many nonprofits. Yet so much of what makes Santa Barbara a vibrant community is the result of efforts by talented individuals—students who attended the university and stayed on, community activists, architects, designers, health-care professionals, and people moved by their love of place and love of community. It was these people—my friends, acquaintances, and colleagues, a mix of people of wealth and stature and others of modest means armed with will, insight, and creativity—who have fashioned the community as it is today.

Santa Barbara's maintaining scale has allowed small businesses to continue and in some cases thrive. By maintaining scale, Santa Barbara has not surrendered its sense of sovereignty to corporate conformity, to bigness just because that's the economic model of much of enterprise today. At the same time the community has not been blind to the benefits that large companies can bring, like a Costco that allows families to buy in bulk and reduce the cost of living essentials and a Trader Joe's that provides affordable and reasonable quality foods, an alternative of sorts to regular supermarkets. We do need the Home Depots that provide tools and building materials, doors, and windows that make home improvements more economically feasible, and Staples for the paper, electronics, and other items that we depend upon to run our homes and home offices. They have their place. But what Santa Barbara has not allowed is a wholesale takeover of the community by large businesses. Its sense of place and its core values are nurtured, even as the forces of greater Southern California, and indeed the globe, press upon it and try to shape it in their mold.

Building on the foundations of community life established decades ago, the CEC's Energy Blueprint and proposals like it suggest that the development of regional renewable energy resources can become the next step in forging a critical transition away from our excessive dependence on fossil fuels. In Santa Barbara's case, though successful in defining and preserving its scale and its physical characteristics, its resource base remains almost completely dependent on a fossil fuel–charged world. The oil platforms, including the infamous Platform A that blew forty-six years ago, remain in the Santa Barbara Channel. And now the tapping of the Monterey shale in Santa Barbara County, like that going on or proposed due to new extraction methods, are signaling perhaps an even deeper dependence on fossil fuels, even as science is demonstrating in manifold ways that the last thing we need to be doing is combusting more fossil fuels.

Communities need to recognize that in a climate-change environment a more localized energy focus is crucial, not only because energy and resource systems they have relied upon are becoming less reliable but because they are contributing to the further depletion of the resources that our lives depend upon. It's becoming an existential consideration for us and our communities. And this is where design, once again, becomes the decisive factor in shaping our future in a climate-changing world.

By definition, design "is an act of intent, of volition."[65] It takes ideas and perceptions and clothes them in matter, cities, parks, buildings, industrial plants—every aspect of the physical world that mankind touches. Recognition of the power of design is ancient; in many mythologies architecture was one of the gifts of the gods to mankind and its powers echo down through the birth of Christianity through the hand of God as described in Creation, and on through the Renaissance and the Scientific Revolutions. The ancient Greek polis was perhaps the most ambitious and far-reaching application of design—a deliberate effort to encompass the entire human enterprise in its highest sense, melding government, art, religion, architecture, work, and play perhaps as seamlessly as has ever happened in the history of the world.

The corporate city of Pudong across the Huangapa River was rice paddies in the mid-1990s.

Design is the most well-woven theme of this work—design of a waterfront, an agricultural valley, gardens, green buildings, recycling and composting and anaerobic digestion plants, green technologies, cradle-to-cradle designed products, and design of a city itself, as well as laws, regulations, and policies. Design is at the center of the Santa Barbara Energy Blueprint that paints one portrait of how a community can forge a postpetroleum future with the architecture, technologies, and the economics of it, not expressed as vague policy abstractions that we've become numbingly used to, but in terms of on-the-ground hardware, the physical artifacts of this future, and the dollars and cents required to build it.

In 1997, I was again in China, standing on the Bund in Shanghai, when the power of design hit me like a body blow. I looked across the Huangpu River to a distant shore beyond which were nothing but rice paddies. Earlier that day, a small group of colleagues from the California Environmental Protection Agency was shown a model of what the Chinese government planned for that distant rice paddy landscape. It was to become a giant corporate city, Pudong, the East Bank of Shanghai, as modern a city as any on earth. Our Chinese hosts told us that it would be built in a few years, an astounding claim, but based on what we had witnessed during our visit we didn't doubt them. That model before us and the irrepressible human energy and financial might behind it underscored the sheer raw power of design that has animated the Asian urban explosion over the past twenty years. Was this to become the design paradigm for our times, massive and concentrated development consuming, in only a matter of decades, the resources that the industrial revolutions of the nineteenth and twentieth centuries devoured over the span of two centuries? Could the world sustain a hundred more cities of a million or more and five megacities of ten million or more—just in China, not to mention the other Asian urban unfolding—a future based on the burning of fossil fuels? I felt completely powerless to influence this design paradigm that was driving development in China, and by extension, much of Asia.

A decade later, I returned to China, this time to Xi'an, and the mind-numbing pace of development was proceeding just as it was a decade ago. A forest of high-rise apartments was under construction, and construction cranes were everywhere on the urban horizon. A subway was being blasted underground next to my hotel and it proceeded night and day. I was made humble once again by the display of energy, will, and execution that China is. And yet when I returned via Los Angeles Airport and made the hundred-mile drive back to Santa Barbara, a psychological shift occurred. Even hurly-burly Los Angeles seemed relatively calm and subdued in contrast to the turmoil I experienced on the streets of Xi'an. The air, though not great, was a far cry from what I breathed over there. The freeways I considered to be in such a state of breakdown before I left were, in fact, looking pretty good, considering California's decimated infrastructure budget. When I awoke the next morning, I walked my dog under clear skies. When I read the Sunday paper, it discussed the rankings of water quality at our beaches tested by Heal the Bay, and all ranked 80 percent or better, a notable improvement over previous years and certainly much better than a decade ago. And then it dawned on me that maybe the ledger card that appears to favor China's ascent isn't as stacked as it might seem. The air one breathes, the land one touches, the quality of water one drinks and swims in, and the conditions under which one works—aren't these in the longer run the most important measures of a civilization's accomplishments, and not just its rate of growth and development?

I noticed on the return home the proliferation of smaller cars, the large number of hybrids, and even a smattering of all-electric vehicles on the streets of LA. And I thought how ironic it is that just as China has embraced the automobile, our love affair with the oil-fueled internal combustion engine is on the decline, as is our dependence on coal and oil that have inflicted such harm on today's environment and incalculable harm on the environment of the future. I appreciated the relative order and calmness of my surroundings and, for the first time, I realized that might be an advantage over the country I had just left.

As China was moving toward bigness and sameness, might the United States and Europe be moving in the opposite direction, appreciating the wisdom offered by Lewis Mumford and E. F. Schumacher half a century ago, the importance of right scale, and promoting design that respects the landscape and the qualities of place, as Ian McHarg taught and practiced? Might we be coming closer to Buckminster Fuller's dream of ushering forth technologies that put people first—technologies that sit lightly on the land and use natural resources sparingly? And perhaps, just perhaps, we were beginning to recognize what Alan Chadwick had instilled in all who,

Los Angeles, California circa 1960. Our smog levels were like China today.

however briefly, came under his spell—that the garden is a transformative force, a place as much in the heart and mind as a physical creation.

Just maybe the time has come when these once embryonic, outlier ideas that had so informed and nurtured me are seeping their way into the hearts and minds of people, especially the young. Hardly any of them even know the names of these luminous souls or their philosophies and ideas. But no matter. What's important is that the values they expressed, the insights and qualities they seized upon, are upwelling in conscious decisions they are making about how they choose to live. And if they take hold within a generation's time, we may indeed witness the necessary end to the once-liberating and, dare I say, magic-making—but ultimately unsustainable—age of oil.

Climate change is starting to haunt us. It stalks us, making us fear for our future and worry about the prospects for our children, giving us night sweats that go away only when the morning light comes and we find our lives seemingly in place. Apocalyptical images of climate events are becoming commonplace in movies and games. All but the most fervent deniers of climate change know that the reckoning is upon us; the forces are in play and we are entering a time of "adaptation," a politically correct word that does little to convey the wild ride into the future that has begun. And now, at last, a New York Times poll finds that two-thirds of Americans are more likely to vote for political candidates who campaign on fighting climate change.[66]

PERSPECTIVE, DETACHMENT, RESOLVE

In the spring of 2014, Elizabeth Kolbert lectured at UCSB about her new book, The Sixth Extinction: An Unnatural History. I must admit that I carried with me a deep sense of foreboding as I made my way to the lecture, bracing myself before the massive evidence that Kolbert sets forth as she makes her case for what's coming our way. The book jacket of her work carries such endorsements as "an epic, riveting story of our species that reads like a scientific thriller—only more terrifying because it is real" and "Elizabeth Kolbert's cautionary tale...offers us a cogent overview of a harrowing biological challenge before us."

Deliberately subjugating oneself to a numbing succession of findings that all point dismally to a biologically deaccelerating world is something only a fervent environmentalist, or a masochist, would do. I have made a lifetime habit of it, so why change? Why and how, in the face of such evidence, should I press on, work on, as if possibilities still exist and outcomes are not predetermined? Why should anyone, for that matter?

As I thought about it in the days after the presentation that was every bit as paralyzing as I expected, and argued even better than I had thought, it occurred to me that, indeed, hadn't I heard all this before? I don't mean climate change and the science behind it. That prospect wouldn't become part of our consciousness for decades. But the threats to the environment that seemed to me, at the time, every bit as chilling as what I heard that night from Elizabeth Kolbert.

When the good earth of my childhood was being torn up around me, I felt loss and bewilderment. When I gazed out the window of that small airplane and looked into the maw of that artesian-like well of blackness spewing into the Pacific Ocean, I saw no hope, only darkness and death. And considering the avalanche of book knowledge, which forecasted our running out of natural resources, the depletion of the fish in the ocean, the poisoning of our land and water, the befoulment of our air, the frightful loss of species, and horror after horror, it all seemed reasonable enough to me: the mounting evidence was there, demonstrating man's proclivities to be blind and bury nature's presence in the modern world. But all this didn't deflate my spirits or unravel me psychologically. Strangely, it had the opposite effect. It awakened a creative spirit and a resolve to bring forth what I thought might be healing influences, like gardens, like community scale, like recycling and green buildings, and, more recently, renewable energy facilities such as anaerobic digesters. The very making of these artifacts, the doing of it, had a synergistic and therapeutic impact on my state of mind. Over time, as I engaged a much bigger world than Santa Barbara, my working environment became an admixture of beauty and toxicity—the gardens of a Chadwick; the majestic beauty of a sweeping, untrammeled coastline; a verdant agricultural valley; toxic landfills; the choking, poisonous smoke from the acetylene torches dismantling the world's electronic waste; the acrid air pollution of Beijing and Xian; the stench from compost piles in the scorching heat of the San Joaquin Valley; and the remembrance of that toxic rivulet that ran long ago into the Ventura River.

So, in a sense, the prospect of climate change, as fearsome as it is, does not change my nature or orientation. Yes, I may prove to be a fool to think that we can still make a difference, to work as if our tomorrows can be influenced by what we do today, when a century of burning fossil fuels is up there in the atmosphere and will be there long after the burning of fossil fuels is no more—long after you and I are no more.

But one thing I do know, and I'm absolutely certain of this: no person, group, or institution knows fully what the future holds. No matter how keen the insights may be, how much the information reveals, life unfolds in surprising, convoluted, and often counterintuitive ways. What seems so certain, so probable, so prone to projection today, far more often than not defies the script.

Who among us can ultimately say that the future is set, that we cannot impact the future of climate on earth? Who is to say that an upwelling of decisions so seemingly small in scale, so disparate in nature, so apparently unconnected, cannot fuse into powerful forces that are built upon entirely different assumptions and suppositions than the dominant ones of today?

Who's to say that within another five or ten years we won't yet break the hold of the fossil fuel age, with its centralized energy plants, its massive and polluting infrastructures, and the consolidation of wealth in the hands of a few companies that have the capital to exploit fossil fuel resources? Why isn't it possible, with the information tools we now have, that the very landscapes we occupy will be transformed into renewable energy landscapes that deliver the energy we need to warm and cool our homes, power our vehicles, and operate our appliances?

I heard many say:

"No way. Why, young man, you can't favor whole grains and wheat bread over white bread. You can't grow a garden without chemicals—the plants won't grow; and besides, the world will starve if you use sustainable growing methods."

"You can't stop growth; it's inevitable like the rain. You can't preserve a coastline in the path of urbanization. Sprawl can't be stopped. You can't prevent Hyatt and Southern Pacific Railroad and the political machine behind them from transforming the waterfront of your city in their image, not the community's."

"You can't get people to recycle or compost; that's for Boy and Girl Scouts. Besides, people just won't invest the time and effort to separate their waste materials."

"You can't eliminate the need for nuclear reactors by imposing energy efficiency standards like making refrigerators or air conditioners use less energy. Such measures are too insignificant to alter the course of energy consumption."

"You can't build green buildings, let alone net-zero energy buildings—they will cost too much and people won't like living in them. You can't meet a third of California's energy needs from renewable energy resources. The renewable energy resources can't be developed."

"You can't build a functioning hybrid or electric vehicle that people will buy. People won't ride bicycles or walk to work, let alone prefer living in towns and cities where they are readily available."

"They won't give up their plastic shopping bags or pay more for organic food. You can't make renewable energy from organic waste, your grass clippings, and discarded food; it's too expensive compared with landfilling the waste."

I have experienced all these "can't be dones," and I remember well all those who told me with their finger-wagging certainty that these were marginal and irrelevant propositions that would never go mainstream. Their views, once so dominant and seemingly inalterable not so many years ago, have receded as more sensible and sustainable ones replace them.

There are green shoots appearing all over the planet even as our dependence on fossil fuels remains so seemingly intractable. They are the creations of people propelled by an inner need to do something, to build alternative constructs, to evolve new means of interaction, new products and services, new technologies that can perform work, make goods, and meet human needs while relying on fossil fuels more sparingly or not at all. The green shoots are beginning to weave a tapestry, a pattern language in the image of a postoil age. It's faint now, but the work underway is incessant, and the will and the means to do more will only build as the urgency of our condition becomes undeniable.

ACKNOWLEDGMENTS

Pico Iyer gave me the inspiration and encouragement to see this project through. His genius helped guide me. Joan Crowder, the first of my editors until her untimely death only a few months ago, was my faithful collaborator for some four years. As errant and unpredictable as I was in meeting self-imposed "deadlines," she kept the project alive when, at times, I wanted to abandon it. And Jenny Cushnie, my second editor who stepped in with her keen intelligence and unflinching eye, gave me inspiration when it was flagging. I owe this book to the three of you. Thanks is due to Dave Davis, President, CEO, and Chairman of the Board of Directors, and Sigrid Wright, Assistant Director of the Community Environmental Council of Santa Barbara, for their content review of my manuscript. Thanks is due also to Lisa Hill who commandeered the preparation of the book, its design and execution through publication, and to Sally Warner-Arnett who obtained permission for the images that accompany the text.

The 1970s were the most dynamic in terms of reach and development of my work. I want to thank two persons of great renown in Santa Barbara for lending me their hands. Pearl Chase was our grand dame; she permeated Santa Barbara's civic life from the 1920s until her death in 1979. Pearl took a curious interest in the formation of the CEC. She commented to one of my great mentors, Robert Easton, that I was "an interesting young man—someone to be watched over." Pearl agreed to serve as the honorary chair of the Committee for Santa Barbara that carried forward her legacy of protecting the Santa Barbara waterfront. Selma Rubin, the midwife of countless Santa Barbara nonprofits, was another inspiration. Whereas Pearl came from the Santa Barbara elite, Selma was working class who, with her husband Bill, came to Santa Barbara in the '60s as an activist. Of her many great achievements in promoting civic life, justice, the environment, and causes like Alzheimer's that had claimed her husband, it was her almost singular effort to protect the Gaviota Coast that earned her a place in Santa Barbara's pantheon of heroes.

Without Maryanne Mott, who was a CEC founding board member and benefactor, our work wouldn't have survived past its first year. Equal to her financial contributions was her keen interest in formulating and cultivating the CEC's projects and programs. Marc McGinnes, Philip Marking, Elaine Burnell, Jim Billig, Judy Patrick, and John Meengs were also among the CEC founders. Their contributions are duly noted in this work.

During the fevered first few years of the CEC's existence, so many people played pivotal roles, such as Betty Stark, who staffed our front office for many years. Living in humble quarters down the street in a retirement hotel, Betty faithfully made her way to the office and cheerfully greeted those who entered the Ecology Center. Beth Amine painted the brilliant murals that adorned the walls of the Ecology Center. Judy Daniel, our talented graphic artist, made the Survival Times come even more alive than it was, and its first editor, Larry Penny, toiled with coeditor Joan Crowder to put out the little magazine that said so much and captured the essence of the early environmental movement.

In 1971, Maryanne Mott introduced me to Hal Conklin, who became co-director of the CEC. Whereas I was a raw work in progress, Hal was polished; he knew just what to say and how to say it. He was tidy, clean-cut—even suave. Over the course of the years to come, he manifested his many talents on behalf of Santa Barbara as councilman, mayor, and a private-sector executive. Damon Rickard was Hal's opposite. This buzz saw of high energy who had attended the Air Force Academy was our workhorse. Moving incessantly about in his baggy and torn jeans that would be a fashion statement today, Damon could build anything, think through any problem, and do it without the slightest interest in recognition.

Others in the community who were not directly active in our work but who contributed ideas and inspiration are Fifi Webster of the Audubon Society, Sue Higgins of the Sierra Club, Elsa Ocskay, Vivian Obern, and June Sunderland.

Those who contributed most to our "intellectual capital" in the early years were Warren Piece and Rich Merrill, whom I have much to say about in the stories of the El Mirasol Polyculture Farm; John and Margie Popper, our irrepressible beekeepers and gardeners and photo documentarians; Randy Wade, whose interest in sustainable agriculture led to his creation of the Santa Barbara Farmers' Market; and Irving Thomas, our brilliant solar engineer who was a force in his own right, one of the true pioneers of solar energy in America along with his cohort Cydney Miller.

Larry Tower and Katie O'Reilly played pivotal roles with the CEC. Larry was our carpenter who built many of our structures, and Katie, a talented graphic artist and fine bluegrass musician, performed at our many celebrations. Kathleen Sullivan helped research and write several key articles that appeared in the Survival Times. Meredith Moore graciously typed about anything that needed typing.

The CEC's reach into the community was facilitated by Selmer Wake, who headed Santa Barbara's famed adult education program, one without equal in the country. Selmer's assistant dean, Dr. Joe Bagnall, gave me an instrument: a lecture series to lead that enabled me to bring to Santa Barbara among the greatest figures of the environmental movement in their time, including Buckminster Fuller, Alan Chadwick, Amory Lovins, Paolo Soleri, Paul Ehrlich, E. F. Schumacher, Norman Borlaug, and Barry Commoner, from whom I learned so much. An offshoot from the lecture series was the "World Game" course that I taught in adult education with Daniel Sisson.

That course led me to meet Robert O. Easton, who took me under his wing at age twenty-four and mentored me up until his death in 1989. No young man could have had a more insightful, generous, and noble role model than Bob. The work of Bob and his friend, the photojournalist Dick Smith, was instrumental in establishing the San Rafael Wilderness. Bob introduced me to James Gildea, who, like Bob, became a great mentor. Jim's life and that of his beloved Ninette, his diminutive French powerhouse of a wife, brought the grace and vision of European salons to Santa Barbara. What a joy and inspiration it was to spend a few hours every month or so talking about our work and our vision for the future or for our town.

Bob and Jim connected me to John Fisher-Smith, a partner in the San Francisco office of Skidmore, Owings & Merrill and his colleague Jerry

Goldberg. They were embodiments of the power of design that featured so prominently in the work of the CEC.

Art Benkaim was perhaps the CEC's greatest volunteer. A retired successful Santa Barbara businessman, he devoted two full days a week for two years as the cashier at our recycling center. Kind and competent, he was a model of selfless work.

Robert Sollen, a reporter at the Santa Barbara News-Press, was our lifeline to the community. He covered all manner of environmental subjects after gaining fame in journalistic circles for his brilliant reporting on the Santa Barbara Oil Spill.

Professors Harvey Molotch and Rich Appelbaum instilled in me a profound respect for the skills resident in the academic world that could be brought to bear on the public sphere, particularly the planning of a city. I was privileged to be one of the five "principals" who authored the Impacts of Growth study that had such a profound effect on Santa Barbara's future. We were joined in that enterprise by Jennifer Bigelow and Dr. Henry Kramer.

Paul Wack, now a professor of urban planning at Cal Poly and UCSB, gave me the chance to become one of the coauthors of the first coastal plans for California. I was joined in that effort by Kirvil Skinnerland, Ruth Ann Collins, Dr. Eugene Bazan, Susan Van Atta, and Kim Schizas.

The creation of the Mesa Project and later the Gildea Resource Center were made possible by Lawrence Thompson, AIA, our architect who went well beyond his professional role in developing our building plans incorporating the theme of sustainability. Many hands built the Gildea Center, including Dennis Allen; Jim Tremaine; Dennis Thompson, AIA; Al Greenstein, of ARCO; Abby Rockefeller; Carl Lindstrom; Brett Hodges, who provided critical financial support when we most needed it; Bob Barrett of the Hewlett Foundation, who shared our sustainability vision; and Arnette Zerbe, who commandeered a volunteer pool.

Lash Construction gave us a big break on grading and paving our access road, and Mr. and Mrs. Wendling kindly allowed us to access the Mesa site from below and across their easement.

Bricks and mortar were the form of the Gildea vision, but equally important was the institutional design, the CEC's "triad" strategy formulated first by

Robert Fitzgerald and Dr. Eugene Bazan. Without communication tools like our white papers and other publications led by journalist/writer Joan Melcher, our work would have not had the reach that it did. No one did more to imbue our work with a loving, generous, and penetrating vision than Dr. Anthony Dominski, who headed our intern program.

The garden at Gildea was first the work of Warren Pierce and then a succession of gardeners, including Lynn Ocone, Rodney Adamchak, and Rob Roy. Geej and Carol Ostroff. And there was Oscar Carmona who worked to make the garden accessible to the larger community with his passion for helping low-income gardeners and the handicapped.

Staff and volunteers at the Gildea Center included Rosemary White, Lutie Fitzgerald, Karen Feeney, Sharyn Main, Heidi Seward, and a slew of interns. Others who went on to play critical roles in the waste field were Karen Hurst, Jenny Gitlitz, and Thomas Outerbridge.

When it came to the community gardens and El Mirasol, inspiration came early on from Jerome Goldstein, who later founded Biocycle magazine, and Robert Rodale, CEO of Rodale Press. Their names are now synonymous with the pioneering phase of organic agriculture.

John Jeavons was an early garden collaborator and an individual who has maintained an indomitable allegiance to his biointensive horticultural vision for more than forty years.

Gary Petersen, Cliff Ronnenberg, Bob Klausner, Steve Young, Cliff Humphrey, William O'Toole, and Nancy Skinner played instrumental roles in developing and implementing our recycling and waste management programs. Neil Seldman, Gary Liss and Richard Anthony were also important influences on the early work. Marc Thomasee managed our recycling programs for many years, followed by Russ Culter. Christine Olsen was our go-to person for arranging early recycling conferences. William O'Toole was instrumental in introducing me to the global waste management arena—especially the waste separation technologies being developed in Europe. William's penetrating insights into recycling and recycling technologies challenged my own, and I benefited greatly from his critiques.

Assisting me in gaining my position in government and working with me during those sometimes trying but fruitful years were Z. Harry Astor of the

California Refuse Removal Council; George Eowan, my volunteer political strategist; Chuck Poochigian, the governor's appointments secretary; Cliff Ronnenberg and Mike Silva; James Strock, California's first secretary of the California Environmental Protection Agency; Brian Runkle, assistant secretary; state senator Gary K. Hart and Joe Caves, who were my political lifeline during my first few years as a political novice; Nancy Michael, staff to the Senate Rule Committee; Senator Pro Tem David Roberti, who presided over my three Senate confirmations; Senator Jack O'Connell; Senator Omar Raines, who stood up for me during Senate confirmation; and Senators Lucy Killea and Marion Bergeson. Byron Sher, author of California's landmark recycling legislation, exemplified a skilled and talented legislator who set a standard for service that I admired so. His all-powerful staffer, Kip Lipper, taught me that government power often resides in those not elected. Not surprisingly, he is known today as California's forty-first senator.

My work at the CalEPA was aided immeasurably by my wonderful staff, Dr. Howard Levenson, Fitz Fitzgerald, and Donnell Duclo. We galvanized into a great team and we remain fast friends.

Industry, environmental, and others who enriched my years in Sacramento include Dorothy Rice and Caren Turgovich; Pat Passwater; John Schmidtz; Loraine Van Kekirix; Sharon Waddell, Laurie Karlstad, and Jeannie Blakeslee; Evan Edgar; my colleagues on the board, Steve Jones and Wesley Chesbro; Sam Eggigian; Kent Stoddard; Jack Pandol, CalEPA undersecretary; Richard Wilson, director of forestry and my roommate in Sacramento for three years; Bob Pestoni; Rudy Vacarezza; and Rich Hayes, Tim Olson, and Jeff Danzinger. Pat Schiavo, formerly in senior management at the California Integrated Waste Management Board, has been an invaluable colleague during my post-government years.

During my years in the private sector, I thank Cliff Ronnenberg for giving me the platform for the beginning of a biogas industry; Michael Silva; David Shawver; Stephen Kaffka; Dan Leppo; Hal Williams; Andy Rose; David Ronnenberg; David Fahrion; the board of the Costa Mesa Sanitation District; Dean Saito; Henry Hogo; Mark Murray and Nick Lapis of Californians Against Waste; Pete Price and Chuck White; Chuck Helgut; Nora Goldstein; Julia

Levin; Sean, Evan and Neil Edgar; Patty Henshaw; Vicki Wilson; Alex Helou; Miguel Zermeno; Reina Peirera and Coby Skye.

Others I want to thank are Carol and Fred Kenyon, Isabelle Greene, Diane Boss, Carla Frisk, Lori Thayer, David Brower, Michael Hathaway, Bob Wilkinson, Kim Kimball, Dr. Karl Hutterer, Mike Noling, Melissa Boyd, Kathy Lynch, Lee Moldaver, Chris Erskine, Rick Stich, Steve Carlson, Steve Guy, Phil Greene, Hugh Prichard, Mark Dawson, Ron Harkey, Marlin Roehl, DeAnne Sarver, Teri Link Cohan. Chen Sheng, Yue Yue Yen, Eugene Tseng, Lee Swenson, Malcom Margolin, Henry Han, Tara Lumpkin Waters, Ron Hubert and Ed France. There were many wonderful people whose names and roles have eluded me and who, by this reference, I honor unnamed. Please forgive my poor memory. No oversight is intended.

Special thanks is due to three UC Santa Barbara students in my ES 172 course who provided research on several of the topics developed in the book; Violetta Muscelli, Logan McCoy and Wei Wei.

The design and publishing of *Out of the Wasteland* was made possible by contributions from the Community Environmental Council, the Gildea Foundation, Maryanne Mott, Diane Boss and Michael Noling.

The stories, the insights, and the views expressed are mine and mine alone and not those of the publisher, the Community Environmental Council.

ABOUT THE AUTHOR

Paul Relis was raised in Long Beach, California. He was a student at UC Santa Barbara when on January 28, 1969 a massive oil spill off of Santa Barbara's coastline helped trigger the modern environmental movement.

He became at 23 the founding Executive Director of the Community Environmental Council. Together with his colleagues they helped shape the future of the Santa Barbara region and went on to pioneer recycling, urban gardening, solar energy, green design and building, programs that were to become the backbone of what we call sustainability today.

Following twenty years as the leader of the Council, he served on the California Integrated Waste Management Board in Sacramento, California, a powerful regulatory agency charged with managing the state's solid waste system and implementing California's nation-leading recycling program.

Today he is engaged in the development of one of the largest facilities in North America to convert municipal organic waste to a carbon-negative fuel to power heavy duty engines, a landmark effort to end our dependence on land filling waste and reduce greenhouse gas emissions.

He divides his time between Santa Barbara and Taos, New Mexico with his wife, Kathy. They have three children.

Photo by Sarita Relis

PHOTO CREDITS

*We gratefully acknowledge the following people and institutions
for the photographs used in this book:*

Front Cover. The Earth seen from Apollo 17 courtesy of NASA.

Front & Back Cover. Landsat Look Image LC80420362014047LGN00 courtesy of the U.S. Geological Survey;

p 11. Platform A Blowout 1969 (hb-nx_203). Courtesy of UCSB Library Map & Imagery Laboratory.

p 14. Crystal Cove, Sept. 1953. https://www.flickr.com/photos/ocarchives/3268121106/. Photo courtesy Orange County Archives.

p 17. "Citizens greeting Senator Muskie at Santa Barbara Airport" February 7, 1969. © *The Santa Barbara News-Press.*

p 21. Whole Earth Catalog, 1969. http://commons.wikimedia.org/wiki/File:WEC-69F-C.jpg. CC BY-SA 3.0.

p 24. City of Santa Barbara. Courtesy of Sarita Relis.

p 26. Santa Barbara Ecology Center, 1970. Courtesy of Hal Conklin.

p 30. Buckminster Fuller. Courtesy of the Estate of Buckminster Fuller.

p 33. E.F. Schumacher and Paul Relis. Courtesy of John Evarts.

p 34. Ian McHarg. From http://earthweek1970.org/. © 1970 Earth Week Committee of Philadelphia.

p 36. Alan Chadwick. Courtesy of UCSC Special Collections. © UC Regents.

p 39. Naples view © William B. Dewey.

p 42. Fish at confluence. Courtesy of Ojai Valley Land Conservancy.

p 46. *Survival Times.* Courtesy of Community Environmental Council.

p 51. Chapala Garden: Hal and fencework. Courtesy of Hal Conklin.

p 55. Bishop Ranch Aerial. Courtesy of Paul Wellman / *Santa Barbara Independent.*

p 65. Cabrillo Boulevard. Courtesy of Sarita Relis.

p 76. El Mirasol Polyculture Farm: children gardening. Courtesy of John Evarts.

p 77. El Mirasol Polyculture Farm: veggie stand. Courtesy of John Evarts.

p 79. El Mirasol Polyculture Farm: John Fry. Courtesy of John Evarts.

p 80. El Mirasol Polyculture Farm. Courtesy of Warren Pierce.

p 91. A "City Farmer" Tends His Vegetables in the Fenway Gardens Administered by the Fenway Civic Association. An Outgrowth of the "Victory Gardens" of World War II, the Association Has 600 Members Who Cultivate a Total of 425 Garden Plots in These Five Acres of Metropolitan Boston 08/1973. By Halberstadt, Ernst, 1910-1987, Photographer (NARA record: 8464447) (U.S. National Archives and Records Administration) [Public domain], via Wikimedia Commons.

p 102. Santa Barbara downtown neighborhood. Courtesy of Sarita Relis.

p 106. Carpinteria Valley. Courtesy of Sarita Relis.

p 116. Earth Tube, Mesa Project. Courtesy of Community Environmental Council

p 131. Gildea Center, winning design drawing, 1983. By Design Works: Principal Architect, Brian Cearnal, A.I.A., with Hugh Twibell A.I.A., Bob Blossom A.I.A., Mark Kirkhart A.I.A. and Mark Shields A.I.A. Courtesy of Community Environmental Council.

p 132. Gildea Center. Courtesy of Brian Cearnal, AIA.

p 147. Santa Barbara Recycling Center, 1978. Courtesy of John Evarts

p 157. Downtown Berkeley. The Oakland - San Francisco Bay Bridge and the San Francisco downtown can be seen in the background. PowerBar headquarters are visible in Downtown Berkeley. Looking from the Berkeley Hills westward. California, USA. 2005. http://upload.wikimedia.org/wikipedia/commons/8/89/Berkeley-downtown-Bay-bridge-SF-in-back-from-Lab.jpg. By User:Introvert (Own work) [CC BY-SA 2.5 (http://creativecommons.org/licenses/by-sa/2.5)], via Wikimedia Commons.

p 170. Waste Incinerator, Tokyo, Japan http://upload.wikimedia.org/wikipedia/commons/b/b5/Tokyo_from_a_train.jpg. By Susan G. Lesch (Own work) [Public domain], via Wikimedia Commons.

p 182. Child Scavenging in Manila's Smokey Mountain Garbage Dump. © Philippe Lissac /Godong/Corbis

p 198. California State Capitol, 10th Street and L Street, Sacramento, California. 23 March 2010. © Steven Pavlov / lovingwa.blogspot.com, via Wikimedia Commons.

p 226. CRT Stanton filter. Photo courtesy of CR&R Incorporated. Photography by Dean and Marjorie Chin.

p 232. Schwartze Pumpe. http://upload.wikimedia.org/wikipedia/commons/c/cd/Sprengung_Schornsteine_KW_West_Schwarze_Pumpe.jpg By SPBer (Own work) [CC BY-SA 3.0 (http://creativecommons.org/licenses/by-sa/3.0)], via Wikimedia Commons.

p 247. Goran Johanssen, Mayor, Gotenborg, Sweden, 2000 http://commons.wikimedia.org/wiki/File:Goran_johansson_02.JPG   http://commons.wikimedia.org/wiki/File:Goran_johansson_02.JPG

p 250. Hammarby Sjostad. http://upload.wikimedia.org/wikipedia/commons/7/71/Hammarby_sj%C3%B6stad%2C_flygfoto_2014-09-20.jpg Johan Fredriksson [CC BY-SA 3.0 (http://creativecommons.org/licenses/by-sa/3.0)], via Wikimedia Commons.

NOTES

PROLOGUE

1. "Welcome to an Engaged Community." Signal Hill, CA. http://www.cityofsignalhill.org/index.aspx?nid=218.

AWAKENING

2. "About Earth Day Network." Earth Day Network Main. Accessed February 06, 2015. http://www.earthday.org/about-earth-day-network.

3. Robert Olney Easton, *Black Tide: The Santa Barbara Oil Spill and Its Consequences* (New York: Delacorte Press, 1972).

4. January 28 Committee, "The Santa Barbara Declaration of Environmental Rights" (Santa Barbara, CA, 1970).

5. Easton, *Black Tide.*

THE REALM OF IDEAS

6. Paul R. Ehrlich, *The Population Bomb* (New York: Ballantine Books, 1968).

7. Donella H. Meadows, *The Limits to Growth: a Report for the Club of Rome's Project on the Predicament of Mankind* (New York: Universe Books, 1972).

8. R. Buckminster Fuller, *Operating Manual for Spaceship Earth* (Carbondale: Southern Illinois University Press, 1969).

9. University of California, Santa Barbara, Environmental Studies, "UCSB's Environmental Studies Program Celebrates 40th Anniversary." News release, April 12, 2010. UCSB. http://www.ia.ucsb.edu/pa/display.aspx?pkey=2214.

10. Bill McKibben, "Earth: Making a Life on a Tough New Planet" Speech, UCSB ES Program's 40th Anniversary Celebration, University of California, Santa Barbara, April 24, 2010.

INSPIRATION

11. William Anders, "Earthrise," December 24, 1968. NASA.

12. "Celebrate Apollo: Exploring the Moon, Discovering Earth." http://www.nasa.gov/pdf/323298main_CelebrateApolloEarthRise.pdf.

13. "The Dymaxion American." *Time* Vol. 83, No. 2 (January 10, 1964).

SMALL IS BEAUTIFUL

14. E. F. Schumacher , *Small Is Beautiful: Economics As If People Mattered* (New York: Harper & Row, 1973).

DESIGN WITH NATURE

15. Ian L. McHarg, *Design with Nature* (Garden City, NY: Published for the American Museum of Natural History the Natural History Press, 1969).

THE GARDEN OF THE HEART'S DELIGHT

16. http://alanchadwick.net/Alan_Chadwick_Archive/Welcome.html.

17. *Journal of the California Garden & Landscape History Society*, Vol. 13 No. 3 • Fall 2010 The Alan Chadwick Garden at UCSC, 2010. http://www.cglhs.org/archives/Eden-13.3-Fa-2010w.pdf.

18. Schumacher, *Small Is Beautiful*.

MR. POLLOCK'S CHALLENGE

19. Robyn Kenney, *Rivers and Harbors Act of 1899*, United States. Retrieved from http://www.eoearth.org/view/article/155764.

DISPUTES AT THE URBAN-RURAL BORDER

20. Buckminster Fuller Institute. "About Fuller." World Game. https://bfi.org/about-fuller/big-ideas/world-game.

21. Elaine Burnell, "Today's Action, Tomorrow's Profit: An Alternative for Community Development" (Santa Barbara, CA: Community Environmental Council, July 1972).

EARTH DAY 1970

22. Christopher Alexander, Sara Ishikawa, and Murray Silverstein, *A Pattern Language: Towns, Buildings, Construction* (New York: Oxford University Press, 1977).

STANDING UP TO POWER

23. Committee for Santa Barbara, "Plan for East Beach" (July 1973).

24. C. M. Cheney and Olmsted Brothers, "Major Traffic Street Plan: Boulevard and Park System for Santa Barbara, California," Adopted by the City Planning Commission, September 30, 1924 and the Board of Park Commissioners, November 20, 1924. On file, Santa Barbara Public Library, Santa Barbara, California.

25. *Survival Times*, February 1973.

26. Robert Olney Easton, *The Happy Man* (New York: Viking Press, 1943).

A FARM IN THE CITY

27. Personal Journal Entry, February 1972.

WHEN YOU'RE BLOCKED, ADAPT

28. Richard Wilhelm and Cary F. Baynes, *The I Ching; Or, Book of Changes* (Princeton, NJ: Princeton University Press, 1967).

HOW BIG SHOULD OUR CITY BE?

29. Santa Barbara Planning Task Force, *Santa Barbara: The Impacts of Growth* (Santa Barbara, CA, August 1974).

30. John Galsworthy, "Ode to San Ysidro," 1912.

IN DEFENSE OF AGRICULTURE

31. D. H. Lawrence, "The Spirit of Place," In *Studies in Classic American Literature* (New York: Viking Press, 1964).

32. "Meet California Flower Grower Rene Van Wingerden." http://www.california-grown.org/img/eis-pdf/Rene%20Van%20Wingerden.pdf.

33. Charles Stewart Mott Foundation. "Our Founder." Mott.org. Accessed February 07, 2015. http://www.mott.org/about/OurOrganization/ourfounder.

BUILDING OUR DREAM

34. Clivus Multrum, Inc.: Manufacturer of Composting Toilets and Greywater Systems since 1973. Accessed February 07, 2015. http://www.clivusmultrum.com/.

BETWEEN THE IDEA AND THE REALITY: EARLY SUSTAINABILITY METRICS

35. The phrase "soft energy path" is a term first used by the brilliant young scientist, Amory Lovins, in his 1976 landmark paper "Energy Strategy: The Road Not Taken." Foreign Affairs, October 1976. http://www.foreignaffairs.com/articles/26604/amory-b-lovins/energy-strategy-the-road-not-taken.

PAY DAY

36. "Village Homes: About Us." Village Homes. Accessed February 11, 2015. http://www.villagehomes.hoaspace.com/cgi-bin/aboutus.pl.

GARBAGE

37. William L. Rathje and Cullen Murphy, *Rubbish!: The Archaeology of Garbage* (Tucson, AZ: University of Arizona Press, 2001).

AT THE GROUND FLOOR OF RECYCLING

38. Paul Relis, Anthony Dominski, and Joan Melcher. *Beyond the Crisis: Integrated Waste Management* (Santa Barbara, CA: Community Environmental Council, 1987).

39. "Diversion Is Good for the Economy: Highlights from Two Independent Studies on the Economic Impacts of Diversion in California," (Sacramento: California Environmental Protection Agency, Integrated Waste Management Board, 2003).

INTO BERKELEY WE DARED TO TREAD

40. Dan Knapp, Urban Ore newsletter. Berkeley, CA, 1982.

41. Berkeley recycling programs also included Urban Ore that recycled a wide range of building materials, under the leadership of a brilliant and vocal entrepreneur, Dan Knapp.

RECYCLING GOES MAINSTREAM

42. Rathje and Cullen, *Rubbish!: The Archaeology of Garbage.*

SMOKEY MOUNTAIN, MANILA

43. Katherine Boo, *Behind the Beautiful Forevers* (New York: Random House, 2012).

USING LESS STUFF

44. Vance Packard, *The Waste Makers* (New York: D. McKay, 1960).

45. Vance Packard, *The Hidden Persuaders* (New York: D. McKay, 1957).

46. Karen Hurst, *The Next Frontier: Solid Waste Source Reduction* (Santa Barbara, CA: Community Environmental Council, 1987).

47. "Municipal Solid Waste (MSW) in the United States: Facts and Figures." EPA. Accessed February 11, 2015. http://www.epa.gov/solidwaste/nonhaz/municipal/msw99.htm.

POLITICS

48. Jim Puckett and Theodore C. Smith, *Exporting Harm: The High-Tech Trashing of Asia* (Seattle, WA: Basel Action Network, 2002).

BIOGAS

49. California Energy Commission: Overview of Natural Gas in California, 2014

50. *The Economist*, "The World in 2015," pages 114, 117.

COMMUNITY ENERGY BLUEPRINTS

51. Tam Hunt and Sigrid Wright, *A New Energy Direction: A Blueprint for Santa Barbara County* (Santa Barbara, CA: Community Environmental Council, 2007).

TRANSPORTATION FUELS

52. "Green Car," which bills itself as the "ultimate guide to cleaner driving, describes the new General Motors Spark EV with an EPA-rated eighty-two miles on a full charge and below the cost of an average new car today.

53. "Governor Brown Sworn In, Delivers Inaugural Address." Office of Governor Edmund G. Brown Jr. - Newsroom. Accessed February 11, 2015. http://www.gov.ca.gov/news.php?id=18828.

54. California Air Resources Board.

55. Brent Kendall, "Justices Plot Middle Course on Business," *Wall Street Journal*, June 30, 2014. http://www.wsj.com/articles/justices-plot-middlecourse-on-business-1404180828.

56. AB 594, AB 1926 (2014).

57. Gladstein and Associates, extrapolation from an analysis provided to the California Energy Commission, March 2014.

SUN

58. "Alternative Energy Developments." City of Lancaster. June 16, 2014. Accessed February 08, 2015. http://www.cityoflancasterca.org/index.aspx?page=1499.

POSTPETROLEUM ECONOMICS

59. William McDonough and Michael Braungart, *Cradle to Cradle: Remaking the Way We Make Things.*New York: North Point Press, 2002.

A POSTOIL PATTERN LANGUAGE

60. Verdexchange Green Marketmakers Conference & Expo, Los Angeles, January 25–27, 2015.

61. Draft Environmental Impact, Planning and Community Development Department, City of Bakersfield, May 2013.

RENEWABLE TECHNOLOGY DIFFUSION

62. Personal conversation with Christian Felske, Environmental Research and Regulation Specialist, City of Edmonton. January 27, 2015.

63. Green Retail Decisions Innovation Summit 2013.

SCALE

64. Lewis Mumford, *The City in History: Its Origins, Its Transformations, and Its Prospects* (New York: Harcourt, Brace & World, 1961).

65. *Webster's New Standard Dictionary of the English Language including Webster's Alphabetized Thesaurus and Webster's Speller* (New York: PMC Pub., 1995).

66. Coral Davenport and Marjorie Connelly, "Most Republicans Say They Back Climate Action, Poll Finds." *The New York Times,* January 30, 2015. http://www.nytimes.com/2015/01/31/us/politics/most-americans-support-government-action-on-climate-change-poll-finds.html?_r=1.

CPSIA information can be obtained
at www.ICGtesting.com
Printed in the USA
FSOW02n0624060415
6221FS